Resurrecting the First
Great American Play

RESURRECTING
THE FIRST
GREAT AMERICAN PLAY

Imperial Politics and
Colonial Ambitions in Frontier Detroit

SÄMI LUDWIG

The University of Wisconsin Press

The University of Wisconsin Press
728 State Street, Suite 443
Madison, Wisconsin 53706
uwpress.wisc.edu

Gray's Inn House, 127 Clerkenwell Road
London EC1R 5DB, United Kingdom
eurospanbookstore.com

Printed in the United States of America

This book may be available in a digital edition.

Library of Congress Cataloging-in-Publication Data
Names: Ludwig, Sämi, 1960– author.
Title: Resurrecting the first great American play: imperial politics and
colonial ambitions in frontier Detroit / Sämi Ludwig.
Description: Madison, Wisconsin: The University of Wisconsin Press, [2020]
| Includes bibliographical references and index.
Identifiers: LCCN 2019019125 | ISBN 9780299325404 (cloth)
Subjects: LCSH: Rogers, Robert, 1731–1795. Ponteach. | Rogers, Robert, 1731–1795—
Criticism and interpretation. | Pontiac, Ottawa Chief, -1769—In literature.
| American drama—18th century—History and criticism.
Classification: LCC PS829.R6 P66 2020 | DDC 812/.5—dc23
LC record available at https://lccn.loc.gov/2019019125

This book is for my son,

JONATHAN

of course

That horrid weapon the scalping-knife hangs by a string which goes round their necks.

ROBERT ROGERS,
Concise Account

He's wild, vain, of little understanding, and of as little Principle, but withal has a share of Cunning, No Modesty or veracity and sticks at Nothing. Be so good to Send me your Advice in what manner he may be best tied up by Instructions and prevent [*sic*] doing Mischief and imposing upon you.

GENERAL THOMAS GAGE
on Robert Rogers in a note to Sir William Johnson, 9 January 1766

I recommended [to the several nations of western Indians] that we might See each others Faces all together & write as one in Clearing the Path & Brightening the Chain of Peace that might extend through all the Nations & Tribes of Indians from the Rising to the Setting Sun—

ROBERT ROGERS,
Michillimackinac Journal

Ponteach is a startling drama, like nothing else written about North America in the eighteenth century, so stark is its condemnation of the colonists, so graphic its portrayal of empire as an institution of corruption, hypocrisy, rape, and murder.

TIM FULFORD

Contents

Conclusions. The Original Backwoodsman?

Illustrations

Acknowledgments

At the origin of this book is my discovery of Robert Rogers's play at the English Department library in Berne, where I was a doctoral student teaching, among other starter courses, an introduction to American drama. Tired of dissecting *The Little Foxes*, I'd heard about melodrama and discovered some of the old American plays like *Metamora* or *She Would Be a Soldier*. In the days before my time in Berne, the matchless Henri Petter, specialist in the American literature of the early republic, had procured a leather-bound series called *America's Lost Plays* that I came across in multiple library revisions. I liked many of these plays, but I was especially impressed by Rogers's *Ponteach* (1766), by his authentic and at the same time weirdly inadequate writing about the Indians of Detroit and their interaction with the English. There was so much substance in this text that I simply couldn't forget it—I always wanted to get back to it and study it more thoroughly.

Fortunately, several decades later that opportunity did finally arrive with a generous CRCT, the French version of a sabbatical, granted to me for the spring semester 2017 by my employer, the Université de Haute Alsace in Mulhouse. Thus my heartfelt gratitude goes to the UHA administration, and especially to Jean-Luc Bischoff for his personal

help and to the Conseil Scientifique over which he presides. My colleagues in the English Department unselfishly stepped in to teach my
courses during my absence and put up with some very tight class
scheduling.

I would not have studied abroad without the kind invitation to
Ann Arbor from David Porter, then head of the English Department of
the University of Michigan, and his team. He showed great interest in
my project and provided me with a coveted library card. My biggest
academic find in Ann Arbor, however, was the Clements Library, with
its ample holdings of historical Great Lakes documents, and where I
found experts to discuss Robert Rogers with during coffee breaks. Brian
Dunnigan responded to my enthusiasm by showing me maps and taught
me how to pronounce Michilimackinac, and Terese Austin helped me
get fancy documents from Hathi Trust and some of the letters reprinted
in this book. I will be eternally grateful for their help and support.

Ann Arbor was also a well-chosen place to spend my three precious
weeks of research in February–March 2017 because it provided me with
a rare occasion to see again my old AFS exchange brother, Joe Tesar,
and reminded me that we had stayed in touch for a solid forty years. It
was good to see his wife, Linda, and their family and the big house he
has renovated. Joe's friends Matthew Shapiro and Susan Garetz generously invited my daughter, Julia, and me to stay at their home, in
walking distance to the campus, as "house sitters"—what an under-
statement for the luxurious accommodation we enjoyed! As another
treat, Julia's former English teacher from Switzerland, Charlotte Jäggi,
happened to be in Ann Arbor as well, accompanying her husband,
Adrian, doing research for the Swiss National Science Foundation. She
lovingly looked after us, drove us to many places, and even brought us
back to the airport (twice).

I received moral support from my wonderful English Department
colleagues of the Upper Rhine universities and their students at our
traditional annual trinational graduate student conference in Basel in
April 2017, where I first presented my *Ponteach* project. Similarly, later
that spring my Polish friend Ewa Lucak and her students and colleagues
were willing to listen to me in Warsaw on the occasion of an Erasmus
Plus teachers' exchange. Looking for samples of Robert Rogers's hand-
writing, I located his fascinating *Michillimackinac Journal* (I use William
Clements's spelling of "Michillimackinac" for discussing this journal)
at the American Antiquarian Society in Worchester, Massachusetts,
and received permission to reprint some of the manuscript pages in my

book. Many thanks for this support. The nonpareil Werner Sollors has played a special role in this project. Even though I didn't respond to his invitation to do research in Cambridge, he agreed to read my manuscript and gave me good advice on reorganizing parts of the text; he even found the precious Nathaniel Potter sermon for me. Finally, I had helpers who assisted me with phonetics and even proofread some of my prose. Thank you Regula Hohl, Jürg Strässler, and Jörg Berger.

Raphael Kadushin found me a great Great Lakes press for my Great Lakes tale, and I am grateful for his confidence in me and in this project. His successor at Wisconsin, Gwen Walker, did equally wonderful work and helped me navigate American sensibilities—an experience which made me realize that my Swiss origin and my awareness of our long history of exporting mercenary soldiers as cannon fodder in European conflicts (the last official vestiges of this practice being the pope's Swiss Guard in Rome) make me see Robert Rogers not merely as battlefield brute but also as a victim of circumstance who tried to excel in a hostile environment.[1] I am also grateful for all the support from the other University of Wisconsin Press staff: Anna Muenchrath, Jennifer Conn, Kaitlin Svabek, Adam Mehring, and of course the hardworking Barb Wojhoski, who is certainly my favorite copyeditor.

My final thanks go to my family at home, to my wife, Beatrice, and our children, Julia and Jonathan, who are always willing to put up with me when I am absentminded and distracted with my academic egghead preoccupations. I love you.

Resurrecting the First
Great American Play

Introduction

From Scalping Knife
to Iambic Pentameter

*P*onteach: or, The Savages of America: A Tragedy, published in 1766, was the first English play written by a North American on an American topic.[1] Though it was published anonymously, critics agree that Major Robert Rogers, a famous military hero of the French and Indian War, had a major hand in its writing, advancing the range of his career from the habitual scalping knife to an artistic project in iambic pentameter. Exotically titled *Ponteach* after its protagonist, the play refers to the Indian leader Pontiac and the Indian uprising of 1763 in a way that is brutally direct and testifies to its author's firsthand knowledge of these ultracontemporary historical events. Pontiac and Rogers participated on different sides in the crucial Siege of Detroit, the last British stronghold in the Old Northwest. This was a major crisis in North American politics because all the other forts had been taken by the Indians and the British Empire was about to lose the vast new territory they had only recently conquered from the French. The play exposes the cheating and corruption of the English colonizers as the cause of

3

this Indian rebellion on the Great Lakes, and there is more authentic ethnographic insight on indigenous local culture in this drama than in any other production about America at that time or even much later.

This alone would already be reason enough to make *Ponteach* a classic of colonial American literature, but instead the play has been ridiculed and neglected. At the time of its publication, genteel English theater critics sniffed at themes of English corruption and frontier brutality. While that same quality later led to some interest in *Ponteach* as a historical document, the focus on its historical significance has eclipsed serious consideration of the play as a work of art. Regrettably, this rejection of its aesthetic qualities has continued, though such an assessment is unjustified: a closer examination of Rogers's much-misunderstood text reveals a work of outstanding artistic craftsmanship. In addition to all the ideological interest, his careful choice of characters and intricate plotting of the events in *Ponteach* live up to the best stage entertainment in English at that time, offering insightful monologues as well as spectacular melodramatic moments. As I shall demonstrate, especially his use of language is innovative (e.g., iambic pentameter in pidgin!) and sometimes exhibits an acoustic finesse that ironically parallels the content of specific statements in ways that are simply outstanding.

Ponteach has also been neglected because of historical developments. Thus the founding of the United States of America redefined the emerging canons of national literatures in a way that has found no real place for this play either in American, English, or Canadian literary histories. Rogers had sided with the Loyalists in the Revolutionary War, and thus he was not a hero in United States; in fact, he was considered a traitor and lost all of his possessions there. As an exile in London, he was seen as an uneducated, exotic foreigner who could not live up to the high standards of the imperial capital. And Canada was no independent nation yet. Furthermore, Rogers was from New England, and *Ponteach* takes place in Old Detroit, Michigan, which is decidedly American territory south of the Canadian border. In short, the play simply fell outside the national categories.

As a result, except for a small number of notes and articles, the critical attention to *Ponteach* has been very limited. Fortunately, Tiffany Potter has produced a highly praiseworthy edition of the play (2010)—which, significantly, comes out of Canada.[2] In short, this play has been treated as a mere footnote to American drama,[3] which in turn has often been reduced to the twentieth century (with many critical works only starting with a discussion of Eugene O'Neill).[4] But even when anthologies have focused on "early" American drama—for example, Jeffrey H. Richards's outstanding Penguin collection—or the all-inclusive, multivolume editions of major publishers such as Heath and Norton, *Ponteach* never made the cut.[5] Elizabeth Dillon mentions, moreover, that the few plays still anthologized today "represent the merest fraction of theatrical performances viewed by the throngs of audience members who regularly attended the theatre in the eighteenth and the early nineteenth century" (20).

Worse, *Ponteach* arguably has never been performed,[6] a fate that it shares with many other early American plays considered aesthetically unattractive simply because they don't live up to our contemporary sensibilities.[7] Thus browsing the internet for videos of old plays, you will find very little. When teaching plays from the precious Richards collection, I could find only simple high school performances of some scenes from *The Contrast*, hefty amateur rehearsals from *The Indian Princess*, and similarly provincial material for *The Drunkard*. At least in the case of *Uncle Tom's Cabin* (the historically influential play version), I found a complete, fairly recent version, and of course all the old racist Hollywood adaptations, with sound and without. Let me make the point that all these plays are immensely teachable and also provide a gold mine of materials for social studies, historical analysis, and aesthetic understanding. We may not always like what they say, but they are the memory of American culture, and in that sense of priceless value. They give us a history of art and how it achieved its aims on the stage. It is lamentable that American institutions have been and still are mostly unwilling to face this important cultural work and that American theaters grossly neglect their own heritage. Not even the many American acting schools, which are rich in talent and produce thousands of new actors, directors, and future producers every year, ever try to revive that rich tradition.

One reason for avoidance may be the fact that *Ponteach*, in particular, forces us to keep our distance from its many elements of violence and racial prejudice that are no longer acceptable.[8] At the same time these hard issues cannot be filtered away by any "correctness" that insists on imposing contemporary values and wants to condemn the sins of the past from the viewpoint of our present. In my opinion it is more important to share this rich material, to make it known and turn it into an object of our discussion. Thus my aim has been to analyze the cultural work done by and to the aesthetics of *Ponteach* in a historical context, mainly by means of honestly positioning myself with my limitations as an author of the twenty-first century while at the same time trying to understand the complex and distant reality of the eighteenth century.

When I visited the University of Michigan in Ann Arbor in 2017, which has an English Department of more than fifty graduate faculty (more than twice as many as all English studies in Switzerland) and some 180 PhD students in language and literature, I couldn't find anybody who had heard of *Ponteach*—even though Robert Rogers made local history.[9] His taking of Detroit from the French makes him, after all, a kind of William Tell or "Founding Father" of the Great Lakes who stands at the very origin of this region's English-language identity. If the play is known in the Clements Library on campus, which even has a copy of the original 1766 edition of *Ponteach* and is one of the best sources for Pontiac materials in general, what remains to be done is to extend that academic interest from the historians to literary scholarship. Let us therefore take a first glance at the play and raise some questions about it.

A Plot Summary of *Ponteach*

Act 1 of *Ponteach* begins with a scene at a trading house, in which the more experienced M'Dole explains to the younger Murphey how Indians can be cheated with alcohol and manipulated scales, a theory that is then put into practice when the Indian customers arrive. The traders decide that the immense profits resulting from such behavior exceed the danger of vengeance. In the second scene, we encounter the English hunters Honnyman and Orsbourn, who complain about the lack of game in the forest, for which they blame the Indians. They shoot two Indians, steal their furs, and scalp them, deflecting their guilt feelings by denying that Indians have a soul and praising the superiority of their own guns. Scene 3 presents the haughty officers Colonel Cockum and Captain Frisk in Detroit and their prejudices about "insolent" Indians. Feeling safe within the walls of the fort, they offend Ponteach with curses. Act 1 ends in a scene with the governors Sharp, Gripe, and Catchum, who revel in their own profits, keeping large shares of the Indian presents for themselves. Ponteach notes this—the French were certainly more respectful partners. He and his chiefs give a warning to the governors and say that they would like to meet the English king in person, but like the traders before, the smug representatives of Britain remain self-satisfied with their profits.

Act 2 opens with a scene of Ponteach's two sons, Philip and Chekitan, returning from a hunt and praising the "unstain'd Fruits of Peace"

PONTEACH:

OR THE

Savages of America.

A

TRAGEDY.

LONDON:

Printed for the Author ; and Sold by J. MILLAN,
oppofite the *Admiralty*, *Whitehall*.

M.DCC.LXVI.

[Price 2 s. 6 d.]

Title page of the original edition of *Ponteach* (London, 1766). (Courtesy of William L. Clements Library, University of Michigan)

(2.1.10) provided by the English occupation (probably a reference to the Royal Proclamation Line of 1763, as T. Potter suggests [2010 ed. 85n]). But then they discuss the worrying dream their father has had about an uprising because the English treat him not like an "Ally" but like a "Vassal" (1.2.36–37). In Ponteach's "*Cabbin*," in the second scene, he tells his sons and his "*Generalissimo*" Tenesco more about his worries and his plans for a conspiracy, emphasizing the complex diplomatic predicaments of the Mohawk alliance with the English and sharing his dream about a "lordly Elk" (2.2.156) predicting victory over the English. Philip and Chekitan afterward show, respectively, optimism and pessimism toward this project, the latter being especially worried about his love for the Mohawk princess Monelia. But Philip suggests that he leave such diplomatic worries to him and serve as military commander instead. In a solus scene, in the end, we learn about Philip's heinous plan to take revenge for a former humiliation concerning a female slave and kill Monelia and her brother, Torax—in order to blame the crime on the English and inherit the Indian empire.

In the third act, Chekitan encounters Monelia and Torax in the forest, where he confesses his love for her but is ridiculed by the maiden's clever retorts and her examples of (Christian) male deception. She first rejects Chekitan and leaves him with Torax, who regrets his Mohawk "Father's wrong-turn'd Policy" (3.1.151). Chekitan continues to worry about the oncoming conflict and especially about the safety of Monelia. In scene 2, Ponteach gets advice from the Indian conjurer and the French priest, who both want to know about his dream and encourage his plans, which the priest sees as an occasion for the French to regain control over the region. But he also has plans to "gain the *Mohawk* Princess to [his] Wishes" (3.2.87). The third scene presents a big Indian council with many chiefs from different clans giving long, formal speeches. They regret the "large Encroachments on [their] common Rights" by the English (3.3.73), and finally decide to go to war against them. The French priest confirms them in their plans, and the scene ends with much hatchet brandishing in a tumultuous war song and dance spectacle.

Act 4 opens in a grove, with the brothers and Tenesco discussing their war strategies and respective duties, and Chekitan still worrying about Monelia's safety; a concern that is confirmed in scene 2, when the French priest tries to rape her. But Monelia is saved by Chekitan and now offers herself to him as his "lawful Prize" (4.2.70). She wishes him good fortune to win laurels in the war. In the third scene, Philip and

Ponteach discuss Chekitan's lovesickness but then are relieved to receive the good news about the uprising, of many victories, forts taken and enemies slain. They toss around the scalps of the English offenders we encountered in act 1 and look forward to torturing their captives, the Honnyman family. In the last scene of act 4, the hunter and his wife discuss their hopeless situation. At the urging of Mrs. Honnyman, her husband confesses and expresses regret for his crimes, pleading with Ponteach for the life of his family. Against the wish of the cruel Philip, the great chief shows mercy; he frees Honnyman's wife and children and decides to kill only "the great hunter *Honnyman*" (4.4.206).

After this emotional climax, act 5 of *Ponteach* continues with more cruelty, when Philip murders the sleeping Monelia and Torax, wounds himself, and blames the English for the murder of this "royal Blood" (5.1.58). In scene 2, the Indians plan a big funeral at the Senate House, and the wretched Chekitan grieves over his loss. Scene 3 shows the Indian wake in a grove, where Chekitan asks himself many maddening questions of reproach, until Torax, who has miraculously survived the attack, wakes up and tells them about the real murderer. The shocked Chekitan vows revenge. Consequently, in the next scene, he kills his brother, Philip, who succumbs without resistance. Chekitan, now without any hope left, kills himself and is found by Tenesco. In scene 5, the final scene of the play, Ponteach is again at the public Senate House, grieving his private loss and learning that the rebellion has failed. Though he has lost his empire, he is not vanquished but will move west to recover. You cannot kill a man who is larger than life: "*Ponteach* I am, and shall be *Ponteach* still" (5.5.102). *Finis*.

A Centrifugal Aesthetics of Contradictions

If *Ponteach* falls between the categories, this makes the play even more interesting because it forces us to reconsider our categorizations and reassess the nature of its "subliterary" qualities. What makes it such a curious play is the fact that, despite Rogers's firsthand knowledge, its plot ultimately moves from realism into a fantasy realm imitating the dominant heroic drama (mostly) and a private plot of the rivalry between two of Ponteach's invented sons, Philip and Chekitan.[10] Obviously Rogers should have known better than to rely on all these European conventions (and I will show below that there are many more). The interesting question therefore is, Why did he do it anyway? Instead of seeing these contradictions in *Ponteach* as an aesthetic weakness, like most of his other critics do, I want to tackle this play text as a rich array of relevant links to issues that reflect real tensions of history, culture, artistic representation, and the role of Major Rogers, that is, this text is constantly pointing beyond its own contained textual nature. In that sense, it is a fascinating aesthetic brew that offers "the works" to any scholar of cultural studies.

This incoherent and even contradictory mongrel script certainly cannot gratify the ideals of any formalist criticism. *Ponteach* forces us to leave the comfort zone of text or logic and to acknowledge that inside it outside influences collide. Thus it gives us access to these impositions and motivates us to understand their impact. Its aesthetic work is not mere deconstruction, about the reshuffling of old representations, but rather it triggers our learning about complexities in the real world. The very contradictions in the script thus make reality "matter" in the literal sense of contextuality, of what is more than text (or its deferred attachment, concept). *Ponteach* is certainly not a traditional *pièce bien faite*. In our case, this would be the wrong yardstick to assess artistic quality. Its many contradictions challenge us in ways that are different from William Empson's seven kinds of ambiguity or poststructuralist undecidability.

Therefore, my approach here will be different. We can make sense of Major Rogers's play only by going beyond textual fusion and confusion. I will not offer any excuses for the disharmonies in this play, but I will show that they are hard and jarring, and I shall examine the text as a referential tool that points beyond itself, as a link to multiple and highly interesting cultural and historical issues at its origins. In that sense, I want to discuss the outside influences on the text that have caused it. Mikhail Bakhtin would probably use the term *centrifugal* to describe this discursive quality, namely, "the uninterrupted processes of decentralization and disunification" that mark the "contradiction-ridden, tension-filled unity of two embattled tendencies in the life of language" (272), or simply "dialogized heteroglossia" (273). As opposed to the modernists and their aesthetic followers, who adore the fusion of opposites within language and work, as Hart Crane would put it, "For the Marriage of Faustus and Helen," Bakhtin does not believe in such weddings or "unitary" language. He rather accuses it of a lack of realism: "Unitary language . . . is opposed to the realities of heteroglossia" (270).[11] And he adds that "a unitary language gives expression to forces working toward concrete verbal and ideological unification and centralization, which develop in vital connection with the processes of sociopolitical and cultural centralization" (271). This is of course exactly the opposite of what was happening in the cultural crisis surrounding Major Rogers in the Great Lakes. Thus we can only appreciate the aesthetic qualities of *Ponteach* once we understand the relevance of the "centrifugal forces" that point outside it. *Ponteach* is an aesthetically rich text because it opens up our interest in a specific time period that has been sadly neglected by scholarly fashions and confronts us with two of its major heroes, the Ottawa chief Pontiac and the colonial ranger Major Rogers, whose lives are as adventurous as it gets and were crucially relevant in their own time. Like any good literary text, this play raises its own questions about ethics, gender, race, class, and all the other topics that literary studies is so fond of. In that sense, *Ponteach* is also a formidable teaching tool in the classroom to learn about the basics of drama, British colonialism, and intercultural relations by way of this specific example from the Great Lakes. We can apply almost any kind of theory to this text and its overflowing richness.

Obviously, *Ponteach* was written at a time of transition. Published a mere decade before the Declaration of Independence, it gives us a vision of the western expansion of the First British Empire at the end of the Seven Years War. But Rogers wrote the wrong play at the wrong time. Because of these historical developments, he was soon ignored. This transnational author will not fit in any canons of national literature. Rogers's voice is about neither Pilgrims nor Cavaliers, and it cannot be justified as a politically correct minority voice. His work goes beyond the categories of our usual expectations.

Part I

Outside *Ponteach*

The Players and
the Historical Context

1

Who Was Pontiac?

When we search the term "Pontiac" in the University of Michigan's Mirlyn catalog, we find over 340 entries, of which the first 120 deal with a town of that name and its history—to a great extent church archives. Pontiac, to be sure, is the name of a city in Michigan famous for its tradition of building a General Motors car also called the Pontiac and of international fame. Yet both go back to the famous Ottawa chief and best known indigenous inhabitant of the area, notorious for his involvement in the Siege of Detroit of 1763 and the general insurgency of the Indians in the Northwest at that time: the historical Pontiac, who knew the historical Major Rogers personally.

Unfortunately, we do not know much about Pontiac. As G. H. Orians writes: "Pontiac first sprang to notice in literature in the journals of Major Rogers" (part 1 146). In fact, he was first put "on the map" of European consciousness in the *Concise Account of North America* (1765): "Ponteack is their present King or Emperor, who has certainly the largest empire and greatest authority of any Indian Chief that has appeared on the continent since our acquaintance with it. He puts on an air of majesty and princely grandeur, and is greatly honoured and revered by his subjects" (Rogers 240).[1] This book was highly praised and raised much interest: it was immediately translated into German by Johann Tobias

Eine kurze Nachricht

von

Nord-America,

enthaltend:

Eine Beschreibung von den verschiedenen Britti-
schen Pflanzungen an dem festen Lande, nebst den
Inseln Neufundland, Cap Breton und St. Johann,

Ferner:

Ihre Lage, Umfang, Himmelsstrich, Erdboden,
Producte unter und über der Er , Regiment,
Religion, gegenwärtige Gränzen und die Zahl der
Einwohner, wie hoch ungefähr jede geschätzt wird.

Darauf folgen:

Die innern, oder westlichen Länder von Nord-
Amerika an den Strömen St. Lorenz, Mißißippi,
Christino und den großen Seen.

Diesem allen ist noch beygefügt:

Eine Nachricht von den verschiedenen Völkern
und Stämmen der wilden Indianer, ihren Sitten,
Gewohnheiten, Regiment, Anzahl, wie auch von
denen d Landen eigenen Thieren.

verfasset

und mit nützlichen und unterhaltenden Anmerkungen, die man nirgends bey andern Schriftstellern
finden wird   von

Robert Rogers,

Königl. Großbritannischen Major.

Aus dem Englischen übersetzt und mit einigen Anmerkungen und neuen Zusätzen erläutert

von

Johann Tobias Köhler

Professor zu Göttingen, Ephorus des Königl. und Chur-
fürstl. Historischen Instituts und der Chur-Maynzischen
Academie der nützlichen Wissenschaften Mitgliede.

Ersten Bandes, erste Abtheilung.

Title page of the German translation of Robert Rogers's *Concise Account*, translated as *Eine kurze Nachricht* by Johann Tobias Köhler of Göttingen University (1767). (Courtesy of William L. Clements Library, University of Michigan)

Köhler, a professor at Göttingen University, who published *Eine kurze Nachricht von Nord-Amerika* in 1767. Later it was reprinted in Dublin in 1769. Since that time Pontiac has mainly been the object of dime novels, savage mythification, and—fortunately—some historical research.

Francis Parkman's *Conspiracy*

For a long time, the course of history and the American Revolution had other priorities than the memory of Pontiac and the colonial Indian uprising, and it was not until the popular historian Francis Parkman wrote his highly successful *Conspiracy of Pontiac* in 1851 that the great indigenous chief became a household name in the United States. Parkman's depiction of Pontiac was clearly racist, and in his emphasis of Pontiac's "conspirational" agency, he both overestimated his power as the single head of the Indian insurgency of 1763 and clearly misrepresented the organizational structures of Indian warfare (an overvaluation that may actually go back to Rogers's earlier depiction of Ponteach's "scheming").[2] Richard White writes that "Parkman created a Pontiac to fit his dramatic needs. He derived Pontiac from Robert Rogers's *Concise Account of North America* and his *Ponteach: A Tragedy*, but even though Rogers had actually met Pontiac, the Ottawa chief of his play was a literary invention" (270). Parkman had of course also read Rogers's other work. But as opposed to Rogers, Parkman describes Pontiac in much more racist terms, as an inscrutable Other,[3] for example, in his negotiations with the interpreter La Butte: "Pontiac stood listening, armed with the true impenetrability of an Indian" (237).[4] But Parkman also projects Christian religious imagery in a negative way, when he finds that "the heart of the savage was unmoved as a rock" (237), or simply talks about "Pontiac, the Satan of this forest paradise [whose] fierce heart would burn with the anticipation of vengeance on the detested English" (217). And in the chapter titled "The Treachery of Pontiac," we read that "the conduct of Pontiac is marked with blackest treachery; . . . He could govern, with almost despotic sway, a race unruly as the winds. In generous thought and deed, he rivaled the heroes of ancient story" (228). If Parkman finds the Indian of heroic stature in the sense of antiquity, he also characterizes his behavior as unreliable and savage: "Pontiac, hideous in his war-paint, leaped into the central area of the village. . . . Warrior after warrior caught the fierce contagion, and soon the ring was filled with dancers, circling round and round with frantic gesture, and startling the distant garrison with unearthly yells" (233). This is reminiscent of the venerable descriptions of "red devils" in the old Puritan captivity narratives.[5] Referring to prophetic signs of calamity and warnings of King Philip's War, Parkman notes that in Detroit, "drops of rain began to fall, of strong, sulphurous odor, and so deeply colored that the people, it is said, collected them and used them for writing" (212).[6] And even when he abstains from metaphysical categorizing, Parkman's racism constantly emphasizes the "glaring faults of Pontiac's character. . . . He was artful and treacherous, bold, fierce, ambitious, and revengeful" (257). Yet artfulness, as I will discuss later, is of course another quality of the powerful antagonist.

At the same time, it is clear that Parkman was inspired by some vocabulary in Rogers's work. In his *Concise Account* the major summarizes his encounter with "Ponteack" as follows: "In short, his whole conversation sufficiently indicated that he was far from considering himself as a conquered Prince, and that he expected to be treated with the respect and honour due to a King or Emperor, by all who came into his country, or treated with him" (243). Rogers had his own reasons to inflate Pontiac's power, and he also characterizes the chief as a typical antagonist schemer: "Nothing was in the way to complete his scheme" (243). Parkman in fact relies on Rogers in many ways, and he even included the two first scenes of *Ponteach* in his book (as reprinted in the appendix of the 1991 Library of America edition), commenting: "The first act exhibits in detail the causes which led to the Indian war" (853).[7] Rogers thus receives the seal of approval from the famous historian.

Yet Parkman's conspirational view of Pontiac probably goes back to Robert Navarre's *Journal ou Dictation d'une Conspiration faite par les Sauvages Contre les Anglais, et du Siège du fort du Detroix par quatre nations différentes.* As M. Agnes Burton writes in her preface of the bilingual 1912 edition: "It is the document upon which Francis Parkman so cleverly built his history of the events of 1763" (7). Even the well-known historian Allan Nevins still writes in the preface to the 1914 Caxton Club edition of *Ponteach*: "Small attention . . . has been paid to Pontiac's life and character, for the obvious reason that Parkman's account of his conspiracy gives an inimitably full and fascinating relation of both, in a book familiar to almost every American home" (n.p.). Only Howard Peckham's *Pontiac and the Indian Uprising* finally corrects this representation from the scheming of a devilish individual "conspiracy" to a general "Indian uprising" with which Pontiac is associated by a simple "and." In a footnote, Peckham states that he is "at variance with Parkman's thesis. Parkman believed that Pontiac was the initiator and strategist of the whole war" (108n).[8] Peckham is the most detailed biographer of Pontiac and based his study on ethnographic insights about Indian warfare: "In the beginning there was only a local conspiracy at Detroit directed by Pontiac, who, however, improvised a more general uprising after his initial tactics failed. . . . It was Napoleon who said that generalship was the art of improvisation" (111). But Pontiac "set in motion the most formidable Indian resistance the English-speaking people had yet faced" (322).

Howard Peckham and Beyond

Though still steeped in some traditional European imagery (also see John C. Dann's foreword on the sometimes antiquated ethnic vocabulary [xvii]), Peckham's *Pontiac and the Indian Uprising* (1947) is a gold mine of cultural and historical information on the great chief's upbringing, tracing his life and the rebellion that made him famous. It was intended as "an investigation of the life and times of Pontiac" (xxi). Peckham discusses the French exploration, the beaver trade, and speculates on the education of Pontiac, on his name (19), and on his younger years. We learn about Ottawa war chiefs and civil chiefs (22) as well as "medal chiefs": "White men would decorate them with medals or gorgets and declare them to be chiefs in the eyes of the great white father across the Atlantic" (23). Peckham explains: "This king-making was an old game in European diplomacy which is still played around the globe" (23). As we shall learn, supporting such chiefs played into the very cultural expectations of gift-distributing chiefdom.[9]

Peckham also reports on the traditional activities of the four seasons, for example: "Summer was the season for making war" (25). Most important, he takes much time to describe the dire economic situation of the Indians after the English takeover of Detroit, explaining the causes of the war. Peckham describes Pontiac as a victim of lies about help from French troops as a "last subterfuge of the renegade French" (235). And he gives us Pontiac's French note of capitulation to Major Gladwin, whom he addresses as *"mon frère"* (237). The historian then minutely traces Pontiac's traveling and trading after the uprising, until his violent death in Cahokia in 1769. Already during his lifetime, the war leader's influence had been overestimated when he was stylized into a chief. Thus Richard White quotes the superintendent of Indian affairs, Sir William Johnson, who remarked: "[The] Indians are very Jalouse of pondiac & want to Chuse another Chief they think we make too much of him" (qtd. 313).[10] As a result, he was alienated from his people: "By 1768, Pontiac was both the most famous Indian in the *pay d'en haut* and a man without a home" (Peckham 313). Thus he "died ignominiously in the dirty street of a French village, his death a monument to the limits of chiefdomship" (313).

Peckham reports on this transformation in Pontiac's speeches as reported by Navarre in French, including some particular phrasings (e.g., "bad birds," 131). We learn about much wampum giving at the peace conference at Fort Ontario—sometimes Peckham uses mere noun phrases to dramatize the repetitive action: "A belt of six rows" (293). Here is his synoptic characterization of the big chief, projecting focalization from within: "He had a cause to defend, a dream of life as it should be, and, gambling on the possibility of success, he struck in the manner he knew best. When he made his peace he kept it and resigned himself to living with the invaders he could not evict. Savage though he was, he never degenerated into a whining beggar" (321).

There are, of course, other works on Pontiac, but many of them are not of much scientific substance. Thomas Guthrie Marquis's *War Chief of the Ottawas* (1920) has a very limited bibliography but provides some beautiful maps of the colonial Northwest; it is still in print, in a 2015 edition. Emil Engelhardt's publication of 1944 abstains from too many racist commentaries in *Pontiac im grossen Indianerkrieg*—probably because Nazi Germany was more interested in indicting the enemy Anglo-Americans. And Clide Hollmann's *Pontiac, King of the Great Lakes* (1968) is a fictionalized popular history narrative that offers a cover picture of Pontiac's first encounter with Major Rogers, courtesy of the Pontiac Motor Division. Hollmann, shown with hunting gear and a dead deer on the book sleeve, writes a whole chapter about that encounter, heavily based on Rogers's own account in the *Concise Account*. A short biography that offers beautiful documentation is Celia Bland's *Pontiac, Ottawa Rebel* (1995) of the North American Indians of Achievement series. Timothy J. Todish and Todd E. Harburn's *A "Most Troublesome Situation"* (2006) is a lavishly illustrated history of the "Pontiac Uprising of 1763–64" by independent history writers with a military interest. These samples give us a sense of the cultural scope of Pontiac research.

But also academic historians who are more aware of the colonial power imbalance have continued writing about Pontiac; more recent

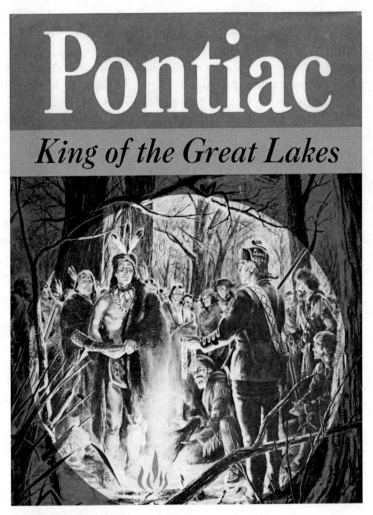

Clide Hollmann's cover (1968) includes a painting from the Pontiac Motor Division: *Pontiac Meets with Major Robert*s.

examples include Francis Jennings's *Empire of Fortune* (1988), William Nester's *Haughty Conquerors* (2000), Gregory Evans Dowd's *War under Heaven* (2002), and David Dixon's *Never Come to Peace Again* (2005). As Dowd summarizes: "The late Francis Jennings, Parkman's severest modern critic, . . . dismisses Pontiac's importance, while Howard Peckham, the most detailed and scholarly biography to date, busts

Pontiac from great chief to local commander. Most recently, William R. Nester has thrown Pontiac out of the title of the war altogether and has renamed it for General Jeffrey Amherst, to whom he assigns responsibility for the disaster" (*War* 5).[11] Dowd notes: "We have so many Pontiacs and counter-Pontiacs because, in part, we have so little evidence for the man" (6). According to him, the "most complete description of Pontiac's appearance—complete with nose rings and imperious bearing" is still provided by Robert Rogers (7). In the same way, he still considers Parkman a "touchstone work" despite its "Anglo-Saxonism and racism," a book "valuable for its many keen insights as well as for its famous prose" (7). Dowd negotiates his position between all these other perspectives: "If Parkman promotes Pontiac to a status he could not have held, Jennings, Peckham, and Nester demote Pontiac too far" (9).[12] He concludes: "In its origins, in its unfolding, in its many endings and turbulent aftermath, [Pontiac's War] revealed spiritual yearnings that led Indians to seek intertribal unity against a British menace" (275).

Dixon primarily reexamines the "broad causes, conduct, and consequences" (xi), emphasizing the role of the frontier settlers in Pennsylvania as an early motivation for the American Revolution:

> Frustrated by their government's inability to contend with the Indians, the backcountry settlers concluded that the best way to insure security was to rely on their own devices. No longer were they willing to depend on an insensitive government in Philadelphia or a monarch three thousand miles away in England. While their urban neighbors along the seaboard fumed over taxation measures such as the Stamp Act and Townshend Duties, frontier folk were more exasperated over land issues and Indian affairs. In the end, the backwoodsman rejoined with the laborer to form the nucleus of George Washington's Continental Army. (xii)[13]

This may be another explanation for Washington's famous retreat to Valley Forge.[14] A very recent study is Michael A. McDonnell's *Masters of Empire: Great Lakes Indians and the Making of America* (2015), which mainly focuses on the role of the Anishinaabe Odawa (Ottawa) at L'Arbre Croche and the mixed Langlade family, emphasizing the role of the chief Pontiac less than the agency and negotiation of their fate ("masters") by the local Indians living near Michilimackinac—a crucial spot of interest for Robert Rogers, as we will see. Generally one can say that in more-recent Great Lakes historiography, the interest has shifted away from great figures like Pontiac and his heroic white antagonists. This trend also manifests itself in McDonnell's important renaming of the French and Indian War and of Pontiac's Rebellion as the First Anglo-Indian War and the Second Anglo-Indian War, respectively, thereby crucially accentuating a ring of imperialist conflict.

As a literature person I still find strong narrative qualities in many of these historical tomes, even beyond Parkman and Peckham. Thus Dixon focalizes through the interior perception of his protagonist when during the Siege of Detroit, "the resourceful Major Rogers noticed intense gunfire coming from one of the houses along the road" (179). And Dowd presents us with the same theatrical signature scene that we already know from Rogers himself (*Journals* 228): "When Belestre formally surrendered Detroit to Rogers on November 29, 1760, ragged blue-coated French troops lined up in the fort's central parade opposite the ragged, green-colored rangers and red-coated Royal Americans. With rolling drums, the red flag of Britain rose, until it floated above the wooden stockade of the fort to be viewed with resignation" (59–60).[15] Librarian Patrick Spero continues this tradition in *Frontier Rebels* with an explicit statement: "Ultimately, I decided that this book was about storytelling" (209). These observations on narrative history writing may serve as a good transition to the powerful fictional legacy about, and in many ways of, Pontiac.

Pontiac in Literature

Richard White emphasizes that the British magnified Pontiac's power as a rebel chief: "They made Pontiac the key to the peace that eluded them. A man whom they had initially scorned and sought to diminish they eventually elevated to near superhuman status" (297). Peckham summarizes the surviving legacy as follows:

> Pontiac's fame is preserved today in obvious forms and curious byways. A motorcar manufacturer has borrowed his name for its product, and a Detroit brewer even markets "Chief Pontiac Beer." Robert Rogers first put the Ottawa leader in a book in 1765 with an inflated and inaccurate account of his power, and first enshrined him in imaginative literature in a dramatic tragedy called *Ponteach*, published in 1766. But it was Francis

Parkman who actually dramatized him and spread his fame
throughout the English-speaking world. (318)

In the popular imagination, Pontiac has also survived in (mainly) dime
novels and children's books. A good source of information about this
legacy are George Orians's two articles titled "Pontiac in Literature."
Orians starts with Rogers and then moves on to Major John Richardson's *Wacousta* (1832) or A. C. Whitney's poetic verse drama *Pontiac, a
Drama of Old Detroit* (1910). It seems symptomatic of the representational situation that Orians mixes Beadle authors (i.e., dime novelists
like Osgood Bradbury) with the historian Parkman (155–56). Similarly,
Albert Black, in his 1959 article "The Pontiac Conspiracy in the Novel,"
presents among other sources Edward S. Ellis's popular *Pontiac, Chief of
the Ottawas* (1897) and writes that Pontiac was a "thorough savage [sic]"
and his faults "were the faults of his race and they cannot eclipse his
nobler qualities" (119). I found Ellis's earlier *Life of Pontiac the Conspirator, Chief of the Ottawas: Together with a Full Account of the Celebrated Siege
of Detroit* also in the Beadle's Dime Biographical Library (1861), a tale in
which whole pages are copied from Alexander Henry (see 70–82). Black
in turn also discusses the Beadle author Osgood Bradbury (1848), who
invented love affairs for Pontiac's fictional daughter Lunette and made
him die a peaceful death: "My noble chief sleeps and will never wake
[sic]" (99). Clarence Andrews offers a good listing of six Beadle and
Adams novels (33) and a long list of other popular novels on the Pontiac
uprising until the 1960s (34–35).

Orians's second article shows that recent representations of Pontiac
have been more enlightened: "To the Indian the concept of private
ownership of the land was preposterous and the ruthless demonstration of game-slaughtering, fence-building and deforestation was regarded by him as insane" (51). Still, we don't really know if Orians is
discussing fiction, history, ethnographic accuracy, or merely another
quest for the noble savage. He also mentions Kenneth R. Roberts's more
substantial 1937 novel *The Northwest Passage* on Robert Rogers, about
which we'll hear more later—though Roberts foregrounds a fictional
plot, he did some research at the Clements Library beforehand. As we
shall see, Roberts provides some interesting ideas about the composition of *Ponteach* as well. In Orians's second article we also read that
Margaret Gray's 1954 novel *Hatchet in the Sky* "was a heavy indictment
of Major Gladwyn, Henry Bouquet, and General Amherst for waging
germ warfare against the Indians, a warfare carried on in times of peace

and in the name of peace" (36). Its title is based on a line from *Ponteach* (1.4.69), when the Indian threatens "Governor Sharp." Orians also mentions a series of novels by Hervey Allan and Neil Swanson's novels *The Judas Tree* (1933) and *Unconquered* (1947): "Pontiac's Conspiracy, claimed Swanson, was rather a conspiracy on the part of such traders as Garth and Croghan to carve out larger empires for themselves" (40). In the mid-twentieth century, the tide of sympathy shifted, and there is an effort to better understand the military strategies of the indigenous. In a reference to the taking of Michilimackinac, Orians writes: "Only if we condemn the wooden horse of the Greeks and cease to regard Ulysses as an epic hero have we the right to condemn the use of a game of lacrosse to gain forts that Indian experience had no resource but ingenuity to secure" (50). Such understanding is appreciated, but it remains a limited piece in the puzzle. More-recent publications about Pontiac overlooked by Orians's survey are Sergeant William H. Bunce's *War-Belts of Pontiac (Red Wampum and White)* of 1943, a novel that wants to "keep alive the spirit of the buckskin man" (back cover), and Mike Roarke's *Silent Drums: Pontiac's Rebellion (1763–1765)* of the First Frontier Series (1994), in "the tradition of *The Last of the Mohicans*" (back cover). Both propagate a rather traditional, unenlightened view of indigenous culture, based on the white man's perspective.

The famous chief has also fascinated writers and readers outside the United States. I cannot go through all the translations and original books written in foreign languages, but one example is the work of the Swiss author Ernst Herzig, who wrote a whole series of novelizing histories about "Berühmte Indianer, weisse Kundschafter" under the pseudonym of "Ernie Hearting," among them volume 13, *Pontiac: Sendung und Schicksal eines grossen Indianerhäuptlings* (1961), based on eight translated sources, among them Kenneth Roberts. Thus the fiction about Pontiac has created even more fiction. In the same adventure-novel category belong Elmar Engel's *Pontiac—Häuptling der Ottawa* and Caspar de Fries's self-published *Aufstand der Indianer*. A French contribution in the same vein is Léon Thoorens's *Pontiac, Prince de la prairie* of 1953.

Yet another intermedial dimension manifests itself in *Ponteach: A Melodrama for Narrator and Piano* (1977) by Lejaren Hiller, who was a "pioneer in the creation of computer music" (Glover 183). Following Rogers's text "with minor editing," the opera begins and ends with a soliloquy by Ponteach. In between we have five scenes with the main white oppressors from act 1 much coinciding with Parkman's selection from the original *Ponteach*. Hiller uses the literary qualities of the play in his selections and is certainly inspired by them in his verbal adaptations that profit from Rogers more than they add. Kallisti Music states on its website:

> The music accompanying all this is no mere background, but a powerfully focused passacaglia based on the Ojibway war song "Scarlet Is Its Head." Other Ojibway and Ottawa music is quoted throughout, as are such contemporary British tunes as "The British Grenadiers" and "Do You Know the Muffin Man"— all in service of the dramatic conception, yet totally integrated into a complex and independent musical structure. One of Hiller's finest works, Ponteach is both a musical *tour de force* and a powerful dramatic experience.[16]

Unfortunately, no recording of any performance can be found.

Children's Books

Another set of curiosa that shows us the scope of mythifications about Pontiac's life are the many children's books. The Ottawa chief is included in Edson Leone Whitney and Frances M. Perry's *Four American Indians: King Philip, Pontiac, Tecumseh, Osceola; A Book for Young Americans* (1904). Kate Dickinson Sweetser's *Book of Indian Braves* (1913) has a chapter on Pontiac, whom she calls (like Peckham?) "this Indian Napoleon" (183). Mary M. Green and Irma Johnson's *Three Feathers: The Story of Pontiac* (1960) is mainly about the city of Pontiac and its automobile factory, though it also mentions Pontiac's childhood as "Little Bear" (37). John William Tebbel and Earl W. De la Vergne's *Red Runs the River: The Rebellion of Chief Pontiac* (1966) addresses "young readers." It shows significant understanding for the situation of the Indians of the Old Northwest: "The French had always been their friends. They sat in the tepees of the red men and ate and drank with them. Sometimes they married the daughters of the Indians. Most important, the French had nearly always been willing to supply the tribes with guns and powder; although the Indians had sometimes used the weapons to make war against the white men (even the French on occasion), they employed them much more often to hunt the game on which their lives depended" (9). And it shows how this situation changed after the Seven Years War, when the English "severely restricted the sale of powder. That meant real

Cover of Howard Peckham's children's book on Pontiac (1963).

hardship for the Indians, who had to hunt with the old-fashioned and less efficient bow-and-arrow" (10). Still there is a teacherly tone, "But Pontiac was a stubborn man, and a proud one" (148), and a final assessment reminiscent of Parkman: "Pontiac left behind him a record of cruelty and horror" (184).

Curiously, Howard Peckham himself contributed to this field: *Pontiac, Young Ottawa Leader* in the Childhood of Famous Americans series (1963) is dedicated to his "dear sister Thelma." It describes Indian

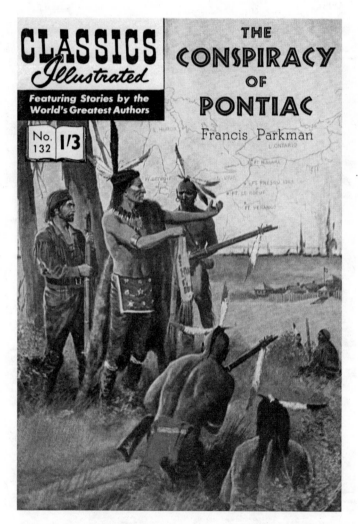

Cover of the Classics Illustrated graphic novel based on Parkman's
Conspiracy of Pontiac (1967).

child rearing, fishing, making maple sugar, the fur trade, and a first contact with whites in a chapter titled "The White Captive." The Indian mother shows empathy for the young captive: "They should let him go. . . . He doesn't want to be an Indian" (139). The book tries to create understanding for the Indians' way of life and treats the war only at the end, when the adult Pontiac meets Major Roberts: "'We need powder for hunting,' Pontiac said. / The officers talked among themselves. / 'We will give you powder,' Major Rogers said. 'After your canoes are packed and you are ready to go hunting, you will get some powder.' / The chiefs were won over" (171). Conflicts are avoided. The book also includes a timeline, "When Pontiac Lived," from 1720 to 1769, and notes contemporary events (193), a pedagogical "Do You Remember?" section with suggested further activities, and "Interesting Words in This Book." Obviously, Peckham felt the need to participate in such an educational project—possibly to counterbalance the influence of books such as *Tom Edison*, *Robert E. Lee*, or even *Jeff Davis* in this Childhood of Famous Americans series.[17]

The life of Pontiac continues to be taught to children. Thus there is a Classics Illustrated graphic-novel adaptation of *The Conspiracy of Pontiac* that claims to be based on Francis Parkman, published in 1967. Matthew G. Grant's *Pontiac: Indian General and Statesman* (1974) of the Gallery of Great Americans series, Virginia Frances Voight's *Pontiac, Mighty Ottawa Chief* (1977), Jane Fleischer's *Pontiac, Chief of the Ottawas* (1979), and Jill C. Wheeler's *Forest Warrior: The Story of Pontiac* (1989) of the Famous American Indian Leaders series are at times beautifully illustrated short biographies that start with descriptions of his childhood and then basically follow the events of Pontiac's life as popularized by Parkman. The latest contribution in this field that I found is the first volume in Jeffery Schatzer's Professor Tuesday's Awesome Adventures in History series, *Chief Pontiac's War*, published in 2009. Also little Pontiac figurines to play with abound (see next page).[18]

Pontiac figurine from a Ferrero Chocolate Surprise Egg
for children.

2

The Adventurous Life
of Major Robert Rogers

If we know little about Pontiac's life, we definitely have more information about Rogers—yet his life was as adventurous and made as
mythified, often by the very same authors. At some point in his life,
Rogers was indeed a celebrity whose military exploits in the French
and Indian War were regularly reported by the gazettes on the East
Coast and in London. The young American was highly respected by his
superiors and envied by many English officers. Several letters *"To Major
Rogers"* which are signed in a language of respect are quoted by Rogers,
for example: "I am, Sir, Your most obedient, *Jeff. Amherst"* (*Journals*
143). Amherst was, after all, no less than the chief commander of the
English troops in North America. He had signed another letter less
modestly: "By his Excellency Jeffrey Amherst, Esq.; Major General and
commander in chief of all his Majesty's forces in North America, & c. &
c. & c." (197).[1] Rogers's contemporaries compared him with British war
heroes such as General James Wolfe or Amherst himself. John Ross reports that

> no North American figure captured the imagination of George
> II's still undivided subjects all around the North Atlantic world
> [more] than Rogers. Newspapers and broadsheets acclaimed his

exploits on snowshoes, in bloody ambuscade, and on grueling long-distance raids. His unmatched—perhaps unprecedented—mastery of the prodigious, untamed North American wilderness not only showed the British how to win but revealed that they could out-match the wood-savvy French *coureurs des bois*, with their long-dreaded mystique, and native warriors of the Eastern Woodlands. In a 1759 issue of *The London Chronicle*, Benjamin Franklin boasted that "one ranging Captain of a few *Provincials*, *Rogers*, has harassed the enemy more on the frontiers of *Canada*, and destroyed *more* of their men, than the whole army of *Regulars*." (353, italics in original)[2]

Ross summarizes: "In the London of 1765, two years after France had been brought to a humiliating peace at Paris, Rogers's fame exceeded that of any other North American, Franklin and George Washington included" (353). No wonder, "Rogers received many invitations from Londoners curious to see the hero of backwoods America" (362). Caleb Stark, son of the famous General John Stark of the American Revolution, who had started his military career as one of Rogers's Rangers, renders a telling anecdote of the Old World about the "highwayman on Houndslow Heath. The robber, thrusting a pistol through the coach window, demanded the purses and watches of the occupants. While others were taking out their valuables, the bold American ranger suddenly seized the man by the collar, by main strength drew him through the coach window, and ordered the coachman to drive on. The captive was an old offender, for whose apprehension a reward of fifty pounds sterling had been offered by the government" (388). This colonial American soldier fired the imagination of his contemporaries. It was during his stay in London that Rogers wanted to boost his career and published his three books in a very short time: *The Journals of Major Robert Rogers* (1765), the *Concise Account of North America* (1765), and the play *Ponteach* (1766).[3]

Biographies

If we want to know more about Rogers's life, we can study his biographies. But we have to understand that after the American Revolution he became (and for many still is) a mere footnote in American history and culture. For more than a century, his books were not reprinted, and his old cartographer Jonathan Carver reaped all the literary laurels for the Northwest exploration planned and financed by Rogers in his *Travels through America, 1766–1768* (1788), which inspired European writers and philosophers like Chateaubriand and Rousseau with notions of the noble savage. As Allan Nevins writes in a footnote: "It is interesting to note that for Carver's description of the beaver, bear, and porcupine, pp. 282, 274, and 279 of the *Travels*, he drew almost verbatim from Rogers paragraphs upon the same, pp. 253, 259, and 263 of the *Concise Account*" (*Ranger* 96n). It was Nevins, the much-decorated Columbia University historian, who rediscovered Rogers after he had been kept under wraps for such a long time. In 1913 Nevins wrote "Introduction to Roger's 'Ponteach'" as his MA thesis at the University of Illinois, which was, however, more a biography than a literary analysis. He later elaborated it into an introduction for the 1914 Caxton Club edition of *Ponteach*.[4] It is highly readable, well researched, and full of solid information. But as far as mythification is concerned, note that nowadays, this biography can also be bought as *Ranger: The Adventurous Life of Robert Rogers and the Rangers* in Leonaur's Military Commanders Series (2011).[5]

John Cuneo's *Robert Rogers of the Rangers*, an Oxford University Press biography of 1959, is another good read, full of facts describing the major's colorful life. As a lawyer, Cuneo also understands the predicaments created by Rogers's debts. He includes very personal information about Rogers's marriage and the relations with his superiors who destroyed his career. A more fiction-inspired biography published as a popular paperback is John Ross's *War on the Run: The Epic Story of Robert Rogers and the Conquest of America's First Frontier* (2009). It offers many maps, a list of dramatis personae, and a detailed chronology. This book is obviously the stuff of hero making and triggers our imagination by conjuring up much of the historical context of Rogers's life. In that sense it borders on Kenneth Roberts's fictional re-creation of Rogers. But in a significant way, Ross's book, like the recent Nevins reprint, indicates renewed interest in Rogers as a historical figure, mainly from the perspective of military historians, who are fascinated by the Ranger's exploits. A typical example of the latter is the 2002 Purple Mountain edition of Rogers's *Journals*, annotated by Timothy J. Todish and lavishly illustrated by Gary S. Zaboly. One sortie after the other is documented, and background is provided in great detail. Both Todish and Zaboly have published several other books on colonial military warfare. And like them, many other post-Vietnam writers have adopted Rogers as the original American "green beret" (see Loescher's multivolume history of the Rangers).[6]

Becoming a Ranger

It is not easy to summarize Robert Rogers's life in a few paragraphs.
Rogers was born in 1731 in Methuen, Massachusetts, into a family of
Northern Irish, that is, Protestant, immigrants. He grew up on a farm in
New Hampshire, which was at one point destroyed by Abenaki Indians,
who had fled to Canada and were incited by the French to return and
raid the new English settlers.[7] Norman Gelb describes the Rogers family
as "simple folk," for whom "Poverty and French and Indian marauders
were a constant threat" (14). After getting involved in counterfeiting,[8]
young Robert was arrested, but he found the need for volunteers in the
New Hampshire militia to be a useful way out of this difficult situation.
He soon became a successful fighter and commander in the French and
Indian War and started hiring his own so-called Rangers, among them
his two brothers, James and Richard, and several men who later became famous Revolutionary War heroes, such as the Generals Israel
Putnam and John Stark.[9]

Caleb Stark writes in the memoir of his father, John, that Rogers
"was from his youth inured to the hardship of frontier life, from which
circumstances he acquired a decision and boldness of character which
served him in after years" (387). He describes the Ranger as follows:
"The enemy dreaded him and his daring followers with good reason. . . .
They penetrated into the enemy's country, and destroyed French settlements and Indian villages, sometimes at four hundred miles' distance.
They were in truth the most formidable body of men ever employed in
the early wars of America, and in every regular engagement proved
themselves not inferior to British troops. To their savage and French
foes they were invincible" (387). Ross almost seems to echo this, adding
a crucial intercultural note: "It would be Rogers's signature genius to
see how a higher synthesis of Old and New World practices could create
a new and formidable mode of warfare; the invisibility and sweeping
range of the forest peoples would be cleverly united to the newcomers'
technologies, strategic vision, and cultural appetite for innovation"
(81). The same aspect already appears in Parkman: "Rogers's Rangers,
half hunters, half woodsmen, trained in a discipline of their own, and
armed like Indians, with hatchet, knife, and gun, were employed in a
service of peculiar hardship" (1994 ed. 161–62). And Cuneo writes:
"Rogers' Rangers, as they soon came to be called, often fighting behind
enemy lines and inflicting severe damage on enemy morale, comprised
the first organized corps of elite assault troops in American history"

(15). He notes that, although "many considered Rogers a boorish yokel and widely criticized the lack of traditional forms of discipline in the ranks of the Rangers, their achievements were for the most part much admired by the British command" (16). Todish observes in the illustrated Purple Mountain edition of Rogers's *Annotated and Illustrated Journals*: "It is known that at least for the 1758 campaign, Rogers's Rangers Companies were issued, for the first time, an official green uniform" (88).[10] Susan Glover also states: "Rogers' Rangers were not red-coated regulars. Garbed in a drab green wool that faded through the spring and summer, they quite literally melted into the landscape" (183). This element of camouflage manifested a totally different attitude toward warfare from the open-field group discipline of the regular redcoats that had proved so disastrously ineffective in General Braddock's campaign against Fort Duquesne. The internet is full of images contrasting green "rangers" and red "regulars." In that sense, Rogers and his Rangers stand at the origin of a self-consciousness of the colonial troops that would later lead to American independence. As Howard Peckham observes: "The inadequacy of British regiments for wilderness fighting was obvious to all but the most bullheaded British officers" ("Introduction" vi).

Guerilla Fighting

Caleb Stark relates how General William Alexander "gave Captain Rogers . . . a commission to recruit an independent corps of rangers" and quotes the orders "to use their best endeavors to stress the French and their allies by sacking, burning and destroying their houses, barns, barracks, canoes, batteaux, &c., and by killing their cattle of every kind; and at times to endeavor to waylay, attack and destroy their convoys of provisions by land and by water, in any part of the country where they could be found" (397). Dixon calls Rogers a "master of irregular warfare" (59). The Ranger writes on 2 February 1756 in his *Journals* about "setting fire to the houses and barns of the village, with which were consumed large quantities of wheat, and other grain," noting, "We also killed about fifty cattle, and then retired, leaving the whole village in flames" (12). He also lists orders from General Abercrombie "to penetrate into Canada, and distress the inhabitants, by burning their harvest (now nearly ripe) and destroying their cattle" (26–27). No wonder Rogers diligently enumerates in the *Journals* how many barns they burned and how many cattle they killed in their various forays. His feats were reported in the newspapers, for example, in the *Connecticut Gazette*: "Boston, March 29: On Tuesday Evening came to Town from Fort William Henry, at lake George, Captain Robert Rogers, who has made himself famous in these parts of America by his [illegible] and Activity with his Scalping Parties near Crown Point" (cited by Todish in Rogers, *Annotated and Illustrated Journals* 43). Ross calls the Rangers an "irregular military unit": "They were not provincial soldiers, because the crown paid them and they served under the rules and regulations of the British army; but neither were they regulars. While ranger officers drew pay approximately equal to their regular counterparts, privates drew twice as much pay as provincial soldiers, who themselves earned more than regular privates. Most important, the company served at the pleasure of the commander-in-chief, who could dissolve it at will" (113). The Rangers stood for a new kind of hit-and-run tactics in the French and Indian War, destroying military and civilian infrastructure. In that sense, Rogers has been celebrated as an inventor of modern warfare.

In 1756, John Campbell, the 4th Earl of Loudoun and then commander of the British North American forces "asked Rogers to write down the principles of successful bush warfare" (Todish in Rogers, *Annotated and Illustrated Journals* xix). This resulted in the famous twenty-eight "Rules of Ranging," recorded in Rogers's *Journals* (60–70). They still exist in several versions that inspire military enthusiasts.[11] Todish comments: "Rogers' Ranging rules are rightfully remembered as one of the first *written* manuals for irregular warfare in North America" (*Annotated and Illustrated Journals* 78). And Ross observes: "The genius of the rules lies in their complete simplicity and clarity, statements and principles that any soldier might comfortably hold in his head, to be summoned up and naturally put to use when a man was tired and scared" (157). He explains: "Rogers used long-standing Indian techniques that acknowledged the savage randomness of warfare in a trackless geography" (159). And further: "Here was a new kind of self-belief arisen among the New Englanders, whom the French and Canadians had long found to be ponderous and flat-footed in the woods" (160–61). The Rangers had to learn the twenty-eight rules so "as to be ready on any emergency to march at a minute's warning"—which Ross calls "a pioneering example of the Revolution's minute men" (145). Wikipedia offers a lavish page on the "Rules" as well. Not surprisingly, William Nester observes: "His twenty-eight 'Rules for Ranging' are still taught by today's American army rangers" (*Struggle* 23).

Bronze statue at the Rogers Island Visitors Center, Fort Edward, New York, dedicated to "Major Robert Rogers, Founder and Commanding Officer of Rogers Rangers in the French and Indian War. Author, in October of 1757, of the *Rules of Ranging*, which have been in use by the U.S. Army since that time." (Courtesy of the Rogers Island Heritage Development Alliance, Inc., Fort Edward, New York)

Glover also mentions Rogers's "particular talent for reconnaissance and scouting missions" and the Rangers' "ability to scout, gather intelligence, adopt the irregular tactics of the enemy, and engage in what we now call guerilla warfare" (180). But their relationship with the regular troops was complicated. This shows in the December 1757 mutiny on Rogers Island, outside Fort Edward,[12] which was prompted by illicit rum drinking: "Surrounding the guardhouse, the mob demanded the release of the prisoners therein, probably the two comrades earlier flogged" (Ross 151). The mutiny had much to do with the inhumane kind of discipline expected by British military commanders, a kind of

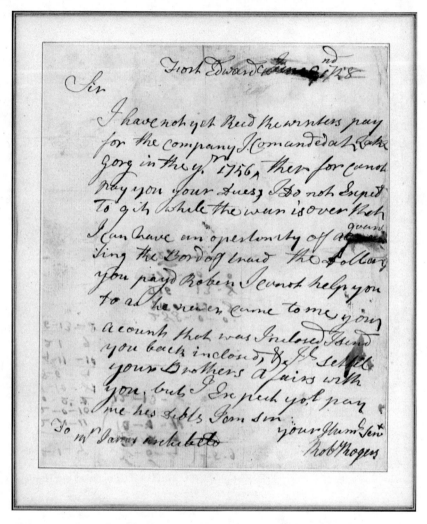

Letter by Robert Rogers, written at Fort Edward, 2 June 1758, in which he indicates his problems of not getting reimbursed for his Rangers' services. (Courtesy of William L. Clements Library, University of Michigan)

Kadavergehorsam, or blind obedience, that the Rangers rejected. As Ross reports: "Flogging proved the most common punishment. . . . On the parade ground stood the whipping post" (149). He explains: "British corporeal punishment particularly galled the entirely volunteer provincials, who viewed themselves in essence as short-term contract workers, hired to protect the immediate interests of their community"

(150). Obviously, there was a different military culture among the Rangers. Because they were often "the third and the fourth sons of the usual large frontier New England families, they knew that their eldest brother would inherit the ill-surveyed claims and brutally hard work of the farm" (147–48); as a consequence, "kinship and community ties softened military hierarchy, deeply alarming British officers with their democratic implications" (150). Todish writes of the social fabric of these colonial troops: "Rogers showed a genuine concern for his men, and in return earned their affection and loyalty" (*Annotated and Illustrated Journals* 17). The Rangers' success stemmed from their solidarity, mutual respect, and voluntary support, rather than mechanical obedience. It is similar to, and possibly anticipated, the militia culture of the independence movement.

Though the Rangers rebelled against redcoat discipline, they were certainly no choirboys. Their fighting was brutally violent, and they took no Indian prisoners. Ross writes: "From the outbreak of the war Indian prisoners taken by either side had never lived more than a few minutes from their capture: their very portable scalps possessed vastly greater value than their live bodies would have" (273–74). Scalping was a common habit. As Zaboly comments on his illustration of the 13 March 1758 Battle on Snowshoes: "The rest of Rogers' men remained to scalp the dead and dying on the brook. Rogers himself . . . vigorously engaged in such trophy-taking on this occasion and no doubt on many another. Scalps meant bounty money, and the memory of the Fort William Henry bloodbath, just seven months before, was still very fresh in the Rangers' minds" (Rogers, *Annotated and Illustrated Journals* 93). In the same volume, Todish also quotes an extract of a "Letter from Albany" in the *London Magazine* (October 1758): "Rogers pursued the enemy two miles but could not come up with them. The next day he buried his dead and scalped the enemy" (qtd. 142). The *Gentlemen's Magazine* gives us another taste of this kind of warfare: "They counted upwards of 100 dead bodies and believe there might be many more, but the stench was so great they could not stand it. *Rogers* buried all his dead" (qtd. *Annotated and Illustrated Journals* 142). And here is the *London Chronicle* for May 8–10, 1759: "By an express from Fort Edward last Saturday night, we have an account, that Major Rogers was on his return from a great scout, with upwards of 300 men, that he has taken five prisoners and six scalps, and killed about 30 of the enemy; our loss, it is said, is three men killed, one Mohawk wounded, and about 14 men frost-bitten" (qtd. *Annotated and Illustrated Journals* 157–58). Ross

"Scalping Ranger," figurine by John Jenkins. (Permission by the artist, http://www
.johnjenkinsdesigns.com/SRR-03.htm).

provides the most graphic description of scalping: "Despite the general
alarm that was bringing the enemy to them, Rogers had drawn his long
knife; then, pausing to grab his enemy's greasy hair with one hand, he
made a quick circular slash with the other. The scalp came off with a
pop, leaving a bright flash of bright skull. Carrying the bloody trophy
in his hand, with a battle scream emerging from his lips, Rogers ran
after Putnam" (93).[13] He adds: "The scalp created a sensation back at
camp; indeed, word of his turnabout trophy rippled back to the settled
lands, earning Rogers his first newspaper mention in *The Boston Gazette*
of 3 November 1755: 'Capt. Rogers . . . kill'd and scalp'd a Frenchman
within 70 Rods [385 yards] of said Fort [Carillion?]'" (93). Scalping did
of course happen on all sides, English, French, and Indian, and one of the
memorable tragedies of this practice is a result of the smallpox epidemic
at Fort William Henry (not reported in Cooper's *Last of the Mohicans*),

when the victorious "Odawa and Potawatomi warriors opened the graves of fallen English troops and scalped their corpses. Some of the fallen soldiers had died from smallpox, including Richard Rogers" (Widder, *Beyond* 34). Rogers's younger brother, Richard, had died during the siege of the fort, and his pathogen-laden scalp, together with others, turned the faraway Indian village L'Arbre Croche into a ghost town: "The windswept village, spreading for a mile or two along the shore, had been nearly exterminated in 1757" (Ross 386).

Superhero

The tales of the Rangers' sorties and their wilderness battles are innumerable.[14] Memorable is certainly the Battle on Snowshoes of 13 March 1758, which teaches us about winter warfare on the New England lakes and the use of *raquettes*, famously described in Thomas Brown's captivity narrative, which also includes a description of the gruesome scalping alive of Captain Speakman (or Spikeman) and his death and includes his last message to his wife (7–9). Another memorable incident of this period is "Rogers' Slide" down "Rogers' Rock," already described by Parkman: "The steep mountain called Rogers' Slide, near the northern end of Lake George, derives its name form the tradition that, during the French War, being pursued by a party of Indians, he slid on snowshoes down its precipitous front, for more than a thousand feet, to the frozen lake below" (1994 ed. 164). Ross writes: "After the battle, Bald Mountain became forever known as Rogers' Rock, and the face itself as Rogers' Slide. The legend of a superhuman escape spread across the trading routes of British North America" (181). As Glover notes, "It was not Rogers' engagements with 'the enemy' in his *Journals* but his overcoming the perils of snow, ice, rapids, dense forest, mountainous terrain, and starvation that engaged the imagination" (185–86). Rogers's reputation at that time must be seen as that of a superhero.[15] Even the historian Nester claims in 2017 that "Robert Rogers was not just America's greatest combat officer of the colonial era but arguably of all time" (*Struggle* 23).[16]

A particular battle to note is the attack on the Abenaki Indian village of St. Francis of November 1759, some two hundred miles into enemy territory, and back. Ross comments: "The brilliance of Rogers's idea to undertake the raid lay not in any massive tactical effect but in its strategic ability to rob the enemy of his nerve" (270). The major himself describes the attack in his *Journals* as follows:

> At half an hour before sun-rise I surprised the town when they
> were all fast asleep. . . . A little after sun-rise I set fire to all their
> houses, except three, in which there was corn, that I reserved for
> the use of the party.
>
> The fire consumed many of the Indians who had concealed
> themselves in the cellars and lofts of their houses. About seven
> o'clock in the morning the affair was completely over, in which
> time we had killed at least two hundred Indians. (147)

Rogers certainly had a desire for revenge against the Abenakis, who
had once destroyed his parents' farm. But today we are shocked by the
brutality of this guerilla warfare. Stephen Brumwell writes that "a new
generation of scholars has condemned the episode as a colonial Sand
Creek or My Lai" (186). As Francis Jennings observes, "The weapon of
deliberate, calculated terror was used extensively by powerful men on
Our Side as well as theirs" (xx), noting on St. Francis "that the depraved
Rogers was lionized in London when he published his boasting *Journals* there" (200).[17] Yet he continues: "On the other hand, Rogers own
casualties were dreadful" (200n). Rogers's men looted the local church
for silver and didn't take enough provisions along for their trip back,
which resulted in a "Starvation March" and even cannibalism (see
Zaboly in Rogers, *Annotated and Illustrated Journals* 186–88).[18] Because
the relief party of Lieutenant Samuel Stevens had left the appointed
meeting point early, Rogers had to organize a spectacular rescue mission with rafts across the Ottaquechee Falls and did save some of his
men—an event that well illustrates the loyalty and responsibility he felt
toward his own corps. Thus his enthusiastic biographer Ross compares
Rogers to "the Norwegian polar explorer Roald Amundson" (255). No
wonder this raid became the material for King Vidor's heroic 1940 war
propaganda film *Northwest Passage*, starring Spencer Tracy as Major
Rogers.

In Detroit (Peace)

After the fighting against the French was over, in 1760 General Amherst sent Rogers to Detroit to take possession of the northwestern
French territory. The major managed to make a long journey in whale-
boats from Niagara up the St. Lawrence and along Lake Erie, losing
only a single man on the way. The trip is well described in the *Journals*
and in the *Concise Account*, thought the most important point, Rogers's

encounter with Pontiac, is not mentioned in the former, where Rogers writes:

> [At the] mouth of Chogage River . . . we met with a party of Attawawa Indians, just arrived from Detroit. We informed them of our success in the total reduction of Canada, and that we were going to bring off the French Garrison at Detroit, who were included in the capitulation. I held out a belt, and told them I would take my brothers by the hand, and carry them to Detroit to see the truth of what I had said. . . . That evening we smoaked the calamet, or pipe of peace, all the Indians smoking by turns out of the same pipe. The peace thus concluded, we went to rest, but kept good guards, a little distrusting their sincerity. (*Journals* 214–15)

In the *Concise Account*, however, we get detailed information about Pontiac and the "Lake Indians": "They are formed into a sort of empire, and the Emperor is elected from the eldest tribe, which is the Ottawawas, some of whom inhabit near our fort at Detroit, but are mostly further westward towards the Mississipi. Ponteack is their present King or Emperor, who has certainly the largest empire and greatest authority of any Indian Chief that has appeared on the continent since our acquaintance with it. He puts on an air of majesty and princely grandeur, and is greatly honoured and revered by his subjects" (239–40).

This is the famous personal encounter as described by Rogers: "In the year 1760, when I commanded and marched the first detachment into this country that was ever sent there by the English, I was met in my way by an embassy from him. . . . His ambassadors had also orders to inform me, that he was Ponteack, the King and Lord of the country I was in" (240). He continues: "At first salutation when we met, he demanded my business into his country, and how it happened that I dared to enter it without his leave? . . . I informed him that it was not with any design against the Indians. . . . I at the same time delivered him several friendly messages, or belts of wampum" (240–41). Pontiac also provided Rogers with provisions: "At our second meeting he gave me the pipe of peace and both of us by turns smoaked with it, and he assured me he had made peace with me and my detachment; that I might pass through his country unmolested, and relieve the French garrison; and that he would protect me and my party" (241).[19] The contrast between these two accounts has led to all kinds of doubts about

A CONCISE

ACCOUNT

OF

NORTH AMERICA:

CONTAINING

A Defcription of the feveral BRITISH COLONIES
on that Continent, including the Iflands of
NEWFOUNDLAND, CAPE BRETON, &c.

AS TO

Their Situation, Extent, Climate, Soil, Produce, Rife,
Government, Religion, Prefent Boundaries, and
the Number of Inhabitants fuppofed to be in each.

ALSO OF

The Interior, or Wefterly Parts of the Country, upon the
Rivers ST. LAURENCE, the MISSISSIPI, CHRISTINO, and
the Great Lakes.

To which is fubjoined,

An Account of the feveral Nations and Tribes of Indians
refiding in thofe Parts, as to their Cuftoms, Manners, Government, Numbers, &c.

Containing many Ufeful and Entertaining Facts, never before
treated of.

By Major ROBERT ROGERS.

LONDON:
Printed for the AUTHOR,
And fold by J. MILLAN, Bookfeller, near Whitehall.
MDCCLXV.

Title page of Robert Rogers's *Concise Account* (London, 1765). (Courtesy of William L.
Clements Library, University of Michigan)

Interview between Captain Robert Rogers of the "Rogers Rangers" and the Indian Chief Pontiac. Mural painting by Charles Yardsley Turner (1912), Cuyahoga County Court House, Cleveland, Ohio. (Courtesy of the Cuyahoga County Archives, Cleveland, Ohio)

the veracity of Rogers's first encounter with Pontiac.[20] But they certainly did have personal contact, even on several occasions.

After complicated negotiations with the French captain Belestre, Detroit capitulated. Several letters were exchanged in English and French (see *Journals* 217–28) until the English flag went up in the fort. Rogers had officially taken control for the English of the whole, though mostly unmapped,[21] French Northwest: "I consulted the Indians about a journey to Michlimakana across by land; but they decided it impractical by this season without snow-shoes, and to our great mortification we were obliged to return to Detroit" (230–31). Nevins writes that after taking Detroit, Rogers became famous: "Everywhere he went he was known, stared at, and sought after, for every news agency for five years had rung with his exploits; everywhere he was introduced and referred to as 'the famous Major Rogers'" (*Ranger* 54). The hero returned east and in June 1761 married Elizabeth Browne from Portsmouth, New Hampshire.

Again in Detroit (War)

Rogers next military venture was the Cherokee Wars of 1761–62 in the Carolinas, where he encountered slavery and extreme brutality against Indians, for example, the "execution of 22 Cherokee chiefs held hostage" inside Fort Prince George (Ross 322). Nevins also writes that "in the Carolina campaigns, he had been suspected of an illegal participation in the very traffic with the border tribes which it was his military duty to regulate; and his open concern with it now brought him under the direct displeasure of Sir William Johnson at Johnson Hill. . . . The exact nature and extent of his derelictions in Indian commerce are dubious, but they had sufficed to make for him powerful enemies" (*Ranger* 71). By that time, Rogers had become involved in different investments and land deals to make up for the financial losses of running a militia for which he was not being properly reimbursed.

In 1763 the Treaty of Paris had been signed, but in the meantime relations with the Indians of the Northwest had deteriorated and a rebellion erupted, the famous "Pontiac's War," which is the topic of the play *Ponteach*. As Rogers describes it, "In fifteen days time, [Pontiac] reduced or took ten of our garrisons, which were all we had in his country, except Detroit; and had he carried this garrison also, nothing was in the way to complete his scheme" (*Concise Account* 243). Most famous is the fall of Michilimackinac in an attack based on the ruse of a "baggatiway" (lacrosse) game, described in gruesome detail in the captivity narrative of Alexander Henry (78–94). And now Detroit itself was under siege. Rogers came to the rescue, but on arrival honored his old friend and new enemy Pontiac with a bottle of brandy—another anecdote among superheroes: "In 1763, when I went to throw provisions into the garrison at Detroit, I sent this Indian a bottle of brandy by a Frenchman. His counsellors advised him not to taste it, insinuating that it was poisoned, and sent with a design to kill him; but Ponteack, with a nobleness of mind, laughed at their suspicions, saying it was not in my power to kill him, who had so lately saved my life" (*Concise Account* 244). Once he had arrived in Detroit, Rogers participated in the Battle of Bloody Run, where he was instrumental in covering the English retreat back into the fort after a disastrous sortie by the unlucky Captain Dalyell: "Had it not been for the courageous stand made by Major Rogers, many more men would have been overwhelmed and killed by the Indians" (Dixon 180).[22] There exists a "Journal of the Siege of Detroit" dated "8th Augt 1763," sent to Sir William Johnson and signed by Robert Rogers, reprinted in Franklin B. Hough's *Diary of the Siege of Detroit* (121–35). It ends with the death of the corpulent Captain Campbell, who had accompanied Rogers on his first trip to Detroit: "Half an Hour after the Savages carried the Man they had Lost before Captain Campbell, striped him naked, and directly murthered him in a cruel manner, which indeed gives one pain beyond Expression" (135). The text was probably intended for publication in a second volume of Rogers's *Journals*. But we are getting ahead of things.

Off to London

After the siege was over and the Indian uprising had collapsed, Rogers again went east, where he was for the first time arrested for debt in New York but liberated by some of his own men. Cuneo writes: "A great many of the soldiers were debtors who had been driven to the service by the dismal alternative of jail and it is easy to guess at their feelings to see a favorite officer treated in this manner. . . . A group broke into the jail on Sunday evening, 14 January [1764], and hurried Rogers out at pistol point while he protested—according to the *New York Gazette*— 'Indeed I am afraid gentlemen, you will ruin me'" (171). He had to escape to Connecticut to be safe from New York prosecutors.[23]

Obviously, Rogers had to sort out his business. He was a hero and at the same time in financial trouble. He had a family now, and he had visions. Because in America his career was blocked, he decided to try his luck in London, where, as we have already learned, he quickly became a celebrity. According to Ross, "London's *Public Advertiser* reported that 'this Gentlemen was the first person in America who raised a Body of Troops at his own Expence, and headed them against the Indians who were in the service of our enemies.—His regard for the Welfare of his Country, however, utterly exhausted his private Fortune'" (354). Norman Gelb writes: "Unable to resolve his difficulties, Rogers looked to London for respite and a change of circumstances. In 1765, he crossed the Atlantic in an attempt to exploit his fame, which had spread to England" (15). Nevins gives us more information on the personal motivation: "For some time past he had seen junior officers elevated above him merely because they had found time to present themselves at London, and opportunity to secure the influence of court friends" (*Ranger* 72). He continues:

> His chief activities in London, therefore, were political and literary. His exploits had well advertised him, and his advent attracted general notice. Old military friends crowded about him, and with the recommendations to various gentlemen of prominence which he had brought with him, he shortly became known among the lesser notables of the season. In the magazines of the time is found frequent mention of his career and his person, and upon the streets, his tall, sturdy figure, carried with an easy boldness of demeanor, was frequently pointed out. He resorted to parties and clubs at which officers, retired and active, were found, and won speedily a deserved reputation for joviality and good fellowship. (73)

Rogers wanted to profit from this popularity. Nevins lists different anecdotes, starting with the infamous episode on Houndslow Heath already mentioned:

> Tradition has still perpetuated stories of how, when accosted one lonely night by a highwayman on Houndslow Heath, he peremptorily knocked him down and dragged him away to justice; of how he appeared, on a wager, at a fashionable ball in the uncouth garb of a backwoods hunter; of how once, deep in his glasses with a merry company, he bet he could tell the greatest lie, and, relating the strange but true story of his father's death,

> was vociferously awarded the palm. Indeed, he laid at this time
> the real foundation for a very considerable and lasting popularity
> in London—one which endured through all the compromising
> vicissitudes which later brought him an exiled petitioner to the
> capital. (73)

In the capital of the British Empire, he quickly found friends. Among
his mentors, Cuneo mentions a Dr. John Campbell (174), Benjamin
Franklin, who happened to be in London and promised to help, and the
politician Charles Townshend (178); Norman Gelb mentions William
Fitzherbert of the Board of Trade, and even the then Mayor of London
(16). William Clements adds "the Earl of Hillsborough, President of the
English Board of Trade" (6).

Becoming an Author

In London, Rogers published his three books with John Millan, a bookseller whose work is not well documented today. We don't know if Millan merely sold books or if he typeset them as well.[24] Judging from the
advertising, he was mainly known for militaria;[25] no wonder he offered
to publish Rogers's *Journals*. As the contact was already established,
Millan also printed the *Concise Account* in the same year and, though
this didn't really fall in his domain, a year later, the play *Ponteach*. All
three books were "Printed for the AUTHOR, And sold by J. Millan,
Bookseller, near Whitehall." Rogers probably paid at least part of the
printing costs; Armour writes, "published at his own expense" (*Treason*
3)—today we would call this "vanity publishing." Ross observes: "As
the economics of book publishing then dictated, Rogers paid a small
cash advance for work to begin" (361). In fact, subscriptions for second
volumes of the first two books were offered.[26] Riding on his success,
Rogers must have decided to write and publish *Ponteach*, which was
only published after he had departed for America again.

As Charles Townshend, Lord of the Admiralty, wrote: "Major Rogers
marches thro' the prints in a thousand various Shapes" (qtd. Cuneo
178).[27] Rogers's first trip to London was a big success: "As final evidence of royal favor Rogers was presented at Court on 17 October and
kissed the King's hand" (Cuneo 180). He returned to America appointed
to a new governorship at Michilimackinac.[28] On his way to the Great
Lakes, Major Rogers and his wife, Betsy, stopped in Oswego, where
he participated in the peace conference presided over by Sir William

Johnson in Fort Ontario. Cuneo writes: "They met Pontiac en route
easterly for a conference with Johnson at Oswego. 'We smoked a pipe
together and drank a bottle of wine,' wrote Rogers to Johnson" (190).[29]
In his elaborate description of the peace talks and belt giving at that
conference, Peckham also confirms that Pontiac and Rogers met (*Indian
Uprising* 289). Dowd writes: "By June 28 Pontiac was at Fort Erie, where
he crossed paths, smoked a pipe, and drank a bottle of wine with Robert
Rogers, himself en route from England to Michilimackinac. It is tempting
to speculate that Rogers told him about his play, *Ponteach, or The Savages
of America*, which he had already seen staged in London" (*War* 250).[30]
The meeting is fictionally elaborated by Kenneth Roberts in anticipation of future plans; the novelist has the big chief tell his white friend:
"Michilimackinac has nothing in common with any other British post.
In importance it's like the sun compared with the blaze of a pine knot.
It's the uttermost fort, from which the soldiers of the Great King look
out on a vast territory of which they know nothing" (502).[31] If the winter
had blocked him the first time he had been in Detroit in 1760, now Rogers
was on his way to the westernmost outpost of the British Empire. As
historian Michael A. McDonnell confirms: "From Michilimackinac,
anything is possible" (21).

Governor in Michilimackinac

At Michilimackinac, Rogers worked for the first time as a civilian. He
organized contact with the local Indians and also included the Sioux
tribes further west in his negotiations. One of his main aims was to keep
relationships between the Sioux and the Ojibwe peaceful in order to
further western trade. Ross comments: "Rogers's greatest focus at
Michilimackinac had been upon bringing peace between these habitu-
ally warring peoples, so that trade could be significantly opened up"
(400). In order to improve relationships, he used soft power, contact,
socializing, the exchange of gifts. We read that "during the two years
that he was governor, Rogers drew to Michilimackinac the largest congregation of Indians that history records" (Morsberger 241). According
to Zaboly, the Great Council held outside the fort in Michilimackinac
in July 1767 was "attended by Chiefs of the Menominee, Winnebago,
Sauk, Fox, Sioux, Chippewa, Ottawa and Missisauga: a congregation
that would have made Sir William Johnson himself proud to have
conceived and supervised" (in Rogers, *Annotated and Illustrated Journals* 291). In his introduction to the *Journals*, Todish writes: "The conference at Michilimackinac was attended by over seven thousand Western

Indians, and was the largest ever held up to that time. The resulting peace saved the Crown costly military expenses and also advanced British trade" (19–20). And here, finally, is Rogers's own reporting on the Grand Council, as described in his *Michillimackinac Journal* (publ. 1918)—another fascinating source on his life:[32]

> A grand . . . Council was Held outside the Fort at this were present the Chiefs of the Bay the Fallavines Puans Sakes Renards Soux, Chippewas Ottawas Messissagas
>
> The Matters of Complaint on either side & the Grand affair of Peace and War were briefly touched upon and Canvassed and after many Short Speeches Replys and Rejoinders of no great Consequence it appeared that there was a general disposition to peace and Amity prevailing among them which I had before recommended to them Separately—I lighted the Calumet or Pipe of Peace which was smoaked with the Formality usual on such occasions by the Chiefs of all the Tribes and Nations, who gave one another the strongest assurances of Friendship and Love, Promised to forgive and forget all past Injuries and Affronts, to keep down and restrain the Fire of their young Warriors and use their utmost endeavors to prevent mischief on all sides for the future and to live in Harmony Concord & good Agreement like Brethren and Children of the same Father, begging that they might all be Treated as Children in Common, have Traders sent amongst them and be Supplyed with necessary goods in their Several distant villages and Hunting Grounds which I assured them should be done. (36)

As Ross concludes: "Within a year Rogers had stabilized British relations with the Western Indians, which had been dangerously off balance since Pontiac's War" (392).

All of this culminated in Rogers's project of a new colony in the Northwest. Thus we find in *Michillimackinac Journal* the "following Plan," which he "humbly" submits "to he better Judgment, of his MAJESTY & the Government of Great BRITTAIN . . . especially at this Glorious period, of the Brittish Annals" (50). He wanted the following:

> That Michillimackinac & its dependencies, shoud be erected onto a Civil Government; with a Governor, Lieutenant Governor, & a Council, of twelve; chose out of the Principal Merchants, that carry on this valuable branch of Trade with Power to enact,

> such Laws, as may be necessary & these to be transmitted, to the
> KING; & for Approbation: That the Governor should be Agent
> for the Indians & Commandant of the troops, that may be
> order'd to Garisson, the Fort who must not see a divided power,
> which the Savages laugh at & Contemon: and have Authority to
> leave the Lieut. Gov., his Deputy, when the service may, require
> him, to Visit the Indians at a distance. (50–51)

Rogers did of course insinuate that he himself would be the proper
person to fill this position of governor, Indian agent, and military commandant of what Armour describes as his "dream of a vast interior
colony" (*Treason?* 4). From Michilimackinac he wanted to expand the
trade to the West beyond the Great Lakes.

Accordingly, the other big project at Michilimackinac was the discovery of the Northwest Passage to get "the reward of twenty thousand
pounds the British Admiralty had offered" (Gelb 16).[33] In North Carolina, Rogers had met Governor Arthur Dobbs, who was a friend of Sir
Robert Walpole and "obsessed" with the Northwest Passage (Ross 327).
Dobbs had written a book about the Passage in 1744 and showed Rogers
his own map, "largely based on the word of a métis fur trader named
Joseph La France, whom he had met in London around 1742" (329).
Thus R. E. Morsberger notes that "Rogers had a greater plan than to be
a mere governor and Indian agent. He proposed nothing less than to
direct a search for the Northwest Passage, which had lured explorers
since the days of Frobisher, Davis, and Hudson" (241). Morsberger
explains that Rogers's plan was to "find across the North American
continent a waterway which men could travel by barge and canoe"
(241)—a strategy that significantly follows, just like Rogers's soft-skills
diplomacy (which I will discuss later), the French explorative strategy
of using waterways. Jonathan Carver, whom he sent on this expedition,
together with Captain Tute, explains in his famous book that the Northwest Passage is "a passage for conveying intelligence to China and the
English settlements in the East Indies with greater expedition than a
tedious voyage by the Cape of Good Hope or the Straights of Magellan
will allow of" (58–59). As Cuneo observes: "The *Concise Account*'s emphasis on North America's interior created a favorable atmosphere in
which to cast Rogers's proposal to discover the Northwest Passage"
(177). In his proposal of 1765 ("First Proposal"), Rogers writes: "The
Rout Major Rogers proposes to take, is from the Great Lakes towards
the Head of the Mississippi, and from thence to the River called by the
Indians Ouragon, which flows into a Bay that projects North-Eastwardly

into the (Country?) [mutilated] from the Pacific Ocean, and there to Explore the said Bay and it's Outletts, and also the Western Margin of the
Continent to such a Northern Latitude as shall be thought necessary"
(102).[34] Michilimackinac was the perfect place to launch such a project.
Carver describes it as "the uttermost of our factories towards the northwest" (63). Leaving the fort on 3 September 1766, the expedition went
up the Mississippi, but unfortunately meeting points were missed, provisions lost, and they got stuck and failed. Zaboly comments: "Unfortunately, unlike Lewis and Clark 40 years later, Rogers' expedition
was sadly underfinanced and undermanned, and thus ill-equipped to
fulfill his grand dream" (Rogers, *Annotated and Illustrated Journals* 289).
The money he had, once again, advanced himself was spent, and Rogers
didn't get a second try, though he submitted a second proposal.

A Hero's Downfall

Because of his ambitious plans, Rogers had made himself enemies in in
the East who didn't favor this kind of competition. As Cuneo writes:
"Johnson was righteously indignant that Rogers should probably use
his position to aid himself and his friends in the fur trade. Both Johnson
and his commissaries used their positions in the same way. The state of
public morality may be seen in the fact that General Gage, who passed
on Johnson's accounts, was soliciting the latter's assistance to add to
his personal fortune through land speculation" (294). Sir William Johnson, who wanted to control Indian trade from Johnson Hall in New
York, and Thomas Gage, the new commander of the British troops in
North America, refused to reimburse Rogers for paying his old Ranger
bills and sent the equally ambitious Benjamin Roberts west to obstruct
Rogers's business plans.[35] The expenses for the Grand Council at Michilimackinac were not reimbursed either.[36] The exploration of the Northwest Passage had failed. Thus the grand vision collapsed. London responded to neither the memorandum nor the petition. A fascinating
source on Rogers's time at Michilimackinac is his handwritten journal
of that stay, stored at the American Antiquarian Society and edited by
William Clements, who notes that Rogers's plans were "never presented
to the English Board of Trade as far as records show" (9).[37] Clements
calls his "scheme [for a new English colony in the Northwest] a wild
one for the conditions and times, and both his Government and trade
plans were creations of a disordered brain" (9)—an assessment that we
may want to reconsider later. Rogers was arrested, put in chains, and
brought east.

Michillimackinac 4th of Sepr 1767

Sir

I do myself the Honour to Inclose you the State of this Country which I have wrote Since my arrival at this Garrison and hope it will meet with your Approbation, And as I have always Ever Since that I have been in his Majesties Service Given you Every Intelligence that I thought Could tend to your Honour and Advantage, and did all the last war Lend my weak Indeavours to Support the Great Character that you by your own Vallour and Assiduity &c Justly Gained —

I hope Sir that you will be pleased when I am Injured to not Reflect upon me for Representing my Greaviencies to you which I do by Incloving the Affidavits of Some Persons that was Present when Mr Roberts the Commissary of Indian affairs Was pleased to give me Very Abusive Language, and the Reason of my not Sending him down the Country was wholly on your account, I hope you will be pleas to Remove him from this Garrison which I dont in the least doubt you will be pleas to do after Perusing the Affidavit —

I Beg Sir that your Consider me as a

Above and right: Letter from Robert Rogers to Sir William Johnson, written at Michili-mackinac on 4 September 1767, shortly before his arrest. (Courtesy of William L. Clements Library, University of Michigan)

Person that has always done my duty while in the
Service, and Pray for your Recommendation
home for Some Preferment

   I am Sir with the greatest Respect
  and Esteem Your most Obedient and
  Most Devoted Humble Servant

         [signature]

P.S. M.rs Rogers presents
her Respects — I beg You'd
Interest yourself in getting
my accounts past —
I have more accounts to send
you of this Country but Cannot
Compleet them this Fall —

   D.r Sir William Johnson

Major Rogers was a disbanded off.r

The quality of the newspaper coverage at that time and what it did to his reputation can be seen in the *Scots Magazine* reporting on "British North America": "*London, Feb.* 6. [1767.] They write from *Quebec*, that Major Rogers, of Michigan settlement, had given in marriage forty white women to the like number of Indians; and also presented the bridegrooms each with a new tomahawk, a brace of fuzees, powder, shot, &c. as a nuptial gift" (99). Or in the *Gentleman's Magazine*'s report of 1768 that Rogers was ambushed by Indians and had escaped back into Fort Michilimackinac (301)—a piece of fake news that we find doubled up in the *London Magazine* (330). But the *Gentlemen's Magazine* also reported Rogers's arrest: "The famous major Rogers has turned traitor to his country, and is now in irons for conspiracy" (348). Also the *London Magazine*'s "Foreign Affairs" knew that "Governor Rogers of Michilimackinac [was] brought to New York in irons" (384). They even knew of his plans to murder the English officers and give the fort of Detroit to the French. Though in October 1768 Rogers was exonerated in a trial in Montreal, he was now without a job, in debt, and without friends in America.[38] He had to run away from his creditors—even his own father-in-law had sued him.[39] And his wife wanted a divorce—no wonder when her husband was never at home, had no money, and his reputation had crumbled.[40]

The records of his whereabouts after Michilimackinac are murky; Rogers probably went back to the Old World. Nevins writes about the second trip to London: "His liabilities totaled thirteen thousand pounds, and to keep himself from falling into a debtor's prison was his immediate care" (*Ranger* 119). In London Rogers again petitioned for reimbursement of his patriotic expenses and tried to finance a second Northwest expedition, this time via the Missouri River—the correct route that would later lead Lewis and Clark to find the Pacific.[41] To no avail. The treasury was drained, and nobody was motivated to finance new American projects after the exorbitant expenses of the Indian rebellion in the former French territories on the Great Lakes.

Rogers was stuck. His being jailed for debt in Fleet prison is mentioned in several biographies. Nevins even reports "Rogers' unverified statement of a later date to President Wheelock of Dartmouth College, that he had fought two battles under the Bey of Algiers" (*Ranger* 127).[42] When the American Revolution broke out, Rogers again returned to America and offered his services to General Washington, who didn't trust him and had him arrested. As Nester writes: "Being treated like a traitor rather than a hero eventually made him one" (*Struggle* 25). The major escaped to New York and changed sides, now fighting with the Loyalists, but his new unit of "Queen's Rangers" was not very success- ful. He was now with the wrong side. Moreover, all his American land claims were lost after the war. Via Quebec and Halifax, Rogers returned to London and "never touched American soil again" (Nevins 141). He lived off "half-pay" (a military pension), drifted into alcoholism, and died in obscurity in 1795. Again Nester: "It was a sordid end for a once great American warrior whose life reads like a Shakespearean tragedy" (*Struggle* 25).

Rogers's reputation has suffered as well. Thus in a review of Cuneo, Milton Hamilton complains that this biography is too positive and in- stead characterizes Rogers as follows: "A great fighter, the ideal and prototype of the modern commando, he was an opportunist, who was concerned only with his own advancement, with no particular principles or ideals" (383). Even worse is Elliott, who attributes to Rogers "thirty years of more or less continuous debauchery of both mind and body, when his audacity in dealing with superior officers and in seeking per- sonal preferment and gain was astounding, and his duplicity, marital infidelity, and disloyalty to relatives, friends and country were disgust- ing" (92). There is much to be explained about this person.

The Myth of Major Rogers in Fiction, Films, Graphic Novels, and More

The figure of Robert Rogers has been appropriated by many. John Ross calls his life *War on the Run*, and it is no coincidence that, like Pontiac's, Rogers's life has also provided material for fictional adaptations. Susan Glover emphasizes that Rogers's "military journals . . . gripped the popular imagination, and for two and a half centuries, the narrative of Rogers' dominion over a hostile natural environment continues to be retold and reimagined in new genres and media" (180). Still, in Alexan- der Macomb's patriotic American play *Pontiac: or The Siege of Detroit* of 1835, Rogers is merely a provincial underling to Commandant Gladwin and wearing a blue uniform (probably anticipating the Union army in contrast to the redcoats); he follows orders and has little to say. Rogers does, of course, also appear in some of the Pontiac fiction mentioned by Orians, and even in a children's book by Jennifer Quasha, *Robert Rogers: Rogers' Rangers and the French and Indian War* of the Library of American Lives and Times, advertised as "a series of biographies for grades 4–8" (also available on CD for youngsters who prefer listening to reading);

and in Bradford Smith's contribution to the illustrated Penguin Random House "middle grade" Landmark Books series. This shows the kind of academic neglect on which Howard Peckham comments in the 1961 edition of Rogers's *Journals*: "He was written about for boys" ("Introduction" ix).

The first revisionist fiction that tried to change Rogers's bad reputation as an American traitor significantly is a piece of fiction, Kenneth Roberts's *Northwest Passage* (1938), a fat adventure novel that presents the Ranger as larger than life. It sports a Mark Twain epigraph about Satan "on account of his not having a fair show. . . . We have none but the evidence for the prosecution, and yet we have rendered the verdict." Thus after his first encounter with the hero, the I-narrator Langdon Towne suggests that Rogers "might have been a greater prince than Ienghiz Khan" (3). Roberts leads us on and off through the major's career and also spends many pages in book 2 on Rogers's first stay in London and his writing of *Ponteach* together with his secretary Natty Potter, presented as a "Cambridge graduate" (367), often drunk, a nephew of the archbishop of Canterbury—"but the Archbishop's not boasting" (368). Roberts, who quotes dozens of lines from *Ponteach*, provides some interesting interpretations and has Rogers say about his publications: "These books aren't intended to be read so much as they are to prove what I can do" (369). He also describes a lengthy encounter between Rogers and Pontiac at the Oswego conference and has the Ottawa chief even inspire the major's future plans on the Great Lakes: "One family can't travel for three months, in winter, to reach Michilimackinac and replace a gun lock: to buy another package of powder" (502). Not surprisingly, this observation echoes some of Rogers's own argumentation in his *Michillimackinac Journal* known to Roberts. Thus the fictional Pontiac continues: "If English traders aren't allowed to travel westward from Michilimackinac, then the tribes'll invite French traders and Spanish traders to winter in their towns. . . . The English King will lose the trade of the Western tribes. He will lose their furs. . . . And in the end they'll become dangerous enemies of the Great King in England" (503). Though the fictional Rogers also ends up as a debtor in Fleet Prison in the last chapter, the narrator and his wife decide that he must be deathless—as Ann says: "You can't kill what was in that man!" (709). Naturally, Rogers still triggers novelists' imagination; one of the latest fictions about him is James Trump's print-on-demand *Rogers Rangers and the Raid on Fort Michilimackinac 1758: A Novel of the French and Indian War*, of 2014. As Susan Glover, looking for the "'Real'

Poster advertising King Vidor's Hollywood adaptation of *Northwest Passage*
(1940), with Spencer Tracy as Robert Rogers.

Robert Rogers," notes: "His heroic identity was resurrected in the following century and has remained perennially under (re)construction
ever since" (180).

This aspect of mythification is also apparent in the fact that Allan
Nevins's biography appears in the Leonaur Military Commanders Series
(see page 33), and in the 1940 film *Northwest Passage* (with Spencer Tracy
as Major Rogers), based on Roberts's novel, which does, however,

Scottish actor Angus Macfadyen as Robert Rogers in the
AMC Network series *Turn: Washington's Spies* (2014).

mainly focus on the St. Francis raid and the hardships of the heroic return trip. Rogers's Rangers show their wartime-propaganda bravery in
green, slightly modified old U.S. Army uniforms,[43] fighting the enemy
and crossing the St. Francis River in a human chain.[44] This is certainly
not one of King Vidor's best films. Yet it even inspired a continuation in
the NBC TV series of the same name with Keith Larson as Rogers,
which dramatized the adventures of the major and his men through
several episodes.

The latest film version can be found in the AMC Network series
Turn: Washington's Spies (2014–17), a "historical drama" in forty epi-
sodes based on the story of the Culper Ring during the Revolutionary
War, as portrayed in the novel by Alexander Rose. Rogers appears as a
somber figure and intelligence expert played by the Scottish actor
Angus Macfadyen. The first episode opens with a victory of the Queen's

Rangers over a detachment of young Revolutionaries, whose half dead are bayoneted while Rogers and the other Rangers have a repast.[45] In later episodes, Rogers is seen walking in the woods, accompanied by a taciturn Indian brave. Whereas the English are depicted as mindless disciplinarians in this production, Rogers is stylized as the most intelligent (but immoral) opponent of the revolutionaries, with close ties to the Native people.

Turn also produced two spin-off graphic novels: one by Steve Ellis (illustrator) and Latoya Morgan (text), called Turn: Origins (2014), the other by Chris Hunt (illustrator) and again Latoya Morgan (text), called Turn: Rivals (2015)—the latter is a prequel of the spy story, about the relationship of Rogers and Washington in the early campaigns of the French and Indian War. Both graphic novels are available only online, but earlier comics versions of Robert Rogers's life exist as well.[46] Thus there is a Classics Illustrated volume of Rogers' Rangers, which is a very racist version of Rogers's adventures. Many analogies to Cooper's Natty Bumppo are emphasized: "As a young man I used to roam through the woods with my Indian friends and became accustomed to life in the wilderness. I hunted and fished with them, and when I grew older, I led them on revenge attacks into French-held territory" (1). The Classics Illustrated Rogers also accompanies English travelers on treks through he woods: "So I was put in charge of security, particularly with regard to transport columns" (2). The booklet incudes a sanitized version of the St. Francis attack. They burn the supplies but spare the women and children (29). Rogers is shown ice-skating instead of using snowshoes (5). The graphic novel ends with the conquest of Quebec: "From now on, that exceedingly large land mass, Canada, belonged to the British Empire and would be under the protection of the British Military. The settlements of North America would be accomplished in peace and without disturbance" (32). In the same category, we have Ted Spring's sketchbook on Rogers Rangers. John Silbersack's science fiction novel of 1955 finally even extends the range of Ranger mythification into the realm of Buck Rogers.

Not to be forgotten is Robert Rogers's international reputation as a bandes dessinées (comic strip) character in the work of Giorgio Cavazzano, whose career is mainly associated with his work as a Disney illustrator in Italy. Cavazzano produced a series of eight volumes that appeared in several languages, among them Italian, French, and German. In these comics, Rogers is a kind of Robin Hood fighting together with the Americans (among them Benjamin Franklin, whose electrical

Cover of the Classics Illustrated graphic novel about Rogers's Rangers (rpt. 2010).

kite tweaks several English officers) against the inept redcoats. The stories are in the popular style of a wily Astérix fighting against the Romans.[47]

On yet another note, we also find many enthusiastic groups of weekend Rangers who organize themselves in historical reenactment groups, wearing Rogers's green uniforms, and roaming the woods. They have their own Facebook pages (see also "Reenacting," "Jaeger's Battalion of Rogers Rangers," among others).[48] Their activities are lavishly documented on the internet—I have counted dozens of Ranger

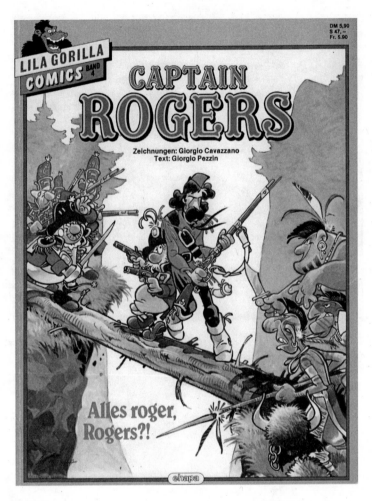

Cover of the German edition of the first volume of Giorgio Cavazzano's
fumetti series on Captain Rogers (1987). (Courtesy of Giorgio Cavazzano)

organizations. There is also a Facebook page with 1,578 members,[49] and
some of them can even be found in Germany, with their own Pinterest
downloads.[50] Rogers Rangers also inspired tin-figure friends in Leipzig
(see next page).[51] America's History LLC (formerly Stars and Stripes
Events) even offers tours with themes such as "Rogers' Rangers and the
French and Indian War." Like his nemesis Pontiac (or was he rather a
partner, or even a friend?), the historical Major Rogers has been re-
created into a creature of the imagination. This makes it even more
fascinating to find his voice in a fictional drama.

Rogers Rangers tin figures cast and painted by Alexander Glöckner (Germany).
(Courtesy of Alexander Glöckner)

3

The Historical Background
of *Ponteach*

N ow that we have learned some facts about the awesome, daunting, and often puzzling lives of our main performers, both the playwright and his protagonist, and the ways in which their lives were appropriated by followers and enemies, it is necessary to learn a bit more about the historical context in which the play supposedly takes place. What is the background of the story of *Ponteach*? Since the play obviously has referential traces that are not merely fabricated but document real experiences, we need to relate these aspects to the situation in the Old Northwest, and generally the area west of the Appalachian Mountains, as we know it from historians. If this play is full of challenging contradictions in which different attitudes, value systems, and perspectives collide and seem to cancel one another, this is not merely a failure but also reflects the situation of the very territory that our story describes. The Northwest was a contested area of extreme social and cultural hybridity, where traditions were constantly being negotiated and reinvented.

Refugees on the Great Lakes

Richard White describes this place of constant migration in *The Middle Ground* as already contested among the Native peoples before the

French Jesuits arrived, let alone the first English traders. To understand the references in the play, we need to know more about the fur trade, how both the French and the English related to the native peoples, the French and Indian War, the complicated alliances, and how the tribes existentially came to depend on European products for survival. As the play narrates history, we need to know what caused these conditions and how they developed—and we also need to contextualize them in the global events of international relations and the First British Empire in order to further understand some of the polemics of the debate.

White offers crucial insights into the experience of the early inhabitants of the Old Northwest. He starts with Indian-Indian conflicts and defines the Algonquin society encountered by the French as one of "refugees." This reminds us that the European arrivals on the American East Coast caused population movements comparable to the Great Migration at the end of the Roman Empire, when Northern European and even Asian tribes crisscrossed the Old World, pushing one another around, and in some cases ending up in Spain and North Africa. Thus White opens his report with "the onslaught of the Iroquois, who may appear initially as a deus ex machina," but he immediately explains that we "should not mistake their warfare for 'normal' Indian warfare in North America. It, too, was a complex product of European expansion" (xv). He writes that the "Iroquois desired beaver and the hunting lands that yielded them, and they wanted captives to replace their dead or to atone at the torture stake for their loss" (1). They had "obtained iron weapons from Europeans when their enemies to the west still relied on stone" (2). White talks of "horrible years" and "nightmares" (2), when "refugees moved west to avoid the Iroquois hammer" and "encountered an anvil formed by the Sioux, a people whom the Jesuits called the Iroquois of the West" (11).[1] As a result traditional tribes and clans were fragmented, adopted, or subjugated, and tenuous new alliances were constantly forming. What White labels the "Algonquians" of the Great Lakes was certainly a physically and culturally syncretic population.

Often the exact geographical location is unclear in these earliest Jesuit reports. We read that at Green Bay, "far from their original home, Hurons adopted by the Iroquois attacked refugee Hurons" (White 3) and learn of a band of Seneca destroying a Miami "village" with guns and being in turn killed by the pursuing Miamis (4).[2] Both the Indians and the French had authority problems in that territory of migration, where

tribes intermingled and the geographic notions of home changed constantly. White makes it clear that "not all the peoples of the *pays d'en
haut* were Algonquin speakers," but "with the onslaught of the Iroquois,
the Algonquians forged a collective sense of themselves as people distinct from" the Five Nations in the East, on the one hand, and the Sioux
in the West, on the other (xi). He specifies that "this clustering of diverse
peoples had its own social and environmental consequences. It disrupted
older notions of territory; geographical boundaries between refugees
became difficult to maintain" (11). He adds: "The precise mix of the area
changed constantly as some groups moved away and others entered.
The region became a hodgepodge of peoples, with several groups often
occupying a single village" (14).

In short, this was a multicultural territory even before the arrival of
the Europeans: "The whole logic of Algonquian actions was that dangerous strangers had to be turned into either actual or symbolic kinspeople,
if the refugees were to survive hunger, disease, and Iroquois attack"
(White 15). This was accomplished through intermarriage, which weakened patrilineages (17).[3] The calumet was "a more overtly political and
ceremonial way of achieving peace" (20). Ironically but not surprisingly, it was also an imported cultural practice: "The calumet had origi-
nated beyond the Mississippi among the Pawnees who claimed to have
received it from the sun. It had spread to the Sioux and to the Illinois
and was, during the mid and late seventeenth century, adopted by the
nations of the Great Lakes" (21).

A New Kind of Government

White writes that, "together with the Frenchmen, [the Algonquians]
pieced together a new world from scattered pieces" (2) on what he calls
a "middle ground," that is, a new culture of invented traditions where
neither the Indians nor the French could completely impose their old
ways on the other. As a result, "the boundaries of the Algonquian and
the French worlds melted at the edges and merged" (50). Thus White
presents a "more complex and less linear narrative," in which he tells
"how Europeans and Indians met and regarded each other as alien, as
other, as virtually nonhuman. It tells how, over the next two centuries,
they constructed a common, mutually comprehensible world in the
region around the Great Lakes the French called the *pays d'en haut*"
(ix–x).[4] In this world, "the older worlds of the Algonquians and of

various Europeans overlapped, and their mixture created new systems of meaning and of exchange" (x). This is how White describes the new interculture:

> On the middle ground diverse people adjust their differences through what amounts to a process of creative, and often expedient, misunderstandings. People try to persuade others who are different from themselves by appealing to what they perceive to be the values and practices of those others. They often misinterpret and distort both the values and the practices of those they deal with, but from these misunderstandings arise new meanings and through them new practices—the shared meanings and practices of the middle ground. (x)

Neither side could enter this encounter culturally intact. The new contact was not a formal negotiation of tribes or nations but happened on the local level of mixed villages: "This was a village world. The units called tribes, nations, and confederacies were only loose leagues of villages. . . . Nothing resembling a state existed in the *pays d'en haut*" (16). White writes: "Without a clear national territory and lacking even the most rudimentary national government, villages of the same nation, often located in separate refugee centers, could and did pursue independent policies" (17). Neither the French governor of Canada nor the Indian elders could impose their authority: "What Rousseau thought about Indians matters, but to understand the *pays d'en haut*, it does not matter as much as what the inhabitants of Vincennes or Kaskaskia thought, or what Onontio, the French governor at Quebec thought" (xiv). Because neither side had the power to impose its ways and "official French supervision of exchange became a mirage, . . . most trade was the work of small groups of Frenchmen traveling to Indian villages" (57). And since, in turn, these traders could not count on protection by their own government, they "had to find means to protect themselves either through force or by establishing personal ties within the communities in which they traded" (57). White sees the notion of the French trader Le Parisien that *"Nous sommes tous sauvages"* (We are all savages) as an opportunity to escape subordination: "Frenchmen in the West could to a remarkable degree act independently, if only temporarily, in reaching accommodations with the Algonquians among whom they traveled and lived" (58). Both sides were weak, and within both groups, the French and the Indians, the internal authority of their respective elites was being challenged.[5] Thus they "often negotiated largely on a face-to-face level within the villages themselves, and . . . these relations were not what either French authorities or Algonquian elders might have preferred them to be" (60).

An acceptable rhetorical solution to patch up the new relationship was the benevolent rule of the French "father": "During most of the time between 1680 and 1763, the vast majority of Algonquians remained Onontio's loyal children" (xv). When we look at this naming of the French governor at Quebec, we have to be aware of the complex use of family metaphors in this intercultural context, one that has repercussions all the way into our understanding of *Ponteach*, as we will see later. In the context of local knowledge and the spread of information, White also makes an interesting observation about European literacy, observing: "Long after it ceased to govern the actions of those who actually lived among Indians, the idea of Indians as literally *sauvages*, or wild men embodying either natural virtue or ferocity, persisted among intellectuals and statesmen in France. Assimilated into European controversies, these imaginary Indians became the Indians of Chateaubriand and Rousseau" (51). Curiously, such formal knowledge, philosophy, literacy, theory, in short, education, was a hindrance to acknowledging the real experience on the territory and its accommodation to a pragmatics of facts that could not so easily travel across the Atlantic.

Necessary Cultural Compromises

White gives powerful examples of cultural encounters that established the middle ground, a "new set of common conventions" (52) that was, however, never formally standardized. Crucially, it "depended on the inability of both sides to gain their ends through force." He reports on the Indian conflicts with the Jesuits negotiated by French commander Antoine Laumet de la Mothe, Sieur de Cadillac, and the Indian leaders, particularly a "Huron chief known as the Baron" (53),[6] who told a story of an old man's communications with the Master of Life, "who is one in three persons, who form but one spirit and one will" (54). The Indian thus interlaced his own supposedly authoritative Indian tradition with elements of Christian doctrine in an effort to accommodate his interlocutor—a tendency that would continue with many more Native American prophets to come, among them the Delaware prophet so crucial to the Pontiac story, as we shall see.

Values also clashed concerning the role of women: "European conceptions of marriage, adultery, and prostitution just could not encompass the actual variety of sexual relations in the *pay d'en haut*" (White 63). Already the ironic Lahontan wrote in his *New Voyages to America*: "A Young Woman, say they, is Master of her own Body, and by her Natural Right of Liberty is free to do what she pleases" (2:453). And Cadillac noted that girls "are allowed to enjoy themselves and to experiment with marriage as long as they like and with as many boys as they wish without reproach" (qtd. White 64).[7] Observing the "badly skewed sex ratio" in the *pay d'en haut*, White notes that "sexual relations with the coureur de bois offered an alternative to polygamy" (65). But he also mentions an interesting case of Algonquin women who chose sexual abstinence as part of the Jesuits' cult of the Virgin Mary and joined "a congregation composed largely of women, particularly young women and older girls" (67), citing the case of a chief's daughter, Aramepinchieue, who against the will of her father refused to marry a dissolute Frenchman named Accault, who was an enemy of the Jesuit missionary Father Jacques Gravier (72–74). This refusal both challenged her parents' authority and compromised Father Gravier's relations with the Indians. The Jesuit relented when Accault became a practicing Catholic, and in finally accepting the marriage, he "made the Kaskaskias the most Catholic of the Western Algonquians" (74). He had succeeded in finding a local solution.

Another crucial cultural issue to settle was punishment. The Europeans also had a "doctrine of revenge," but it was negotiated by a tribunal, whereas the Indians preferred either, "in their words, 'to raise up the dead,' that is, to restore the dead person to life by providing a slave in the victim's place, or 'to cover the dead,' that is, present the relatives with goods that served as an equivalent" (White 77). White gives the example of the murder of two Frenchman in Green Bay, which threatened tenuous alliances because the execution of the Indian culprits would have caused revenge on the French (79). He explains:

> Blood revenge was appropriate in each society but for different
> categories of killing. For the Algonquians there were two kinds
> of killings—deaths at the hands of enemies and deaths at the
> hands of allies. The appropriate response depended on the identity of the group to whom the killer belonged. If the killer belonged to an allied group, then the dead were raised or covered.
> If the murderers refused to do this, then the group became

> enemies and the price appropriate to enemies, blood revenge,
> was exacted. For the French also there were two kinds of killings—
> killings in war and murders. Killing enemies in war theoreti-
> cally brought no retribution once the battle ended. (80)

The Algonquians now pleaded for mercy for their allies with the commandant at Michilimackinac because in an earlier case, the French had
spared an Iroquois prisoner of war: "The French insistence on blood
revenge in an inappropriate category, therefore, created great confusion" (80). In the negotiations "neither French nor Algonquian cultural
rules fully governed the situation" (81), and certainly the wrong person
was executed.

In another case the French governor Vaudreuil stated that "the
blood of Frenchmen is not to be paid for by beaverskins" (qtd. White
85), delegating a delicate case to the commandant at Detroit, where "a
cultural fiction was agreed on. Cadillac and the Ottawas agreed to act
as if Le Peasant [the culprit] were a slave being offered to the French in
compensation for their dead" (87), and in turn the "notoriously obese
and nearly seventy years old" Indian miraculously escaped. Through
this "accident," both sides were able to keep face. Practice had to over-
rule formal argumentation, and thus "killings the French once considered solely their own concern became issues to be settled on the middle
ground" (90–91).

White points out that most of this intercultural argumentation was
by analogy: "This ritual of the middle ground . . . operated by analogy"
(93).[8] Thus he finds examples where the Indians plead in terms of the
Ten Commandments, and the Kaskaskia chief Kiroueria argued: "I
know that the Great Spirit, the Spirit Creator, God, forbids us, my father,
to kill our children" (qtd. 92). Hence, White concludes, the "members of
both cultures established an alliance that they both thought furthered
interests generated within their own societies. They maintained this alliance through rituals and ceremonials based on cultural parallels and
congruencies, inexact and artificial as they originally may have been.
These rituals . . . helped bind together a common world to solve problems, even killings that threatened the alliance itself" (93).

Obviously this French and Indian culture was different from British
jurisdiction—here is, in contrast, Francis Parkman's description of "the
French, the English, and the Indians." Regarding the French, he sees
only "plumed cavaliers" who "scorned to lay aside the martial foppery
that bedecked the camp and court of Louis the Magnificent" (1994 ed.

70) and deplores the fact of superficial Romish conversion by the Jesuits who merely "contented themselves with sprinkling a few drops of water on the head of the proselyte" (73). Parkman contests that while the French "filled the woods with a mongrel race of bush-rangers . . . , the slowly-moving power of England bore on with silent progress from the east" (63). For the American thinker this culture of negotiation was altogether insubstantial.

A Business of Gifts

The main engine of the middle ground was the fur trade, and this is what Parkman has to say about it: "The fur-trade engendered a peculiar class of men, known by the appropriate name of bush-rangers, or *coureurs de bois*, half-civilized vagrants, whose chief vocation was conducting the canoes of the traders along the lakes and rivers of the interior; many of them, however, shaking loose every tie of blood and kindred, identified themselves with the Indians, and sank into utter barbarism" (1994 ed. 78). Thus, not surprisingly, Parkman describes the middle ground as follows: "The renegade of civilization caught the habits and imbibed the prejudices of his chosen associates" (78). In contrast, "the borders of the English colonies displayed no such phenomena of mingling races" (79). Some of Parkman's French-bashing goes all the way back to the founder of Detroit, La Motte-Cadillac: "There was much congeniality between the red man and the Canadian. Their harmony was seldom broken; and among the woods and wilds of the northern lakes roamed many a lawless half-breed, the mongrel offspring of the colonists of Detroit and the Indian squaws" (215). Marriage even becomes a metaphor for the French attitude toward the Indians: "France labored with eager diligence to conciliate the Indians and win them to espouse her cause. Her agents were busy in every village, studying the language of the inmates, complying with their usages, flattering their prejudices, caressing them, cajoling them, and whispering friendly warnings in their ears against the wicked designs of the English" (75). Hence Parkman concludes: "They met the savage half way" (75). And later: "As Charlevoix observes, the savage did not become French, but the French became savages. Hundreds took themselves to the forest, never more to return" (77–78). Parkman's was the nationalist Anglo-Saxon perspective.

White's analysis is more differentiated. He elaborates on the symbolic dimension of trade for the Indians, and the different logic of the Algonquians, about the issue of *besoins*, namely, the "needs of each party. . . . both sides framed the exchange in terms of gifts rather than trade" (98). He explains that "Algonquians, as individuals, did not accumulate wealth. . . . Goods, in effect, only paused with a recipient and then flowed on through established social channels" (101). For example, White quotes Nicolas Perrot on the large distributions at the Feast of the Dead (Perrot 78–88): "They reduce themselves to such an extreme of poverty that they do not reserve for themselves a single hatchet or knife" (103; Perrot 88). This is a version of the famous potlatch ceremony of the Kwakiutl Indians. According to John Steckley and Bryan D. Cummins "potlatch" means "to give": "While giveaway is a major component of native ceremonies of North America, the amount of giveaway in a potlatch was on a scale unequalled elsewhere" (170). They note an element of competitive power in this tradition: "One proof that a high-ranking man was worthy of his position was how much he could give away at a potlatch, particularly to other people of high rank, who would be given the largest number of gifts" (170). Political power thus involved gift giving and providing; for the Indians, the material goods themselves were associated with the building of relationships. The two things simply could not be separated. White explains: "Symbol and utility merged here to give European trade goods an influence far beyond their simple use value" (104).[9]

This is where family metaphors come in: "Like the model of the alliance, the model for exchange was familial. The French were fathers and the Algonquians their children. . . . The obligation of Onontio to provide for the needs of his children became the basis for trade, and this in turn obligated the Algonquians, as good and satisfied children, to obey and aid him" (White 112). Family, political power, and economics overlapped. McDonnell writes: "The key to turning foreigners into relations . . . was through kinship building" (93). If in the European world this meant that the father commanded and the children obeyed, in "the Algonquian world, a father was generous, kind, and protective" (94). According to White, in the intercultural context, this meant that "presents had become, and would remain, a critical component of French attempts to hold Algonquian loyalty in the face of English trade advantages" (113). Thus "gifts of powder or blankets given in the fall before a hunt would be reciprocated in the spring with furs. The French gradually reinterpreted these gifts as loans to be paid back regularly" (114), but ultimately, Indians "treated credits as a gift" (480).

White explains this logic of Algonquian *besoins*: "The term had a special resonance in their society because, once an appropriate social relationship had been established, an assertion of need for something

could become a special claim on the thing needed" (129). Thus the Algonquians would argue that "they deserved to have those goods that
the French possessed but did not themselves immediately require"
(129)—because *"besoins* took precedence over profits. They [the Indians]
had an obligation to visitors, and the French had an obligation to them"
(131). He concludes: "Conceptually, trade and gift exchanges were different, but in actual social practice they could no longer be disentangled
without the collapse of the entire exchange network" (141). White thus
tells us about alliance chiefs or "medal chiefs": "Medals were the visible
marks of alliance chieftainships" and used to "recognize a man who
had already attained status in his village as an intermediary between
that village and the French" (179). With gifts the French could make
chiefs important: "Gifts gave the chiefs the ability to be liberal, and
liberality was the great mark of chieftainship" (179). In short, "the status
and influence that came from bestowing goods on others meant much.
Obtaining French recognition as a chief thus became an important aspect
of village politics" (180). White continues: "In one sense, presents bound
the chiefs to Onontio, but in another sense, presents made Onontio but
a large version of a chief. . . . These gifts . . . were the fruit of the French
acceptance of the Algonquian interpretation of patriarchy" (180). He
mentions the amazing cost of "20,000 livres granted annually by the
king" (180). Though gifts were connected to a system of vassalage, ultimately they were also a way of imposing Indian economics on the European colonizers.[10]

White Technology:
Profiting from the European Conflict

If the colonization of America created pressure from the East and a
"hammer" that fragmented Indian culture in the Algonquian Northwest even before the arrival of white people and their culture, the fur
trade created even more migration, in particular because the demand
for beaver and other pelts increased and the ceaseless hunting had de-
pleted the forests of the East. As Peckham writes: "By 1640 the beaver
supply for the Iroquois trade was exhausted," and as a result, the Iroquois started attacking the Hurons (*Indian Uprising* 2). No wonder
Robert Rogers writes about the Northwest in his *Concise Account*: "This
country, if any in America, will always have the advantage of the fur and
peltry trade; on account of its large lakes, and the extended uninhabit-
able country to the north-ward of it, both of which will tend to keep up

that valuable and lucrative branch of commerce here to the end of time" (182–83). Hunters had to go further west, which increased travel distance to the eastern buyers and created an influx of further white trading posts, and as a consequence more appropriation of white culture by the Indians. The importance of the fur trade manifests itself in the term *buck*, still in use today, which goes back to the prize for a buckskin, the main currency of trade at the time.[11] Yet because the animals had become rare, hunting with bow and arrow became difficult and the native people depended increasingly on guns and ammunition; worse, "the bow and arrow fell into disuse, and new generations lost their skill for lack of practice" (Peckham, *Indian Uprising* 11). Much of this of course concerned technology transfer and the introduction of new European products. This is how White describes the French trader Nicolas Perrot's arrival at a Miami village: "The gun, he said, was for the young men, the kettle was for the old; and he tossed a dozen awls and knives to the women, adding some cloth for their children. The French expected gifts of beaver in return" (7). White notes that "individual French traders quickly discovered that their most effective tactic was to claim that trade alone made victory in the war against the Iroquois and the Sioux possible" (25). The Indians now depended on support from the whites for that technology, that is, for the products themselves as well as their maintenance: a broken gun had to be fixed at the local fort. Thus when Rogers left Detroit after he had taken it from the French, the "Indians . . . requested that a gunsmith and physician be kept at the fort for service to them" (Peckham, *Indian Uprising* 66).

The conflict between the English and the French actually favored the Indians. Because the two European powers competed for allies, the native people had a choice and could make demands. They could pick the better offer, whereas the Europeans had to make investments and compete against each other. Especially the weaker French now had to support their allies with gifts. White calls this "an odd imperialism where mediation succeeded and force failed, where colonizers gave gifts to the colonized and patriarchal metaphors were the heart of politics" (145). Parkman quotes a letter by Sir William Johnson to the Board of Trade (13 November 1763):

> The French, in order to reconcile them [the Indians] to their encroachments, loaded them with favors and employed the most intelligent Agents of good influence, as well as artful Jesuits among the several Western and other Nations, who, by degrees,

prevailed on them to admit of Forts, under the Notion of Trading
houses, in their Country; and knowing that these posts would
never be maintained contrary to the inclinations of the Indians,
they supplied them thereat with ammunition and other necessaries with abundance, as also called them to frequent con-
gresses, and dismissed them with handsome presents, by which
they enjoyed an extensive commerce, obtained the assistance of
these Indians, and possessed their frontiers in safety; and as
without these measures the Indians would never have suffered
them in their Country, so they expect that whatever European
power possesses the same, they shall in some measure reap the
like advantages. (1991 ed. 851)

In the French and Indian War, both sides had their allies, basically
the Iroquois or Mohawks on the English side and the Algonquians or
Hurons on the French side. Of course the situation was much more
complicated because tribes had migrated and been fragmented and
joined into new alliances. But basically the rough dividing line was as
fiction readers know it from Cooper's *Leatherstocking* tales.

And as contacts intensified, so did cultural dependency. In *Pontiac
and the Indian Uprising*, Peckham explains:

> The effect of these contacts upon the Indians was subtle and far-
> reaching. Aside from the new and engulfing market for furs
> created by the white man, his culture was so much richer than
> that of the red man, of course, that new appetites and demands
> were created among the Indians. Some of the elements of the
> Frenchman's material culture consisted simply of improve-
> ments over the Indian's. Thus the French had steel knives and
> axes while the Indians had stone; the former had brass kettles,
> the latter clay; the French had steel needles, the Indians used bone;
> the former had various and superior fabrics, and the savages
> had only furs and hides and rush mats. (10)

Peckham quotes a long list of merchandise sent by William Johnson
to Amherst, which he describes as "illuminating of their needs and
tastes":

> Strouds (coarse blankets) of blue, black, and scarlet; French and
> English blankets, the former being preferred; walsh cottons or

> pennistons for stockings; green-napped frieze for stockings;
> worsted and yarn hose with clocks; flowered serges of lively
> colors; calicos and calimancos for gowns; ribbons of all sorts;
> linen for shirts and ready-made shirts; threads, needles and
> awls; clasp knives and scalping knives; vermilion and verdigris
> for painting themselves; Jews harps and hawk bells; stone and
> plain rings; silver gorgets and trinkets; small beads, brass wire,
> corn combs, scissors, razors, and looking glasses; brass and tin
> kettles, large and small; tobacco and pipes and snuff boxes;
> tomahawks and small hatchets; black and white wampum; red
> leather trunks, pewter spoons and gilt cups; flint, lead, duck
> shot; beaver and fox traps; iron fish spears; and rum. (*Indian
> Uprising* 71)

The alcohol is mentioned at the end because Johnson knew full well
that his superior, Jeffery Amherst, was against the rum trade. But the
list gives us a good sense of the comprehensiveness of the Indian con-
sumer needs and of the extent to which the colonial European traders
were ready to accommodate them.

English Rule

The conflict described in the play *Ponteach* concerns the situation after
the English victory in the French and Indian War. The English now had
a monopoly on regulating trade, and the Indians could no longer profit
from the earlier competitive environment. The English considered themselves the new owners of Canada and no longer saw any reason to spoil
the native people. The war had cost a fortune, and the purpose of colonialism was, of course, not to pay the colony but to exploit it.[12] This created all kinds of conflicts about the very nature of this occupancy. For
example, the Indians had let the French set up trading posts and forts in
order to profit from an alliance built on an economy of gift giving. And
the French had provided them for more than a century with highly appreciated and useful European technology. As Ross explains: "For generations Indian cultures had regarded Europeans' gifts as the central
mark of appreciation and respect from a grateful people to those who
had generously opened their lands. The gifts . . . acted symbolically as a
means of preserving a fragile hierarchy of power" (337). In the Indian
understanding, the Great White Father was paying tributes. Hence the
French were not conquerors but tenants. Peckham writes:

> The Great Lakes tribes had not yet been crowded by farmer
> settlers. . . . They regarded [the land] as theirs to hunt on, and
> the French as tenants who had been allowed a few acres here
> and there on which to establish trading posts and forts as much
> for the convenience of the Indians as for the profit of the French.
> The land was not theirs to transfer to the British, although they
> might assign them the forts agreeable to the Indian landlords.
> The English had to all appearances accepted this view by noti-
> fying the Indians of their intended occupation of the forts, by
> assuring them of generous treatment and advantageous trade
> (rent, in a sense), and by seeking their friendship. In other
> words, these savages believed that the British had succeeded
> the French at the western posts by permission of the Indians.
> (*Indian Uprising* 103)

The English, however, would treat Canada and its Indians as if it had
legally belonged to the French—they had conquered it, and now they
owned it.

Middleton talks of the "refusal of the British to resume gift giving"
and "the continued obsession of the British government with economy"
(*Pontiac's War* 204). The English no longer saw any need to favor the Indians as allies, to give them gifts, or to treat them particularly respect-
fully. Concerning the British victory over France, White writes that "the
Indians had always been children, but now they were being infan-
tilized" (256). He describes chaotic business relationships: "When gain
rather than 'love' ruled the trade, exchange remained chaotic. Theft,
after all, procured grain as readily as trade. The British cheated and the
Indians stole" (265). And "Amherst . . . cut scalping and clasp knives,
razors, tomahawks, gunpowder, flints, fowling pieces, and rum from
Johnson's list of trade goods to be carried by traders in Detroit" (265).
Alcohol was an issue as well because it had long been used to destabi-
lize the Indians in the West: "The problem was that the British had
pushed the rum trade for years, and its sudden curtailment simply became another example of British arbitrariness and stinginess" (266).
Ross writes that the "dangerous economizing of gifts confirmed the Indians' worst fears that the British came not as friends and equals but as
conquerors" (338–39). Cuneo comments:

> Wave after wave of discontent had swept the Indian tribes along
> the British frontier since the ending of the war. Contrary to

> promises, trading goods had failed to become plentiful and cheap: settlers were encroaching on hunting grounds; British officials severely curtailed the presentation of gifts. No summary expresses the Indian point of view better than 'Ponteach's' speech in the play of the same name which appeared in 1766 and was attributed to Robert Rogers. (160)

As we shall see, this context is very important to our understanding of the play.

Peckham writes that the English treated the local tribes according to contemporary international law and "never recognized the Indian tribes as sovereign nations" (*Indian Uprising* 103). He notes that "international law was not constructed by European colonial powers as conferring any rights on savage or even unchristian nations" (104) and explains that from the point of view of this Eurocentric framework of jurisdiction, the "United States of America was in fact the first non-European country admitted to the family of nations" (104).[13] In an effort to understand the situation in the Northwest from the contemporary perspective of imperial colonization, Peckham then observes: "The savages were clearly in the right. The French were tenants and maintained themselves in peaceful occupancy by frequently making presents to the Indians. The British government, however, professed to be governed in such transactions by international law, which as we have seen was not universal law. Indian nations not being regarded as members of the 'family of nations' had no rights at the bar of international justice" (285). He concludes: "The Indians had no more rights than the wild animals that roved over the land" (286). Peckham's bestiary comparison of this legal perspective emphasizes the dehumanizing cynicism of the Eurocentric codification of entitlement.[14]

Certainly the English would no longer provide the Indians, many of whom had previously sided with the enemy, with weapons, guns, bullets, or powder or arm them in any other way. Even Parkman, who was no friend of the Indians, observes their dismal situation: "With the downfall of Canada, the tribes had sunk at once from their position of importance" (1994 ed. 184). They no longer held the balance of power between the French and the English: "The English had gained an undisputed ascendancy, and the Indians, no longer important as allies, were treated as mere barbarians, who might be trampled upon with impunity" (185). Peckham notes that Sir Jeffrey Amherst, the commander-in-chief of His Majesty's forces in North America, had little understanding of Indian culture: "His lack of imagination was no handicap in fighting this war, although it became a fatal weakness in the task of pacifying the French-allied Indians" (*Indian Uprising* 57). Amherst saw the French gifts as bribes, as unnecessary expenses that he could do without. Thus he wrote on 9 August 1761 to Sir William Johnson: "You are sensible to how averse I am, to purchasing the good behavior of the Indians, by presents, the more they get the more they ask, and yet are never satisfied; wherefore a Trade is now opened for them, . . . that will oblige them to supply themselves by barter and of Course keep them more constantly employed" (qtd. Widder, *Beyond* 104). Indians were supposed to become part of the colonial work ethic. Parkman quotes from a letter by Amherst to Colonel Bouquet in January 1763: "As to appropriating a particular sum to be laid out yearly to the warriors in presents, &c., that I can by no means agree to; nor can I think it necessary to give them any presents by way of *Bribes*, for if they do not behave properly they are to be punished" (1994 ed. 174n). Peckham summarizes the situation as follows:

> The Indians were not slow to realize that actually the English had no liking for them. The arrogance, or reserve, toward native peoples which has usually characterized British colonial administrators was typified in Amherst. The Indians had been useful pawns during the war, and it was a stratagem of warfare to lure them away from the French. Now that Canada had surrendered and peace was in sight, the Indians had no further military value. They were not only to be dismissed, but insofar as possible ignored. Their "begging" was a nuisance and an expense, and Amherst thought he could humble them with discipline. (*Indian Uprising* 102)

The war had been won through military discipline and not negotiation. Thus the new English administration was used to giving orders rather than compromising.

Peckham continues with a description of personal relationships:

> That arrogance was further expressed in the orders forbidding the soldiers to mingle with the Indians. Neither were the savages welcomed in the forts. They were expected to state their business and get out. Gladwin [the English commandant of Fort Detroit] himself was accused of showing contempt for Indian customs.

> Intermarriage was frowned upon. All this in marked contrast to
> the French, many of whom had found the Indian maidens attrac-
> tive enough to take as wives. (*Indian Uprising* 102)

Though the historian Peckham's wording about "maidens" jars our
contemporary sensibilities, he has a point in observing that interper-
sonal relations with the English were different. As the older Parkman
observes: "The borders of the English colonies displayed no such phenomena of mingling races" (1994 ed. 79). Not only was the power distribution different now, but the new rulers didn't want intimate relationships. They shunned fraternization, to use the modern term—a negative
attitude that certainly had an impact on the family metaphors that tradi-
tionally defined Indian relationships.

Causes of the Rebellion

Keith Widder observes: "Regrettably, Amherst did not understand the
complicated relations between Indians, French-Canadians, and metis,
who made up the fur-trade society of the upper country" (*Beyond* 72).
And Peckham notes: "Amherst's posture as a stern parent was ridiculous"; moreover, "he stupidly regarded the giving of presents as a kind
of bribery, and he would have none of it" (*Indian Uprising* 72). Even the
Anglo-Saxon nationalist Parkman notes that the British profited from
the lack of competition after they had conquered Canada: "The presents,
which had always been customary to give to the Indians, at stated in-
tervals, were either withheld altogether, or doled out with a niggardly
and reluctant hand; while, to make the matter worse, the agents and
officers of government often appointed the presents to themselves, and
afterwards sold them at exorbitant prices to the Indians" (1994 ed. 173).
In trying to explain the causes of the Indian rebellion, he notes in particular that because of the long cultural contact, "the latter had forgotten
the weapons and garments of their forefathers, and depended on the
white men for support. The sudden withholding of these supplies was,
therefore, a grievous calamity. Want, suffering, and death were the
consequences" (174). There was a long and hierarchical chain of command in the English system, and the local English representatives, even
when they understood the situation and were sympathetic toward the
Indians, had their influence curbed. William Johnson, who was the Indian agent for New York, married to a Mohawk wife, and with very
close business ties to the (Iroquois) Indians, was also unsuccessful in

pleading with Amherst: "There is in my opinion a necessity for putting some clothing, ammunition, etc. into the hands of the commanding officers at Oswego, Niagara, and Detroit, etc. to be occasionally given to such Indians as are found deserving and serviceable, and as they have been used heretofore to receive presents in great abundance" (qtd. Peckham, *Indian Uprising* 88–89). But "General Amherst replied that he did not think presents necessary" (89).

In discussing the causes of the Indian rebellion in the Northwest, even Parkman uses the word *rapacity* to describe the new business relations: "The English fur-trade had never been well regulated" (1994 ed. 174). The Harvard man specifies: "Many of the traders . . . were ruffians of the coarsest stamp, who vied with each other in rapacity, violence, profligacy. They cheated, cursed and plundered the Indians, and outraged their families; offering, when compared with the French traders, who were under better regulation, a most unfavorable example of the character of their nation" (175). Unfortunately the English redcoats, who had imbibed a sense of military and cultural superiority (for which later they would dearly pay in some battles, e.g., at Bloody Run), also showed much disrespect to the native people—so much so that for once even Parkman takes the Indian perspective: "Formerly, when the warriors came to the forts, they had been welcomed by the French with attention and respect. The inconvenience which their presence occasioned had been disregarded, and their peculiarities overlooked. But now they were received with cold looks and harsh words from the officers, and with oaths, menaces, and sometimes blows, from the reckless and brutal soldiers" (175). Note how, curiously, in certain ways our historical source goes in circles in this case, as when Parkman adds in a footnote: "Some of the principal causes of the war are exhibited with spirit and truth in the old tragedy of *Ponteach*, written probably by Major Rogers" (175n). Both of these points are impressively documented in *Ponteach* (see especially scenes 1.1, about the traders, and 1.3, about the officers). But Ross also quotes local eyewitnesses on how Lieutenant Campbell's successor at Detroit, Henry Gladwin, "had antagonized the Indians by calling them 'hogs and other names' and telling them to leave because he 'would not hear them'" (339). In a chapter section titled "On Bad Terms," Dowd mentions that the same Gladwin ordered the public hanging of an Indian woman and only afterward realized that this affected "the Temper of the Indians" (qtd. *War* 65). Obviously, there was little cultural sensibility on the English side.

As Calloway writes in a curious use of theatrical metaphors: "America in 1763 was a crowded and often confused stage. The actors on stage did not have a script spelling out how the story would unfold, nor did they even have a clear view of everything that was going on. . . . Different people experienced the same events, the same year, in different ways" (17). The English reluctance to provide the Indians with essentials, and in particular with hunting gear, created hardships and a real existential crisis for them. They had neglected their resources and provisions during the war, new white settlers were encroaching on their hunting grounds, and game was scarce. Not only had they mostly lost the skills to hunt with bow and arrow, but the new rulers now refused to provide them with the very technology they needed to get food. Ross, who is mainly interested in the military aspects of Indian relations, has this to say about ammunition. After stating that "British relations with the Great Lakes Indians had deteriorated badly," he mentions the

> paternalistic relationship in which the French lavished their "children" with presents and ammunition. Over a half century the cultures had melded and morphed their ways by intermarrying and extensive trading. That changed overnight with the British victory. Squeezed by the extraordinary costs of the war, Whitehall had pulled the purse strings tight, and Amherst dutifully instituted a set of trade and settlement policies that were not nearly as generous as the French had been. The war years and the recent Cherokee action hardened Amherst into a resolute Indian hater, who now often referred to the tribes as "vermin" in correspondence. (337)

Ross also quotes Lieutenant Campbell, who had been left in charge in Detroit immediately after Major Rogers's departure, writing to Amherst on 28 November 1761: "The Indians Sold all their skins at Niagara for Rum, and are now in a Starving Condition for want of Ammunition, Which I'm afraid may drive them to Dispair. They apply to me daily and cannot be convinced I have no ammunition for that purpose" (338). At some point the issue simply became one of hunger.

The English knew that the situation was provocative and had deteriorated since their takeover in 1760. Peckham also mentions the problem of settlers and "lawless squatters" (*Indian Uprising* 103). He explains:

> It is unfortunate that the frontier has always attracted some of
> the worst examples of white mankind. The congenitally dissatis-
> fied, the fugitives from justice, the army deserters, the debtors,
> the swindlers, all were churned out of seaboard society and
> thrown to the frontier. Some of them were squatters who had
> seated themselves without title on lands acknowledged as In-
> dian property. Others traded with the savages and cheated at
> every turn. Not all the frontier settlers can be regarded as inno-
> cent victims of unprovoked cruelties. A hatred of Englishmen
> individually had been built up in the Indian mind at the same
> time that British policy was proving so exasperating. (219)

As Parkman states, the 1763 Royal Proclamation "came too late" (1994
ed. 196).[15] Following the end of the French and Indian War in 1760,
when Major Rogers had taken formal possession of the French outposts
on the Great Lakes, settlers had moved into the new territory, thus by
the time the Proclamation finally was made in 1763, hostilities had already broken out. As Peckham writes: "His Majesty's ministers knew
where Detroit was . . . and recognized a full blown Indian revolt when
they saw it. They had been discussing the desirability of a boundary
between red and white settlements in America, both as a gratification to
the Indians and as a curb to English migration for fear that interior
towns might set up manufacturing in competition with the mother
country" (*Indian Uprising* 178). He continues: "News of Pontiac's war
caused the ministry to hasten its deliberations. The crest of the Appala-
chians was set as the western limit of white settlement, and the line was
announced on October 7 by royal proclamation" (179). But "it came too
late to prevent a war and its effectiveness was promptly offset by the
refusal of westward-pushing frontiersman to observe it" (179). All hell
broke lose, first with the Indians and later with the disgruntled American settlers from the East Coast who would use the Royal Proclamation
Line as an argument to start the American Revolution.

On the Indian side, the power of the traditional chiefs, the negotiators of peace, had been systematically weakened by English stinginess.
Thus White tells us of Colonel Bouquet deriding the chief Beaver for
having "so little . . . influence among his own People" (266, ellipses
original), and comments that the English officer did not understand
that to deprive chiefs "of presents was to deprive them of influence"
(267). In short: "All over the *pay d'en haut*, those chiefs who tried to
mediate with the British lost influence" (267). The result was chaos, lack

of diplomacy, and greater influence of younger and more violent war chiefs.

The Indian Uprising

In the context of our understanding of *Ponteach*, the preceding discussion explains the outbreak of hostilities at the head of which historians have long seen Pontiac, even though it is clear today that this Indian insurrection was not masterminded by a devilish antagonist as Parkman suggests in his *Conspiracy*. Yet the onslaught was devastating, and the English lost all their outposts in the Northwest except Detroit, the most famous takeover being the one achieved through the ruse of a lacrosse game at Fort Michilimackinac, described in great detail in Alexander Henry's popular captivity narrative.[16] Middleton writes: "In the first few weeks of the conflict, Pontiac and his allies captured nine forts, killed nearly three hundred British troops, slaughtered or captured several hundred settlers, displaced many thousands more, pushed the frontiers back 50 miles in many places, and seized £100'000 worth of merchandise" (*Pontiac's War* 201).[17] The list includes Fort Sandusky, Fort St. Joseph, Fort Ouiatenon, Michilimackinac, Fort Venango, Fort Le Boeuf, and Fort Presque Isle. Fort Pitt and Detroit were put under siege. Peckham writes that "not a single British post remained in the western Great Lakes region except besieged Detroit" (*Indian Uprising* 166). He adds: "Besides attacking forts, the Indians raided the lonely cabins of settlers exposed on the western edge of Pennsylvania, Maryland, and Virginia" (214). This resulted in a general war and collateral retaliations, most infamously by the notorious "Paxton Boys," who attacked, killed, and scalped a group of innocent Christian Indians in Conestoga, Lancaster County, who had not been involved in this violence at all (see Peckham, *Indian Uprising* 219).[18] The tense relations had turned into an all-out war.

General Amherst, who after winning the war against the French had expected his remaining service in North America to be peaceful, was furious. Even Parkman writes that "Sir Jeffrey Amherst . . . held the Indians in supreme contempt, and his arbitrary treatment of them and total want of every quality of conciliation where they were concerned, had no little share in exciting them to war" (1994 ed. 195). Peckham writes that Amherst had a fit at his headquarters and suffered from culture shock: "He disliked America and particularly New York in the summertime. He wanted to go home now!" (*Indian Uprising* 171).[19]

Here is Peckham focalizing inside Amherst: "Those mad savages! Was he going to have an Indian war on his hands?" (174). In contrast to this statement in free indirect discourse, the historian concludes that Amherst himself "never tried to understand Indians, and he was ignorant that they felt themselves mistreated and reacted to it in their own fashion" (177).

Cultural misunderstandings about the very rules of warfare further exacerbated the situation. Peckham observes: "In the eighteenth century war was definitely a professional business, with its rules of correct behavior. Soldiers engaged in it; civilians did not," but the Indians "violated part of this military code. They attacked civilian settlers, they laid traps for unwary British soldiers and fired from cover, and they tortured and sometimes ate their prisoners" (*Indian Uprising* 220). He suggests that this "conflict of basic concepts of war explains the extreme measures of revenge which General Amherst came to advocate" (220). One of the commander's main allies in this ruthless fight was the Swiss mercenary General Bouquet, to whom he wrote in a letter: "I am fully convinced the only true method of treating those savages is to keep them in proper subjection and punish, without exception, the transgressors" (qtd. Peckham, *Indian Uprising* 173). It was in such a punitive expedition that Bouquet vanquished the combined Indian forces in the decisive battle of Bushy Run (1763, near present-day Harrison City, Pennsylvania), ending the siege of Fort Pitt.

The English commander even suggested the use of biological warfare. Peckham notes that Amherst "wrote to Bouquet that he wanted to hear of no prisoners being taken on his march westward to relieve Fort Pitt," and he quotes the general's postscript: "Could it not be contrived to send the small pox among the disaffected tribes of Indians? We must on this occasion use every stratagem in our power to reduce them" (*Indian Uprising* 226). Peckham continues: "Bouquet answered that he would try to spread an epidemic with infected blankets and mentioned a wish to hunt 'the vermin' with dogs. Amherst replied on July 16: 'You will do well to try to inoculate the Indians by means of blankets, as well as try every other method that can serve to extirpate this execrable race" (227).[20] Clearly the desperate high commander refused to apply his own high standards of warfare; when Native Americans were concerned, he favored genocide. He added: "You will therefore take no prisoners, but put to death all that fall into your hands of the nations who have so unjustly and cruelly committed depradations" (qtd. Peckham, *Indian Uprising* 227).

Bouquet's negotiation with the Indians after the victory is reported in Rev. William Smith's *Historical Account of Colonel Bouquet's Expedition against the Ohio Indians in the Year 1764*, which was appended to the Dublin 1769 edition of Rogers's *Journals*. As a "preliminary condition" Bouquet demanded that the Indians deliver "all the prisoners in [their] possession, without any exception; Englishmen, Frenchmen, women and children; whether adopted in [their] tribe, married or living amongst [them] under any denomination and pretence whatsoever, together with all negroes" (19–20). Smith gives a heartbreaking account: "The Indians . . . delivered up their beloved captives with the utmost reluctance; shed torrents of tears over them, recommending them to the care and protection of the commanding officer" (34).[21] The author notes these human emotions even though he doesn't believe in Indian marriage. Yet he comments: "They exercise virtues which Christians need not blush to imitate. . . . No woman . . . need fear the violation of her honour" (35). We learn that for some of the white children who had been adopted by the Indians and bonded with them, this surrender was like a second captivity: "Among the children who had been carried off young, and had long lived with the Indians, it is not to be expected that any marks of joy would appear on being restored to their parents or relatives. Having been accustomed to look upon the Indians as the only connexions they had, having been tenderly treated by them, and speaking their language, it is no wonder that they considered their new state in the light of a captivity, and parted from the savages with tears" (36). Smith was especially worried that this distress was sometimes also the case with adults, who even went on hunger strike: "But it must not be denied that there were even some grown persons who shewed an unwillingness to return. . . . Some who could not make their escape, clung to their savage acquaintance at parting, and continued many days in bitter lamentations, even refusing sustenance" (37).

The peace after the conflict named after Pontiac was settled at a big congress with Sir William Johnson at Fort Ontario in today's Oswego. Peckham describes the ritualized speeches and belt giving in great detail. He quotes Pontiac professing loyalty: "Father, while my father of France was in this country, I held him by the hand and never did him bad action. Now he is gone, I this day take you by the hand in the name of all the nations, of which I will acquaint those at home, and promise as long as I live no evil shall ever happen about Detroit, if in my own power to prevent it" (*Indian Uprising* 292). This is a lesson in shifting family politics. Peckham calls it a "climactic appearance on the stage of Indian diplomacy" and suggests that perhaps "Johnson cunningly kept [Pontiac] in the limelight" to rouse the jealousy of other chiefs (297). The Ottawa chief would soon be alienated from his own villagers and later assassinated. The loss in battle also initiated a further loss of cultural control, as White argues. It initiated the end of the middle ground.

The Imperial Perspective

To understand the historical significance of these events beyond the local situation of the Great Lakes, we have to be aware of the globalist ambitions of and in the British Empire at that time. The end of the French and Indian War was also the end of the Seven Years War in Europe and thus correlates with world events that placed England at the head of Old World imperialist ambitions. Britain was expanding east and west. After Scotland and England had been unified in 1707, the East India Company had progressed against the Mughal Empire and won the Battle of Plassey in 1757. In this First British Empire (before the loss of the American colonies and the arrival of Napoleon), the gigantic possibilities of American expansion matched and even rivaled its Asian ambitions. Native American chiefs had visited London and been a popular sensation.[22] In his book on Sir William Johnson, Fintan O'Toole discusses the visit of the four Mohawk chiefs, emphasizing the theatrical dimension of their stay, and notes that the most glamorous of them was the youngest, whom the Dutch had called Hendrick Peters. He "delivered the Mohawks' speech to Queen Anne" (10). O'Toole mentions a performance of *Macbeth* at the Haymarket, where the audience "paid their money, not to see the play, but to see the Indian Kings" (11).[23] Ross writes about the older Hendrick, with whom the young Robert Rogers had fought against the French general Dieskau under Johnson, that "the wise 75-year-old Mahican sachem Theyanoguin (also known under the Dutch name of Hendrick), who had preeminence among the Iroquois," was a "corpulent figure of great grim competence in two worlds, he wore English clothes, had visited London twice, and bore a savage knife scar across the length of his left cheek" (75). It is not clear why Ross changes the tribal affiliation to "Mahican," but in any case, the interest in imperial contact was immense and thoroughly covered by the press in the capital.

Ross writes about this crucial historical moment:

> When Rogers performed the rough and perfunctory ceremony
> of accepting Belestre's surrender of Detroit, the symbolic center-
> piece of the French west, he officiated over one of the most
> transformational moments in modern Western history. A nearly
> unimaginable swath of the continent had changed hands, the
> largest international transfer of land in history. When the peace
> was formalized in February 1763, the British Empire would
> swell larger than that of Imperial Rome, most of its vast gains in
> the New World, where it now reached from the Atlantic west to
> the Mississippi River and from Hudson Bay south to the Gulf of
> Mexico. Large swaths of this land lay unmapped and largely
> unknown to the colonists and Europeans, the contours of the
> geography not defined in paintings, maps, or travel writings or
> even yet imagined in novels or plays. (307)

Rogers himself was certainly influenced by this historical context. He
opens the "Introduction" to his *Concise Account* as follows:

> The British Empire in NORTH AMERICA is become so extensive
> and considerable, that it is presumed any attempts to transmit a
> just notion of it to the public will be favourably received by
> every Englishman who wishes well to his country; for, without
> a right knowledge of a country, new and unsettled, as a great
> part of this is, so distant from the seat of empire, it is not likely
> that attention will be paid to the defending and peopling it, and
> to the encouraging commerce in it, which is indispensibly requi-
> site to render it advantageous to the nation in general, as well as
> to those individuals who become adventurers in it. (iii)

Also the £20,000 offered to the finder of the Northwest Passage that
fired Major Rogers imagination are a symptom of this grand vision of a
Western part of the British Empire. There were vast possibilities for
geographic expansion and riches to be made.

Whereas the U.S. Americans later mainly wanted to settle in the
West and pushed back the (American) Indians, in London and within
the empire, the general picture was one of the colonial exploitation of
foreign nations—even Rogers, who should have know better about Indian tribal organization, calls "Ponteack" the "present King or Emperor"
of the western Indians in the *Concise Account* (239).[24] This knowledge is

significant for our understanding of the play *Ponteach* and its neglect by critics: after the American Revolution, the British hype about American expansion ceased, together with the interest in colonial heroes like Rogers himself. America was written off as a loss of no further concern; the British would in the future focus on trade and their "special relation," as it would later be called, with the young Anglo-American nation. And for the new Americans of the young republic these episodes became ancient colonial history—from their point of view only interesting as a harbinger of the United States. All of this explains American lack of interest in Rogers and his play, which doesn't fit into the new cultural framework of a national legacy.

The Post-*Ponteach* Northwest

Still, it may also be interesting to consider the further development of the Great Lakes area after Major Rogers's play and career in order to bring the Native American experience into better focus. White emphasizes the conflicts and shifting alliances of the Indians with the English against the Americans (again, they were on the losing side).[25] He also emphasizes the increasing intolerance and brutality, of both of the "Big Knife" settlers from Virginia and the Algonquians. Traditional chiefs, who formerly took care of their people's *besoins*, were increasingly replaced by war chiefs. The case of Pontiac seems to be representative, as "already in 1764, and increasingly in 1765, Pontiac was metamorphosing in predictable Algonquian fashion from a war leader into a chief. This was the normal life cycle of a leader" (White 300). But his transformation, anticipated in the conclusion of *Ponteach*, did not pay off—as we know, Pontiac the trader was soon assassinated.[26]

The western Indians came under more and more pressure by colonial settlers. William Johnson writes in a letter to the Earl of Dartmouth of 4 November 4 1772 "that the back[country] inhabitants particularly those who daily go over the Mountains of Virginia employ much of their time in hunting, interfere with them therein, have hatred for, ill treat, Rob and frequently murder the Indians, that they are generally a lawless sett of People" (qtd. White 315). Relationships steadily deteriorated from the French to the British and now the Americans. White writes that the new colonials who moved into the West were ignorant about and uninterested in the Indians: "Unlike the earlier Frenchmen, these British settlers did not believe that their lives depended on good relations with Indians" (317). As a result, he notes the "declining authority of British chiefs, [who] found it impossible to control the discontented" (322). Moreover, "not only did the British fail to support the chiefs as they should, they actively undermined the peace of the villages through the liquor trade, which created havoc among the Algonquians" (322). Thus there are historical issues at the origin of Rogers's opening scene with the traders in *Ponteach*: "A drunken Indian would agree to what a sober Indian would never consider. . . . Rum, by resolving social restraints, very often produced violence. But since the consequences of trading in rum did not always fall on the trader, and because the gains it could produce were so spectacular, the trade persisted" (White 342). One almost gets the impression that the historian is paraphrasing *Ponteach* (1.1).

Because the agreements of the middle ground were no longer honored, there was also a crisis of the law. As White notes, "If white settlers fell outside British laws, why should Indians fall within them?" (344). Revenge thus turned into an unrestrained pattern of lynch law: "The Algonquians, who knew well enough the desire for revenge, had buried their desires with their dead in the rituals of peace. The people of the backcountry acknowledged no such rituals" (345). The English were confronted with the same predicaments as the French had been earlier. Thus White quotes Detroit captain James Stevenson's reaction "on hearing that Captain Brown at Niagara had arrested four Senecas for murder, 'What law will they try them by? & who are to sit as their judges? If they are hang'd the savages will look upon it as murder in cold blood, & revenge will ensue'" (351). White mentions in this context the "mutual weakness of its two major parties: the Iroquois and the British empire. Both spoke for peoples—the Algonquians and the backcountry settlers—whom, in fact, they could not control" (351). The English could not control the American settlers, and the same applied to the influence of the Iroquois, who were considered the legal owners of the land where the Algonquians lived—a situation often described in American literature as the colonization of the Delaware, whom the Iroquois considered "women."[27] This had a devastating influence on land sales and made it easy for the Iroquois to sell the land of others. In the same way, Algonquians would sell the land on which they lived because they were not sure about its legal ownership.

With the final United States control of the Western territories, all traces of middle ground culture were lost. White notes an increase of Indian hating: "Indian haters killed or alienated the very men who were willing to act as alliance chiefs or mediators for the Americans"

(384). And he adds: "Indian haters killed Indians who warned them of raids. They killed Indians who scouted for their military expeditions. They killed Indian women and children. They even killed Christian, pacifist Indians as they prayed. Murder gradually and inexorably became the dominant American Indian policy" (384). White's point is that these new settlers "entered the middle ground only to destroy it" (389). A good example is the Gnadenhutten massacre of 1782. Because the Indians had "white artifacts that the Moravians had adopted" and "their horses had been branded," they were considered thieves and killed (390). For the settlers, it was unimaginable that they would live like whites. Division lines became more specifically racial: "By such killings, Indian haters kept their boundaries firm" (391).[28]

In the new Northwest Territory under an American governor, we still find a "deep animosity and endless cycles of revenge. The similarities between white and Algonquian social and political organization served only to make both sides capable of pursuing local and private vengeance with little fear of hindrance" (White 416). Even Secretary of War Henry Knox summarized "the situation for the Continental Congress in the summer of 1787" as follows: "The deep rooted prejudices, and malignity of heart, and conduct, reciprocally entertained and practiced on all occasions by the Whites and Savages will ever prevent their being good neighbors" (qtd. White 416). At this point, White finds the rise of the myth of the American frontier, of figures like the literary Dan'l Boone.[29] The Indians were vanquished. Their resistance fell apart. White mentions a delegation of chiefs who "agreed to go to Philadelphia [to meet President Washington]. The delegates survived attempts by the Kentuckians to murder them, but more than half of them succumbed to smallpox" (460). There were more famines: "Wholesale depletion of large animals became obvious only in the very late eighteenth and early nineteenth centuries" (489). He continues: "In southern Indiana, Ohio, and Illinois, whites, not Indians, were the main agents of the slaughter" (489)—also because they had encouraged the Indians to overhunt their territories and kill animals mainly for their hides.[30] The Indians were forced to radically change their way of life: "The increase of domestic livestock and the decline of game became a major indicator of the changes overtaking Indians in the early nineteenth century" (493).

There were more ill-fated alliances with the British against the Americans, but the Indians were betrayed in 1794 at Fort Miami (468), beaten by Washington's general "Mad Anthony" Wayne, after whom the fort's name was later changed to Fort Wayne.[31] His influence on the

American Western myth continues in the career of actor Marion Robert Morrison, who named himself Anthony Wayne for the silver screen, but Fox Studios rejected this because it sounded too Italian and re-named him "John Wayne." Any compromise culture in the old Indian Northwest ended with the defeat at Tippecanoe by William Henry Harrison, the new governor of Indiana Territory and later president of the United States. White ends his long study with an 1824 interview of the Shawnee prophet conducted by ethnographer Charles Trowbridge and the stylization of the two brothers Tecumseh and Tenskwatawa as the "hero" and the "witch" (520). The Indian medicine man now "had reverted to a *savage*. . . . Algonquians had become objects of study in a world of white learning" (522). And the Indians themselves became alienated from their original homes and "trapped in their dreams" (523). Stereotypes shifted from evil to noble; referentiality was objectified and kept in check. There was no longer any dialogue or interest in the subjectivity of the "other" (lower case). Rogers's play is so precious because it negotiates all the attitudes that were instrumental in this change.

Part II

Inside *Ponteach*

The Play Text and
Its Literary Qualities

4

An Artistic Failure?

Robert Rogers's play opens up many of the above-mentioned dimensions, and in its contradictory nature reflects the tensions and contradictory forces that had an impact on its author and his possible collaborator(s). My main contention is that this quality, which I have called "centrifugal," is not an aesthetic weakness but rather can be read as a richness that reflects multiple dimensions of referentiality that "matter" significantly as realistic elements referring to historical experience. This makes us take a closer look at the text itself, which will yield further fascinating issues and an artistic richness that justifies our rediscovery of the much-neglected literary side of Major Rogers as well. The following chapters, therefore, will first focus on referential issues in *Ponteach*, but beyond that, they will also discuss its form and content, elaborating on the play's aesthetic dimensions, its language, its composition, and its genre affiliations and innovations, and discuss some of the arguments and issues the play addresses in its imagery. Let's start with textual issues surrounding its production.

Negative Aesthetic Assessments

As already noted, *Ponteach* was a commercial failure, and it has also been considered an artistic failure, at best useful as a source of historical evidence. Symptomatic is the fact that Nevins's long introduction to the play in the 1914 Caxton Club edition is mainly a biography of Rogers, because "the literary importance of the tragedy does not warrant a studiously critical attention to the task of prefacing and annotating it" (7). Comparing *Ponteach* with the contemporary *Prince of Parthia* by Thomas Godfrey, "a Philadelphian, the son of a member of Franklin's Junto," Nevins observes that Godfrey's play, "beaten out in smooth blank verse, and with considerable merit of construction, . . . was much superior both poetically and dramatically to Rogers work" (15). As we shall see, I will challenge this dismissive assessment. To be sure, some discussions of this play have been very superficial. Clarence A. Andrews, for example, has mainly read Morsberger, but not the play, which is why he makes obvious mistakes: "The play asserts that it's no crime to cheat the Indians, who are 'savage beasts,' and 'don't deserve to breathe Christian air'" (33). As we shall see, this statement is made by a protagonist characterized as evil in the tale. To cite another example, Yale professor Benjamin Bissell considers "the rest of the play" (after act 1) full of "various fanciful and extravagant touches" and consistently misspells Monelia's name as "Monimia" (135).

Also the fact that *Ponteach* seems to be full of contradictory intensions and is in that sense many-voiced has been interpreted as a sign of aesthetic weakness and lack of craft. Thus Morsberger writes that the elements of the play that are not merely historical evidence, that is, the love story and the conflict between the two sons, are "stilted and artificial, with the worst characteristics of elegant eighteenth-century tragedy" (245–46). He concludes: "Except for a few scenes, the play has almost no artistic value" (246). Orians writes of *Ponteach* that "judged by present day standards of stagecraft it was crude and left a great deal to be desired" (part 1 149); Marilyn J. Anderson merely registers "Rogers' technical inability to transform his ideas into an effective dramatic form" (229). Michael Friedrichs, finally, observes that the play mixes contradictory dramatic methods to achieve a failed concoction.[1] And in her fairly superficial discussion, Priscilla Sears mentions *Ponteach* as the first play about Indians but claims that it "follows the un-American, principally European, dramatic and philosophic tradition of portraying the Indian as unrestrained, yet uncorrupted and exemplary, living happily and honorably in harmony with nature" (34–35). She agrees with the critics that they "justifiably judged it 'unreservedly insipid and flat' and 'one of the most absurd productions . . . ever seen'" (35, ellipses original). Note that this late twentieth-century critic still copies

Rogers's contemporaries like the old eighteenth-century "most absurd" argument of *The Monthly Review* and the "insipid and flat" criticism of *The Critical Review* (quoted below) and is simply unwilling to reassess the play's aesthetic value.

An exception in this sea of generally negative verdicts may be Castillo, who finds something positive in the hybridity of *Ponteach*: "The stately rhythm of the blank verse jars against the ignoble behavior of the two traders" (216). She finds New World mestizo elements that she associates with Cabeza de Vaca's captivity narrative—postcolonial qualities also noted by Tiffany Potter, who finds "ambivalent colonial mimicry" inspired by Homi Bhabha in *Ponteach* (34). What remains to be seen is, of course, what kind of aesthetic yardstick we want to apply to this writing and what we mean exactly when we ask for an aesthetic reassessment. This can be done only if we delve more deeply into the play proper.

Limited Abilities? Rogers's Education

The long line of negative evaluations mostly goes back to observations about Rogers's lack of education. Already his contemporaries didn't think much of the major's learning. Norman Gelb writes that "many considered Rogers a boorish yokel" (16). Referring to Rogers's hiring Nathaniel Potter as his personal secretary (about whom we will hear more later), Nevins finds that Sir William Johnson, the Indian agent for New York, "stated in 1767 that he [Potter] had been hired because Rogers was so illiterate as to require someone to do business for him" (*Ranger* 79–80). Much evidence of this comes from samples of Rogers's writings. Cuneo writes: "Like his associates Robert received little formal education. He was a poor speller, although we should not be too critical: his was a society where the primary means of communication was oral and all spelling was treated phonetically" (6). Ross quotes the earliest text we have, a note the youthful Rogers wrote to a friend in a panic because he had been arrested for counterfeiting: "Mr. Gilman for gods sake do the work that you promised me that you would Do by No meanes fail or you Will Destroy me for Ever. Sir, my Life lays att your providence now Ons more I adjure you by your Maker, to Do it for whie should an onest Man be Killed Sir, I am a souned freiend / Robert Rodgers" (66). Cuneo also quotes a letter to his wife that Rogers wrote during the Siege of Detroit: "Dear little Angel . . . Every moment My thoughts are with you My Souls desiar is to be personaly So and am Determened never more to be from you after this War—but will As Surely as I live when I Return continue to be a more Study [steady] Husband as Ever—more loving there canot be" (163). And Ross cites a "heartstruck letter" to his beloved Betsy: "Whenever I Set down to write to you Love and grief beyond degree together with pure gratitud and warm affection which I have for you my Dearest Betsy Invites from my Eyes a Shower. I often bid my passions all be gon and call fro thoughtless Rest but my fanceys Meet you a thousand times Every day" (315).[2] His letter writing even made it into the fiction about Rogers, as this excerpt from Kenneth Roberts's *Northwest Passage* illustrates; a character writes, "He asked me a score of times how to spell it; and I heard him ask Potter repeatedly," yet the major is said to always sign "Your affeconot husband" (380).

At the same time, however, we have to understand that Rogers had many practical language skills. From an early age on, he was able to communicate with Indians,[3] and we may well assume that he could also express himself in French. As Nester writes: "He was an articulate, animated speaker and writer of English, and was conversant in French and Algonquian" (*Struggle* 23). In his *Journals*, Rogers writes that near Carillion, "we were challenged by a centry. I answered in French, signifying that we were friends; the centinel was thereby deceived, till I came close to him, when perceiving his mistake in great surprize he called, Qui etes vous? I answered Rogers, and led him from his post in great haste, cutting his breeches and coat from him, that he might march with the greater ease and expedition. With this prisoner, we arrived at Fort William-Henry, Oct. 31, 1756" (35).[4] And in a chapter section titled "Taunting his Foe," Ross quotes a "billet" Rogers left behind for the French commander after an attack "within 600 yards of the walls of Carillion" (159):

> The next day the French ventured outside to find the rangers long gone and seventeen dead cattle, one bearing between its horns the following note:

> > I am obliged to you, Sir for the repose you have allowed me to take; I thank you for the fresh meat you have sent me; I shall take care of my prisoners; I request you to present my compliments to the Marquis de Montcalm.
> >   ROGER,
> >   Commandant of the Independent Companies (160)

French was also needed in his taking of Detroit in 1760. In the *Journals*, Rogers quotes many original letters from the French commandant "De Beleter" in Detroit and translates them into English (221–25). Similarly, when he made the French inhabitants of Detroit swear an oath to the English, "these painful words [were] read to them in French by Major Rogers" (Widder, *Beyond* 59). In any case, Rogers liked languages and communication. He had a sense of rhetoric and irony and enjoyed company—an aspect that we also find in the many references to his being a brilliant raconteur.[5]

When it comes to his prose style, we even get some very positive feedback. Glover asserts us that "Rogers' matter-of-fact account in his published *Journals* remains riveting, almost defying credibility" (181). And the magazine writer Ross projects in his biography that the bookseller

> Millan was intrigued, finding Rogers' prose clean and direct, a style honed over years of filing reports to busy superiors describing scouts and fights undertaken on terms well outside authority's experience. . . . With a knack for writing succinctly under stress, Rogers had formed a vibrant, immediate first-person narrative style highly unusual for his day. Not until far into the next century would travel writers, foreign correspondents, and such military leaders as Ulysses Grant develop comparative powers of plain exposition. (359)

Especially the writing in the *Journals* and the *Concise Account* is often praised. Ross even claims that "Thomas Jefferson . . . modeled the layout of his *Notes on Virginia* on Rogers's monograph. It would be part of the first generation of natural history texts in the New World" (360). Even Morsberger, who is fairly critical of Rogers's dramatic skills, writes: "His prose style is simple and effective, both vivid and lucid" (245). This is confirmed by Nevins: "Beginning with October, 1755, and continuing nearly six years, all Rogers expeditions, adventures, and exploits, are recorded in his journals;—drily, unambitiously, but with a detail that in spite of itself glows at some passages into vividness" (*Ranger* 33). If in the *Journals* "ill-calculated space given at times to trivial letters and orders betrays hasty composition," the *Concise Account* "bears evidence of more careful literary workmanship" (76). Nevins continues:

> The style of the second book, moreover, is solid and clear, and it
> amasses an amount of information, drawn from observation
> and research, that is far from contemptible. Altogether, there is
> no point at which we are more likely to be surprised into real
> respect for the Ranger than in the reading of his two treatises.
> They not merely exhibit his singular success in self-education,
> but for one of his education and profession reflect every credit
> upon his natural powers and abilities. (78)

Even the great Francis Parkman admits: "His mind, naturally active,
was by no means uncultivated, and his books and unpublished letters
bear witness that his style as a writer was not contemptible" (1994 ed.
162–63). In a footnote Parkman writes about the *Journals*: "The incidents
of each day are minuted down in a dry, unambitious style, bearing the
clear impress of truth" (163n). From all this evidence we can conclude
that Rogers certainly knew how to express himself despite his low origins, that he knew how to name things clearly, and how to tell a good
story.

The *Concise Account*, as the direct predecessor of *Ponteach*, is rich in
facts and provides much information about Indians, the kayak, their
tools, what a sauna is, the bark canoe, and how they make maple syrup.
Rogers also talks about the languages of the Indians, the matrilineal social system, their forms of government, and their religion. In addition
he presents a detailed bestiary of North America, listing its most important animals and their behavior, which he describes in loving detail.
Equally important is the geographically distributed detailed description of rivers,[6] plants, trees, and soil. In addition to honing his writing
skills, all these descriptions necessarily must have influenced the play.

Printing History

Unlike Rogers's earlier two books, *Ponteach* was not a success; it was
never reprinted during his lifetime. The reviews, many of which are
available in the commented Tiffany Potter edition, made fun of the play
or were disgusted by the fact that it showed things that the cultured of
London didn't want to see. The play text proposed to stage unacceptable
things, and these reviews contributed to the outcome that *Ponteach* was
never performed. Moreover, since no archives of the publisher, John
Millan in London, have been found so far, it is unclear what the exact
conditions of the production were; it is highly probable, however, that

the major carried the costs. Cuneo writes that "Rogers' publisher . . . advanced him credit" (174). But with the demise of Rogers's career a few years later, the play, like its author, was forgotten.[7]

It was almost a century later, in 1851, that Francis Parkman reprinted two scenes from act 1 as historical evidence in his *Conspiracy*: "The account of Indian wrongs and sufferings given in the first act accords so nearly with that conveyed in contemporary letters and documents, that two scenes of the play are here given, with a few omissions, which good taste demands" (1991 ed. 853).[8] But the play as a whole was only rediscovered in the early twentieth century by Allan Nevins, who was, like Parkman, a historian fascinated by the Ranger's career. Following his MA thesis of 1913, Nevins edited the first reprint, the Caxton Club edition of 1914. Not surprisingly, he writes in his introduction to this edition: "The importance of Rogers' *Ponteach* does not lie in any purely artistic qualities. It is only the historian, whether of events or letters, in whom it can nowadays inspire more than a transiently curious interest," and he even claims that "it must seem to any reader who picks up the play for its own sake almost pitifully devoid of intrinsic merits. The web and woof of its style never rise from the commonplace to the even faintly poetical, and all too frequently sink to doggerel and empty declamation" (11).[9] Knowledge of the play remained limited to a small group of historical connoisseurs. As Friedrichs notes, it is not a recognized subject of literary studies.[10] The Caxton Club version of *Ponteach* at least made it into the very specialized three-volume anthology of early American drama compiled between 1918 and 1921 by Montrose Moses, who comments in his introduction to the play: "There is no distinct excellence in depicting Indian character as such, after the romantic manner of Cooper, although Rogers, with his English tradition, has been able to lend to his dialogue a certain dignity of diction which is striking, and which gives the play a decided literary value" (1:114).

Otherwise, silence . . . until Tiffany Potter's Canadian edition in 2010, that is, again roughly another century later. Her reprint is lovingly edited, with numbered lines, and contains much comment and extra material such as many of the contemporary reviews and the last part of the *Concise Account* with information on the habits of the Indians, the encounter with the "Emperor Ponteack," and Rogers's memorable description of North American animals. The best source to work with, however, is the PDF version of the original edition available in the Internet Archive, which is both analogic and digital, that is, visually correct as well as verbally traceable for search functions. Also available in the archive are Rogers's other books (and of course much more material from olden times, as many grateful scholars know). I have chosen to cite, wherever possible, page numbers from these first editions, adding the more precise line numbers from Tiffany Potter for *Ponteach*. In quotations from the play, I have bracketed letters to indicate changes in capitalization.

5

The Realistic Dimension

As it is obviously the most striking aspect of *Ponteach*, I will first discuss its many referential qualities and the territorial knowledge that Robert Rogers could contribute to this aesthetic production. Like an ethnographer, he knew about Indian behavior and their habits. He knew the English personnel on the Great Lakes—when it comes to the inhabitants of Fort Detroit, we can almost speak of a *pièce à clé* pointing at historical personages. And he furthermore knew the events, the incidents, which he presents in an unforgivingly direct way. Our preoccupation with such realism will, however, at the same time and by contrast also lead us to note the saliency of unfitting elements where knowledge is overruled by strangely dominant literary conventions—an aspect that will later lead us to much more formal and literary assessments.

Brechtian Didactics

But first things first: the element most praised in *Ponteach* is its stark realism. The author is not mincing words but uses a direct language of fact to criticize the English colonizers on the Great Lakes. The historical position of Major Robert Rogers makes this information particularly relevant, as he knew the Ottawa chief Pontiac personally: they had met

on friendly terms and smoked the calumet together when Rogers first
went to Detroit to make the French surrender the fort; then they had
fought on different sides during the Siege of Detroit; and after the rebellion, they again drank brandy together. As Gordon M. Sayre observes:
"Ponteach's genuinely heroic figure arises, I believe, from the fact that
Rogers was there. He met Pontiac and fought against his rebels, and his
play bears the mark of this experience" (*Tragic Hero* 19).

Nevins claims in his introduction to the Caxton edition of *Ponteach*
that, "altogether, Rogers' picture of the vices and abuses of the soldiers
and traders, lying at the source of the rebellion, of the galled resentment of the Indians, and, in fact, of the whole fundamental characteristics of much of border life, is proved by contemporary documents to be
faithful and authoritative" (14).[1] Rogers knew the facts, and he could
express them clearly. Thus the style of the whole first act is even curiously reminiscent of Brechtian epic theater. Barnard Hewitt, though
wrong on a major fact,[2] writes in *Theatre U.S.A.: 1668 to 1957* that *Ponteach* is "an interesting play because of its sympathetic attitude towards
the Indians and the sharpness with which it portrays the rascality and
cupidity and cruelty of their white oppressors. The early scenes might
have been conceived by Bertold Brecht" (106–7).[3] Like Brecht's "epic
theater," the opening scenes of Rogers's play are of an almost allegorical
didacticism that lays out the social roles of the interaction in an exemplary, direct style controlled by a narrative perspective that foregrounds
the facts and makes no bones about exploitative agency, ideologies,
and responsibilities in a way reminiscent of Marxist exposures of capi-
talist economics. The play shows the events in brutal directness, what
Ross calls Rogers's "powers of plain exposition" (359).

Thus in act 1, scene 1, we encounter "the very Quintessence of
Trade" (1.1.34) and "*Indian* Commerce" (1.1.37). The older M'Dole
teaches the younger Murphey: "But, as you are my Friend, I will inform
you / Of all the secret Arts by which we thrive" (1.1.18–19). There is a
manipulative plan behind this, and it goes as follows: "Our fundamental Maxim then is this, / That it is no Crime to cheat and gull an *Indian*"
(1.1.28–29).[4] Thus M'Dole tells his apprentice how to manipulate the
scales by putting a foot on them and making the Indians believe that it
"exactly weigh'd a Pound" (1.1.42). The actors openly express themselves without much hiding, and this expository stage behavior is now
applied to an economics lesson demonstrating their ideology. When
three Indians arrive, they first get some strong drink for free in order
to induce them afterward buy the overpriced, watered-down rum.

Murphey now thanks his teacher for the "kind instructions": "By *Jove*, you've gain'd more in a single Hour / Than ever I have done in Half a Year (1.1.100–101). M'Dole deflects all responsibility for wrongdoing: "Let their Vengeance light / on others' Heads, no matter whose" (1.1.115–16). Rogers shows here how causality is willingly obfuscated in a deregulated market that ignores the consequences of such injustice and thrives on social irresponsibility. In European fashion it banks on profits and neglects what White would describe as the need for adequate relationships (see above). It treats business partners as opponents one can steal from rather than as allies.

The consequences of this behavior are well illustrated in the second scene, which applies this imbalance to game hunting. We meet a pair of disgruntled Englishmen who blame the Indians for the lack of wild animals: "These hateful *Indians* kidnap all the Game" (1.2.13). Again there is an older Englishman, called Honnyman, who immediately turns M'Dole's logic of dispersed "vengeance" from the previous scene against the Indians: "Cursed revengeful, cruel, faithless Devils! / They kill'd my Father and my eldest Brother. / Since which I hate their very Looks and Name" (1.2.31–33). Retaliation is abstracted to an Indian type of "Looks and Name," and this type is easily transferred to another token in a gesture of attributing collective responsibility. Honnyman makes clear that he is aware of his transfer: "Tho' these are not the same . . . / I abhor, detest and hate them all. / And now cou'd eat an *Indian's* Heart with Pleasure" (1.2.36–39). He even adds his own example of inverted logic by desiring cannibalism, again arrogating to himself behavior usually projected onto Indians. The two hunters then shoot two natives loaded with furs and congratulate themselves for their economic efficiency in obtaining so many pelts with a "single Shot" (1.2.66).[5] They also scalp the Indians for cash, and when the younger one, Orsbourn, has second thoughts about this vicious deed— "I vow I'm shock'd a little to see them scalp'd" (1.2.90)—Honnyman teaches him that "it's no more Murder than to crack a Louse, / . . . / And as to Haunting, *Indians* have no Ghosts, / But as they live like Beasts, like Beasts they die" (1.2.92–95). The natives are not human beings; like animals, they have no soul. There is no guilt involved, and there are no legal consequences: "And think no more of being hang'd or haunted" (1.2.103). Justice correlates with a metaphysical balance curiously denied as an absence of primitive superstitious causality ("haunting") that strangely would apply only to one's own species or race (not to animals and Indians). Agency in this economy only goes in one, deadly, direction: "And bless the first Inventor of a Gun" (1.2.106). This is a demonstration of the rawest and crudest kind of imperialism.

Traders, hunters, officers—Rogers systematically presents us with the whole array of colonial personnel, illustrating the evils of power and prejudice. Colonel Cockum speaks out on the "damned bawling *Indians*" and "their Complaints" (1.3.1–2). And Captain Frisk observes that "their old King *Ponteach* grows damn'd saucy" (1.3.10). The names themselves signal a didactic allegorical mode. These characters are what they are called—a quality certainly compatible with epic theater. Again the scene shows that the complaints should actually be inverted because offensive behavior comes only from the English. Tiffany Potter has observed that some of the officers' complaints of "insolence" (1.3.14) and encroachments of "familiarity" (1.3.16) are actually rooted in the English language of class conflict and its sense of superiority (Rogers, *Ponteach* [2010] 72n).

Enter Ponteach, who complains about his men being cheated by traders. From a class perspective, he would certainly be their peer, but he is rebuffed by Colonel Cockum: "Hold your noisy cursed Nonsense; / I've heard enough of it; what is it to me?" (1.3.28–29). Ponteach's experience of reality is refuted, and the Indian is even denied the very capability to make sense. Also Captain Frisk denies any meaning in the native's discourse and does not want to be plagued with his "cursed endless noise" (1.3.41). The other is excluded from participation in any form of dialogue insofar as his ability to forge logic (rather than "noise") is rejected by the colonialists' racism. The chief responds to this offense in the traditional Algonquian way: "My Bus'ness here is only with your Colonel" (1.3.43). He wants to formalize the interaction by naming the colonel as his proper interlocutor because his concern is with a friendly relationship as the main purpose of economics ("Bus'ness").[6]

After this is straightforwardly denied and the English start cursing—"You maybe d—d, and all your *Frenchmen* too" (1.3.48)—we learn that the innocent Indian chief does not even know such language: "Be d—d! What's that? I do not understand" (1.3.49). According to Tim Fulford, "this language exemplified Rogers's new, shocking and perhaps unconscious realism, which offended polite taste and dramatic convention, and was born of the play's backwoods transatlantic origin" (87). He introduces "to literature language really spoken by men decades before Wordsworth called for poets to do so. His characters speak neither the gentlemanly language of officers' dispatches and governors' reports, nor the language expected on the London stage, but the semi-literate, blasphemous slang of hard men desperate to make their fortunes by any means" (88). Fulford continues: "For the first time, the unofficial language of colonization burns off the page of a literary work: it is greedy, grasping, racist, immoral, cruel. Rogers reveals empire to be dirty work, done with relish by debased men" (88). The censorship of the word *damned* is in the original, which may reflect the printing environment in London at that time. The expression triggers an immediate reference to Manichean metaphysics, as Cockum explains: "The Devil teach you; he'll do it without a Fee" (1.3.50). The play thus exposes a theological layer of absolute Otherness that determines the approach of the English. The concern of the interaction has become more complicated and conceptualist here, explaining the materialist action.

Significantly, Ponteach delivers a counter discourse, his great speech, and insists that he is not a conquered subject, a historical issue we have discussed above:

> So ho! Know you whose Country you are in?
> Think you, because you have subdu'd the *French*,
> That *Indians* too are now become your Slaves?
> This Country's mine, and here I reign as King;
> I value not your Threats, nor Forts, nor Guns;
> I have good Warriors, Courage, Strength, and Skill.
> Colonel, take care; the Wound is very deep,
> Consider well, for it is hard to cure.
>
> (1.3.62–69)

These words are, moreover, very close in content and attitude to the message Rogers reports in his *Concise Account*, when he met "Ponteack" and his "Attawas" on his way to the then French garrison in Detroit: "In the year 1760, when I commanded and marched the first detachment into this country that was ever sent there by the English, I was met in my way by an embassy from him. . . . His ambassadors had also orders to inform me, that he was Ponteack, the King and Lord of the country I was in" (240). Castillo rightly observes: "One wonders to what degree the content of Ponteach's speeches in the play actually reflects Pontiac's personal exchanges with Rogers" (218). Here is again Rogers in the *Concise Account*: "At first salutation when we met, he demanded my business into his country, and how it happened that I dared to enter it without his leave? When I informed him that it was not with any design against the Indians . . . I at the same time delivered him several friendly messages, or belts of wampum" (240–41). The play shows that the attitude of the English officers who took over after Rogers was of a different kind. Rogers had emphasized cooperation: "At our second meeting he gave me the pipe of peace and both of us by turns smoked with it, and he assured me he had made peace with me and my detachment; that I might pass through his country unmolested, and relieve the French garrison; and that he would protect me and my party" (241). In stark contrast, the officers of the play refuse cooperation. They rely on subjugation and relish military hubris: "*Frisk.* Oh! Colonel, they are never worth our minding, / What can they do against our Bomb and Cannon? / . . . / Heav'n be thank'd, we're safe within these Walls" (1.3.76–79). Like the Puritans of old, they want to control the land from behind palisades.[7]

The last scene of the first act again moves into a mode of economic demonstration when we meet three governors in the fort. Again they have allegorical names—Sharp, Gripe, and Catchum: "Here we are met to represent the King" (1.4.1). Note the metaperformative nature of this comment, which invites the theater audience to witness the following events. The scene makes no bones about their greed and directly lays out the superstructural ideology of the governors' stealing from the Crown at the cost of the Indians: entrusted with "these *Indian* presents" (1.4.19), they take half of the "Thousand Pound" (1.4.20), emphasizing that they are profiting from the fact that the Indians do not know mathematics: "*Catchum.* Yes, only these Two simple easy Rules, / Addition and Subtraction, are great Helps, / And much contribute to our Happiness" (1.4.41–43). Superior European cultural technology is being abused. The Indians will also be unable to read the inventory to discover the cheating: "What matters that? They cannot read, you know" (1.4.58).[8] Rogers makes it clear that Ponteach, who has already asked the officers about the intentions of their king—"Did your King tell you thus to treat the *Indians*?" (1.3.52)—blames the Crown's representatives for this behavior, which is shown as the very cause of the oncoming rebellion.

As in the third scene, the first part is an interior discussion among themselves which manifests the attitudes of the English, and which is then followed by an encounter with Ponteach as the Indian representative, illustrating the practice of their ideology. The governors are somewhat more diplomatic than the officers and at least try to keep up a facade of friendly relations. Denying any social forces, they deflect the Indian's grievances to individual human nature: "There's good and bad, you know, in every Nation" (1.4.86). Sharp assures Ponteach of the English king's good intentions: "He like a Father loves you as his Children; / And like a Brother wishes you all Good" (1.4.109–10). But as Rogers presents the situation, Ponteach sees through this excuse and wants to talk to the English king directly, as an equal:

> Your King, I hear's a good and upright Man,
> True to his word, and friendly in his Heart;
> Not proud and insolent, morose and sour,
> Like these his petty Officers and Servants;
> I want to see your King and let him know
> What must be done to keep the Hatchet dull.[9]
>
> (1.4.114–19)

And he has a message for him that would metadramatically address audiences in a London performance: "Let him know then his People here are Rogues, / And cheat and wrong and use the *Indians* ill" (1.4.126–27). Later in the Senate House, he complains again: "Their King is distant; would he hear our Prayers" (3.3.85). In the real world, this message to the King would address the play audience (and possibly even the king himself) and sidetrack the unreliable American intermediaries. As we will see later, Rogers put words in Ponteach's mouth that supported his own personal ambitions for royal office. -

In any case, the economic base of this diplomatic transaction is clear: the Indians notice the meagerness of the English gifts. Thus one chief says: "We think it very small, we heard of more" (1.4.154). Another chief states, "Your King is stingy" (1.4.161). And a fourth one talks about his friend "King Astenaco, the great Southern Chief," who had been to England[10] and told him "that he [i.e., the English king] was generous, kind and true, / But that his Officers were Rogues and Knaves, / And cheated Indians out of what he gave" (1.4.165–69). The play here hammers home its point by repetition. The audience must know about all this American graft and corruption. Ponteach gives belts and furs in return with a message to the king, but he refuses his representatives: "The Calumet I do not chuse to smoak" (1.4.205). His warning anticipates the oncoming war:

> Tell your King from me,
>
> . . .
>
> That I have Warriors, am myself a King,

> And will be honour'd and obey'd as such;
> Tell him my Subjects shall not be oppress'd
>   (1.4.207–11)

Yet when the Indian delegation leaves, the governors still don't understand the seriousness of the situation. Instead they delight in the fact
that the presents from the Indians are much more valuable than theirs—
rich wampum belts and heavy furs. They decide to keep them: "What
would the King of *England* do with Wampum? / Or Beaver Skins d'ye
think? He's not a Hatter!" (1.4.246–47). Note the powerful imagery of
disrespectful familiarity—in the very sense of challenging class at home
(i.e., the king's authority, or "hat"). Thus the dialogue artfully decon-
structs the earlier argumentation of "insolence" about the Indians.

The pattern of greed is sealed when the governors decide to start
their own business venture:

> We throw the whole into a common Stock,
> And go Copartners in the Loss and Gain.
> Thus most who handle Money for the Crown
> Find means to make the better Half their own
> And, to your better Judgments with Submission,
> The self Neglecter's a poor Politician.
> These Gifts, you see, will all Expenses pay;
> Heav'n send an Indian Treaty every Day;
> We dearly love to serve our King this way.
>   (1.4.255–63)

Giddy with their profits, they start rhyming in addition to using iambic
pentameter. The combination of "submission" and "politician" emphasizes exactly what is wrong in this English North American colonial
administration, where public service and private profit are inseparable.
All of this is summarized in another set of triple-rhyming, sarcastic
closing lines, reminiscent of the earlier appreciation of guns, which end
this memorable opening act of the play.

Note that these are type characters who personify causality. They
stand for certain kinds of motivation and behavior. Moreover, there is
a clear exposition of how one specific action will dialectically lead to
another particular reaction. Logic and causality reign supreme. Significantly, Honnyman later recants his own causal diffusions when he is at
the torture pole: "Had I not kill'd their Friends, they might have spar'd /

My Wife, my Children, and perhaps myself, / And this sad dreadful Scene had never happen'd" (4.4.64–66). If today such rationality may smack of Marxist dialectics, it may also reflect the logical thinking of the military officer Rogers—or the theological retribution theory of a coauthor, as I will suggest below.

Real People

The allegorical force of this unflattering portrait of colonial politics in the New World is at the same time supported by historical allusions and not-so-oblique references to real people and events. The heady Captain Frisk in the officers' scene was probably inspired by the unlucky redcoat Captain Dalyell, who died in a reckless sortie during the Siege of Detroit, which ended in the defeat at Bloody Run.[11] Rogers, who had been ordered back to Detroit, had to safeguard the retreat. Ross sees Dalyell as exemplary of a "British officer's arrogance about redcoat invincibility" (346). And Peckham writes about him: "Besides being ambitious and self-confident, the captain had absorbed Amherst's contempt for Indians as intelligent fighters" (*Indian Uprising* 202). Only the partial Parkman reports that "Dalzell raised his clear voice above the din" (1994 ed. 311) and calls him a "gallant soldier" (314).

As to the governors, Tiffany Potter writes: "Ponteach offers detailed criticism of colonial policy and very lightly veiled attacks on individual historical figures, such as Fort Detroit commandant Major Henry Gladwin's apparent embodiment in the acid-tonged Governor Sharp" (32).[12] Sayre in turn suggests that the Governors Sharp, Gripe, and Catchum are "likely based on Sir William Johnson or Jeffrey Amherst" (*Tragic Hero* 154). As Amherst had always supported Rogers's career, he may have been a less likely target, but Johnson, whom Rogers had known for a long time and who had become one of his enemies and would later destroy his career, is very probably a model for these unsympathetic characters. Both Parkman and Peckham write in great detail about the partying and dancing at the first visit to Detroit of the superintendent of Indian affairs in 1761. Peckham quotes from Johnson's journal: "[The ladies] assembled at 8 o'clock at night to the number of about twenty. I opened the ball with Mademoiselle Curie—a fine girl. We danced until five o'clock in the morning" (78–79).[13] Johnson is also a likely role model for the character "Ogden," mentioned by the traders, who was manipulating weights: "By this old Ogden built his stately

House, / Purchas'd Estates, and grew a little King" (1.1.38–39). This "stately House" may well refer to Johnson Hall, Johnson's own Trump Tower in Johnstown, New York. As Calloway writes: "Johnson diverted much of the management of Indian affairs and Indian trade from Albany to Johnson Hall" (64).[14] And later: "Major Robert Rogers, who shared Amherst's distrust of Sir William, may well have had the baronet in mind when he wrote his play, *Ponteach, or The Savages of America*, in which an unscrupulous trader kept a foot on the weighing scales when buying furs from Indians" (64). Thus we find a certain recognition factor, which involves Rogers's propaganda for or against certain powerful players in the English Northwest. But the historical reading of these hints is something we can only speculate about—they were either ignored, or they backfired against the later governor of Michilimackinac.

Also the fiction writer Roberts suggests this association in *The Northwest Passage*, when he has Rogers go over the scene with the governors: "Then Governor Sharp speaks up. He ought to be played by someone like Sir William Johnson—a smug old hypocrite, able to steal your chronometer while telling you he doesn't use chronometers" (439). Later he writes: "Rogers tossed the proofs back on the table: 'ain't that like Johnson?' he said. 'Superintendent of the Six Nations and of all other Northern Indians! Look at Gage, Commander-in-Chief of His Majesty's Forces in America! Look at the two of 'em, thick as two squirrels with the same tail!'" (439). Ross suggests that Thomas Gage was probably jealous of Rogers's military prowess—Rogers had witnessed Gage's cowardice in a battle near Fort Carillion in 1658 (198, 376). When Gage became commander of the English forces in North America, Rogers had many reasons to dislike him.

In addition to these real, slanted, or supposed English impersonations in the play, we have a strong reference to Neolin, the famous Delaware prophet, who exerted great influence in an early pan-Indian movement that was expressed in his famous dream. Widder writes about "Neolin's vision where a Wolf (Delaware) Indian made a trip to heaven" (*Beyond* 99). And Sayre observes that "Rogers' Ponteach includes a character named the Wolf, identified in the dramatis personae as an 'Indian King who sides with Ponteach'" (*Tragic Hero* 151), whose line of argument in the Indian council correlates with the dream of the Delaware prophet. The Wolf reminds the councilors of a golden age, when they

> Liv'd by the Chace, with Nature's Gift content,
> The cooling Fountain quench'd their raging Thirst.
> Doctors and Drugs, and Med'cines were unknown,
> Even Age itself was free from Pain and Sickness.
>
> (3.3.180–83)

He warns that they have become "soften'd Sons, a puny race" (3.3.194), and "poison'd with the Infection of [their] Foes" (3.3.199)—though it is unclear if this infection is medical (smallpox) or cultural, or both. He offers advice: "Dare to be like our fathers, brave and strong, / Nor further let the growing Poison spread" (3.3.203–4). The Delaware prophet argued that Indians should return to their old ways and abandon the influence of white culture. His influence stands as an early example of Native American nationalism that tried to unify different tribes against their common white enemies—a strategy that would move west, continue with the Shawnee prophet Tenskwatawa, and later even lead to the ill-fated ghost-dance movement. Significantly, Neolin's message was expressed in a dream vision about the Master of Life, with three paths to choose from (see the illustration in Sayre, *Tragic Hero* 149), an element that suggests the influence of Christian narratives and what White calls "middle-ground" culture rather than any pristine Indian religion. White insists that "with his references to a Christian God, to heaven and hell, to sin, and to a return to old ways, [Neolin] was part of a growing movement of religious syncretism among the Delawares and Shawnees, [who had begun to] combine Quaker beliefs" with their own (279).[15] Fulford notes that "the God of which the prophet spoke . . . was a post-colonial hybrid of the Great Spirit, in which most North American Indians believed, and the remote heavenly Jehovah, about whom the missionaries preached" (81). Thus his "authentic" Indian heritage already negotiated European notions.[16] Neolin's dream had been quoted (and somewhat bent and appropriated) by Pontiac in his famous speech in the council at the Ecorse River, which Parkman stylized into the beginning of Pontiac's masterminding the insurrection, noting that he "conclud[ed] by the proposal of his plan for destroying Detroit" (1994 ed. 210). Peckham also mentions the Delaware prophet, and Pontiac's appropriation of the story and its message (*Indian Uprising* 113–16), confirming that "Pontiac had altered the Prophet's message slightly to support his own ambitions. . . . Pontiac twisted his meaning to point it at the British and except the French" (116). Significantly, the Wolf's speech in the play is followed by the intervention of the French priest, who "desire[s] Admittance to [Ponteach's] Council" (3.3.222). Thus the referential dimension of *Ponteach*'s personnel opens up all kinds of complicated contemporary political issues. The hybridity of their discourse is both internal and Indian already as well as externally imposed by the obvious influence of European dramatic conventions, as I will illustrate.

Another important Indian character in the play, who never appears but whose influence looms large, is the Mohawk chief Hendrick, mentioned in the second act, when Chekitan objects to the war because "[t]he powerful *Mohawk* King / Will ne'er consent to fight against the English" (2.2.74–75). Worse, he may influence the other chiefs "[t]o muster all their Strength against our Father" (2.2.78). Hendrick is again a topic in the negotiations in Ponteach's "Cabbin," when Philip offers to dissolve the Mohawk's "strong Attachment" to the English (2.3.143). The whole tragedy of the events, which also involves the love story between Pontiac's son Chekitan and Hendrick's daughter, Monelia, is one between the major Indian "nations" (if we may use the word against White's advice), the Algonquians and the Iroquois. The Mohawks, representing the latter, were thick with Sir William Johnson, whom one of his biographers, James Flexner, calls the "Mohawk Baronet."[17] The play correctly describes its own "Hendrick" as an ally of the English, although the real Hendrick was already dead at the time of the play's events. Flexner writes that he had fought in the Battle of Lake George with Rogers's Rangers (147–60). In his book we find several pictures of "the great Mohawk sachem who was Johnson's dearest Indian friend, as depicted by I. Faber in 1710" (41) and "an original drawing by T. Jeffries 1756" (147). So what are we to do when Nevins makes the following assertion in his introduction to the Caxton edition of *Ponteach*?

> The part played in the story by Pontiac's negotiations for Mohawk aid has no basis in fact, for this easternmost tribe of the Iroquois Confederacy was a fast-rooted ally of the English, and would have offered a field of discouragingly scant promise to his emissaries. We know nothing of Pontiac's sons or Hendrick's daughter; Hendrick himself was eight years dead at the time of the revolt; and private calamities had nothing to do with Pontiac's retirement to the Illinois. (14)

There is clearly poetic license in resurrecting this beloved Indian character, probably the one with the highest recognition among English theatergoers familiar with the stellar visit of the "Four Indian Kings" in 1711. Also Tiffany Potter, who even mentions two chiefs called "Hendrick," emphasizes the "recognizability of the Mohawk 'Hendricks' of the two previous generations" (7). But Rogers's didactic point was probably to lay out the basic political conflict of the different alliances between the Algonquian Indians and the French (Ponteach) in the *pay d'en haut* and between the English and the Iroquois (Mohawk) in the eastern colonies (mainly New York), and to make them part of the plot. The resurrection of the ancient chief clearly fulfills this function—and the fact that his children supposedly roam about the Great Lakes is plausible as well in view of the great migrations of Indian refugees at that time.

We may also add to our list of historically referential figures certain stereotypical characters. Thus, as already mentioned, the rapacious traders, murderous hunters, and the haughty officers of allegorical name in *Ponteach* were well-known figures on the frontier, just as were the French priests, the unhappy captives, and the diverse Indian groups, civil chiefs and war chiefs. A formal type of accuracy may be found in Rogers's consistent pairing of protagonists: two traders, two hunters, two Indians killed. Thus in his *Michillimackinac Journal*, Rogers is visited by "Two Chiefs of the Chippeawa" (15 October 1766) and later "Two Chiefs of St. Mary's" (5 November 1766). More crucial to the "culture of revenge," which we also find addressed in the first two scenes of the play, Richard White comments on the killing of La Demoiselle's people in 1752: "Two rebels had died, and now Frenchman began to fall in combinations of two. The Miamis promptly killed two soldiers at Fort Miami. At Vincennes, two Frenchman were killed while making pirogues, and two slaves were also murdered" (229). And later, just when Rogers was writing Ponteach, the following events occurred:

> By the late winter of 1765 and the spring of 1766, killings in the *pay d'en haut*, particularly around the Ohio, were reported with an alarming regularity. At Detroit, two soldiers were killed by the Saint Joseph Potawatomis in revenge, as it turned out, for the rape of two Indian women. . . . In April, at the mouth of the Scioto, two employees of British traders murdered five Shawnee men and women while they slept. The victims died after having fed the starving Englishmen. Robbery was the apparent motive. (White 345)

Thus there is an almost journalistic accuracy in some of the fictional events Rogers elaborates. The rape in the last quote may even add some probability to the melodramatic case of Monelia and the lecherous priest.

Real History

Generally, even in the later part of the play, which has been labeled pure fiction by some critics, we find references to historical events, though often much compressed, as was usual in theatrical representations of that time. Thus it takes a long time for the Indians to start the war, much of which is upstaged by the tragic love affair between Chekitan and Monelia, and the conspiracies of the French priest and Chekitan's evil brother, Philip. But Philip already refers to the historical takeover of Fort Detroit by Robert Rogers in his first appearance. Hadn't his father first favored the English and

> protected them from harm,
> Nay, put them in Possession of *Detroit*;
> And join'd to fill the Air with loud Huzza's
> When *England's* flag was planted on its Walls?
>
> (2.1.28–31)

This is a clear reference to the events also described in the *Journals*, when Rogers took Detroit from the French Captain Belestre: "The French garrison laid down their arms, English colours were hoisted, and the French taken down, at which about 700 Indians gave a shout, merrily exulting" (228). Obviously, Rogers is making the character Philip refer to his own earlier description of historical events.

The play also refers to the intercultural misunderstanding, supported by international law as I observe below, that after conquering Canada, the English would "own" the Indian land. Inverting the accusations of "insolence," Ponteach states that the English are "false, deceitful knavish, insolent, / Nay think us conquered, and our Country theirs, / Without a Purchase, or ev'n asking for it" (2.2.62–64). The plan to negotiate with King Hendrick shows the limitations of the Indian village solidarity. Thus when Chekitan praises his brother's idea of "urging their Attachment to our Cause" (2.2.332), he points to the real complications of Indian alliances in Pontiac's time.

When the insurrection finally breaks out, after the meeting in the Indian "Senate-house" in the third scene of act 3, this corresponds to the famous council of Indian chiefs at the Ecorse River on 17 April 1763, about which Parkman writes a whole chapter: "Having roused in his war-like listeners their native thirst for blood and vengeance, he [Pontiac] next addressed himself to their superstition, and told the following tale" (1994 ed. 203). In the historical council, no Delaware prophet was present, but according to Robert de Navarre, Pontiac "related in the council the story of a Wolf (Delaware) Indian, who had journeyed to Heaven and talked with the Master of Life. He spoke with so much eloquence that his narrative had just the effect upon them that he desired" (22).[18] In the play, we also find a historically prophetic vision by a chief called "the Bear," which actually predicts Manifest Destiny:[19]

> Lo, these proud Strangers now possess the Whole;
> Their Cities, Towns, and Villages arise,
> Forests are spoil'd, the Haunts of Game destroy'd,
> And all the Sea Coasts made one general Waste:
> Between the Rivers Torrent-like they sweep,
> And drive our Tribes towards the setting Sun.
>
> (3.3.159–64)

The Bear also talks of dispersed tribes whose "very name is lost" (3.3.166)—which reflects the situation of the "refugees" described in White's book.

History continues in act 4, in the famous scalp tossing depicted in scene 3, when we hear of Indian victories and "Huzza"-shouting warriors declare: "Three Forts are taken, all consumed and plundered" (4.3.33). Tiffany Potter writes that this is, in a "highly condensed" timeline, a reference to the English forts of Sandusky, St. Joseph, and Miami taken in 1763 (13n).

And finally, in the very last scene of the play, we read that other chiefs have "Patched up a Peace, and lend their Help no more" (5.5.41), which can be seen as a reference to the aborted Siege of Detroit. Tenesco quickly brings news of the final defeat, of "speedy Flight" and "the Fury of a conquering Foe" (5.5.75–77). In his immediately following final grand monologue, Ponteach accepts his defeat, again insinuating Manifest Destiny: "I will not fear—but must obey my Stars; / Ye fertile Fields and glad'ning Fields, adieu (5.5.86–87). Thus the only power left to Rogers's Ponteach is his "unconquer'd Mind" (5.5.95). Against all tragic convention the hero survives, like the historical Pontiac, who shifted his activities from the field of war to efforts in trade. As Peckham reports, when the historical Pontiac arrived in Cahokia, where he would be assassinated in 1769, he "had with him his two grown sons and a few other Indians. He said he came to trade in peace and he did just that" *(Indian Uprising* 309). As we know, the English entertained high but culturally mistaken hopes during the First British Empire to instrumentalize Pontiac's influence over the Indians in order to facilitate western expansion.

Real Ethnography

Fulford writes that Robert Rogers's Indian heroes "became the first Native Americans to feature in English literature who were based on detailed reports of face-to-face colonial encounters and who were complex and rooted in a culture that was portrayed with some verisimilitude" (89–90). Such realism can also be found in all the ethnographic information in the play. Thus when the chiefs refuse the "calumet" (1.4.205), this reference involves knowledge about the complex peace-keeping ritual (see White 21, cited above).

Complementary to this is the use of the "hatchet" imagery announcing war: "To raise the Hatchet from its short Repose / Brighten its Edge, and stain it deep with Blood" (2.2.20–21). Already in his oratory with the governors, Ponteach uses this imagery: "If honourable Peace be our Desire, / We'd always have the Hatchet buried deep" (1.4.63–64), and he warns: "Else we will raise the Hatchet to the Sky" (1.4.69).[20] He states: "I want to see your King and let him know / What must be done to keep the Hatchet dull" (1.4.118–19). *Calumet* and *hatchet* are metonyms for practices well known today. Thus White can write shorthand: "Facing west, Onontio and his chiefs—French and Algonquian—ideally carried the calumet, not the hatchet" (142). But in Rogers's time, such knowledge was certainly new and exciting.

The play also includes references to the Indian tradition of gift giving. Thus when the three governors cheat the Indians in the scene already discussed, this interaction is part of an intended reciprocating negotiation ritual of the middle ground familiar from habitual interactions with the French governor Onontio, as mentioned in part 1. The English king's representatives also receive gifts in return, and as Governor Sharp notes: "By *Jove*, they're worth more Money than their Presents"

(1.4.243). Significantly, the play shows that beyond the issue of profit, this business is supposed to be about relationships. In that context, "wampum" is also mentioned four times, and a wampum belt is even staged in the unequal gift-giving scene, where its symbolic message is not being relayed to the English king.

As already mentioned, there is a long scene based on traditional Indian oratory in the play, in which different chiefs voice their opinions without interrupting one another in an assembly headed by Ponteach. The formality of Indian oratory is famous and has impressed European explorers, missionaries, political negotiators, and ethnographers, and most recently new age environmentalists.[21] Fulford even claims that the play's "heroic speeches are inflected with the characteristic vocabulary and attitudes that, according to witnesses, the real Pontiac and his allies used" (85). While some of the chiefs in the play have names such as Ponteach, Tenesco, or Astinaco, others bear totemic animal names, such as the Bear and the Wolf, which refer to the Indian tribal organization of clans—as in the case of the Delaware prophet.[22] This allows the English reader to sense another kind of social and political organization and the Native American efforts to resist total acculturation.

Ponteach's dream of the Elk offers further ethnographic information about Indian reasoning and the strong influence of visions. Important as a decision-making tool, this dream is first mentioned by his sons, who have observed that Ponteach "shook his mighty arm" (2.1.52) in a theatrical gesture, like a "hunted Elk" trampling "his Assailants down" (2.1.54–55). In the next scene Ponteach himself tells them of "last Night's Dream" about a "lordly Elk" who grew in size and was feared and attacked by other animals: "The fierce Tyger yell'd the loud Alarm, / When Bears, Cats, Wolves, Panthers, and Porcupines" attacked it (2.2.167–68). But the Elk "Trampled and spurn'd them with his Hoofs and Horns, / Till all dispers'd in wild Disorder fled, / And left him Master of th' extended Plain" (2.2.177–79). When comparing Ponteach's dream to dreams in Shakespeare plays, Fulford notes that "this dream . . . is recognizably Indian. It accords with what later witnesses wrote of such dreams among the Iroquois and Ojibwa, as does Rogers's later discussion of the sweat lodge into which shamans retreated to communicate with the spirits" (89). The dream is then interpreted by his own medicine man, another well-known ethnic figure—who has been sweating in a "sultry Stove" (3.2.5), an Indian sauna, and thus yet another ethnographic reference—observing: "You are the mighty Elk that none can conquer" (3.2.48). But Rogers makes clear that he considers this dream business mere superstition and aligns it with the work of the French priest, who confides: "The Conjurer agreed with me to pump him" (3.2.68). Rogers had little regard for both European and Native American priests.[23] We see here how he is using his intimate knowledge of Native Americans while at the same time expressing his own opinion about some of their specific cultural behavior.[24]

As another central ethnographic element, we also have the scalping scene already mentioned, which illustrates this grisly practice in America. I am not sure, though, if Philip's decorative idea to "cover all [the Indians'] Cabbins with their Scalps" (4.3.48) goes back to authentic practice. Though primarily intended to create sensationalist frisson, scalping was a reality among both Indians and whites—as Rogers shows in the hunters' scene of his play (1.2). Adding to this theatrical excitement, the Indian torture scene with Honnyman and his wife and children was probably the first one written for the stage (4.4), and it brings another typical example of colonial brutality to Europe. The experienced hunter tells his wife about the famed Indian stoicism:

> [They] Love Torments, Torture, Anguish, Fire, and Pain,
> The deep-fetch'd Groan, the melancholy Sigh,
> And all the Terrors and Distress of Death,
> These are their Musick, and enhance their Joy.
> In Silence then submit yourself to Fate:
> Make no Complaint nor ask for their Compassion;
> This will confound and half destroy their Mirth;
> Nay, this may put a Stop to many Tortures,
> To which our Prayers and Tears and Plaints would move them.
>
> (4.4.14–22)

But Rogers adds the crucial point that the Indians are not merely slaughtering their captives like animals. After he is killed, the scene ends with a ritual for Honnyman's soul. Ponteach orders the Indians to "Drive hence his wretched Spirit, lest it plague us; / Let him go hunt the Woods; he's now disarm'd" (4.4.201–2) and makes them *run round brushing the Walls, &c. to dislodge the Spirit* (original italics).[25] And he finally addresses the spirit directly: "Go, tell our Countrymen, whose Blood you shed, / That the great Hunter *Honnyman* is dead" (4.4.205–6). The rhyme emphasized the incantatory nature of the statement.

Of further interest is the fact that when Ponteach decides to redeem the wife and children for ransom, this also reflects contemporary North American practice:

> I know her Friends; they're rich and powerful,
> And in their Turn will take severe Revenge:
> But if we spare, they'll hold themselves oblig'd,
> And purchase their Redemption with rich Presents.
>
> (4.4.158–61)

This was the standard procedure of hostage taking in the Indian wars that we know from the narratives of Mary Rowlandson and other captives. At the same time, the particular gesture of wanting to negotiate with the English humanizes Ponteach. Thus for Fulford the "Indians, here, are not ferocious beasts" (89). It is of course hard to differentiate between sensationalism and ethnographic information (especially on the stage), but Fulford insists that Rogers's "characters were a great advance on the feeble stereotypes that preceded them" (90). Though some details may not satisfy our contemporary hunger for authenticity, *Ponteach* offered information that went far beyond the earlier New World dramas by Dryden and others—and it is probably still much more informative about Indian life than many of the plays that came afterward.

Pervasive are also the authentic family metaphors used by Indians to describe their relationship with the whites. Tiffany Potter rightly insists that "these questions of brother, father, uncle, or cousin are crucial" (51). As we have seen in the previous chapter discussing the "middle ground," the father figure Onontio for the Algonquians was a benevolent, generous provider, not a stern patriarch, a differentiation that correlates with the French versus English relations. As Ponteach explains, the French father had adapted to the Indian ways:

> The *French* familiarized themselves with us,
> Studied our Tongue, and Manners, wore our Dress,
> Married our Daughters, and our Sons their Maids,
> Dealt honestly and well supplied our Wants
> . . .
> Call'd us their Friends, nay, what is more, their Children,
> And seemed like Fathers, anxious for our Welfare.
>
> (2.2.50–57)

Ponteach also uses the traditional role of the patriarchal chief and provider for his tribe to describe his own loss of power at the end of the play:

> Kings like the Gods are valued and ador'd,
> When Men expect their Bounties in Return,

> Place them in Want, destroy the giving Power,
> All Sacrifices and Regards will cease.
>
> (5.5.81–84)

By destroying the "giving Power" (an amazingly accurate expression in view of our earlier discussion of the function of presents in Indian culture), namely, his ability to provide gifts for his people, the English have vanquished the great chief. Their governors only mimicked the act of gift giving. If Governor Sharp declares about the English king, "He like a Father loves you as his Children; / And like a Brother wishes you all Good" (1.4.109–10), the meager gifts in act 1 tell a different story. No wonder Ponteach greets the English governors as "Brothers" only: "We're glad to see our Brothers here, the English. / If honourable Peace be your Desire" (1.4.62–63). Since the "father" is supposed to be a provider and the English obviously do not provide, they can at best be seen as brothers. Later Ponteach states that he would like the English "as [their] Friends and Brothers" (1.4.99), but the negotiation of this family relationship is far from clear.[26] Brotherhood further becomes ambivalent in the fratricidal relationship of Chekitan and Philip. Nevertheless, Rogers introduces us to the traditional Native American framework of adoptive diplomacy, teaching us about tribal metaphors of family relationships as well as their historical hollowing out by the English.

Unreal Indian Families?

Yet the authenticity of Indian family relations represented in the play may be questionable. When Chekitan renounces his birthright for the love of Monelia and gives Philip his share of Ponteach's empire, this sounds more like a case of Prince Edward and Wallis Simpson than tribal leadership politics: "Help me, my *Philip*, and I'll be thy Slave, / Resign my Share of Empire to thy Hand, / And lay a Claim to Nothing but *Monelia*" (2.2.282–84). And when Philip responds, "Rewards I do not ask; I am thy Brother" (2.2.285), things do not get much clearer— especially in view of the later fratricide, which will further complicate this concept. We seem to have made a transition to European notions of family relationships. Thus fathers are also seen as dynastic ancestors, for example, when in the Senate House the Bear talks of their "Father's Folly" (3.3.172), and the Wolf (the chief who can be associated with the Delaware prophet) dares his co-councilors "to be like [their] Fathers, brave and strong" (3.3.203). As already discussed, such patriarchal lineage is not the primary function of family-provider terminology among the Indians. A further twist in father imagery is manifested when Ponteach praises Philip, stating that a successful negotiation with Hendrick would "make [him] worthy of [his] Father's Crown" (2.2.146)—though this statement emphasizes Indian values of "worthiness" over inheritance, of earning your reputation, at the same time it reflects a notion of Indian chiefdomship that ignores matrilineality and limits it to the family decision of an elite aristocracy, thus applying the European symbolism of an inherited "Crown."

Furthermore, *Ponteach* also presents a curiously personal notion of family that addresses the constant tension between the private and the public in the play that we shall discuss later. Thus when Chekitan worries that "[t]he powerful *Mohawk* King" may influence the other chiefs "[t]o muster all their Strength against our Father" (2.1.74, 78), he continues spinning the father-motif into an issue of family war:

> Fathers perhaps will fight against their Sons,
> And nearest Friends pursue each other's Lives;
> Blood, Murder, Death, and Horror will be rife,
> Where Peace and Love, and Friendship triumph now.
>
> (2.1.79–82)

This is a vision of disaster that literalizes political relationships in terms of the nuclear family. Yet it may also be seen as a rhetorical way to explain the fragmented refugee family patterns and the politics of village alliances (see White) to a foreign European audience.

A truly European approach can be found in the examples of parental obedience, for example, when Chekitan observes: "When we refuse Obedience to your Will, / We are not worthy to be called your Sons" (2.2.27–28). The same attitude is shown when Monelia can "never disoblige [her] Father" (3.1.139), which makes her lover regret his own "Father's wrong-turn'd Policy" (3.1.151). This certainly goes against the grain of what we know about the liberality of Indian childrearing. These last examples show the impositions of audience expectation on the author(s)—the very cultural tension about the understanding of father imagery between the Indians and the English thus also affects the depiction of Indian family relations in this play.

The European notion of patrilineage manifests itself well in the hunter Honnyman, when he faces the death not only of himself but also of his firstborn son: "Dear *Tommy* too must die / . . . My only Son—My

Image—Other Self!" (4.4.53, 59), who "falls a Victim for his Father's Folly" (4.4.63) and finally his "Father's wretched End" (4.4.177). Then curiously, in the last act, the Indians also use a dynastic definition, namely, when Philip tells Ponteach: "O see, my Father! see the Blood of Princes, / A Sight that might provoke the Gods to weep" (5.1.46–47). This conjures up aristocratic family structures, which are confirmed in the final scene of the play, when Ponteach, solus, laments: "Look on a King whose Sons have died like mine!" (5.5.30). The meaning of the fratricide stands for the end of an aristocratic bloodline. We find thus in *Ponteach* a very contradictory coexistence of, on the one hand, an authentic Indian use of diplomatic family terminology in terms of the fatherly Onontio and, on the other, an encroachment of European notions of nuclear family structures, patrilineage, and aristocratic land ownership. Hence the realism in this play is compromised and challenged by foreign impositions.

6

The Power
of European Conventions

After all this fact-mongering emphasis on realistic referentiality in *Ponteach*, we should not forget that a play is an artistic form with an aesthetic dimension. We have already mentioned some plot elements that are seriously fictional and have little to do with historical events or traditional Indian behavior. Worse, we find the imposition of, or rather submission to, many literary conventions of Rogers's time in which strong European perspectives dominate. Thus some of the very names are European: Philip (who may echo England's old Catholic foe of Armada times, Philip II of Spain—a country now rivaling England for influence among the Indians from across the Mississippi), then Monelia, or also Donata (who even smacks of Italian Renaissance society). Philip's villainy certainly has more to do with the dramaturgy of *Richard III* and the hierarchical organization and succession procedures at European courts than with American Indian politics. As Sayre suggests: "The Indian leaders' nobility, and courage as well as their flaws and their demises were portrayed with all the dignity accorded the greatest characters of the classical and Renaissance tragedies" (*Tragic Hero* 2). He notes the great number of "stage tragedies written by Anglo-American authors between 1766 and 1836. The United States saw a craze for such Indian dramas in the 1830s." Note that our drama *Ponteach*

(1766) comes first in this listing of dates and therefore stands at the very beginning of a powerful new stage tradition.

A World
of Classical References

One of the role models for *Ponteach* is heroic tragedy, which was very popular on the English stage, and exemplified by the master John Dryden, who treated the topic of the New World in *The Indian Queen* (1664) and in *The Indian Emperour, or the Conquest of Mexico by the Spaniards, Being the Sequel of The Indian Queen* (1665). The taste for the exotic was also appealed to in *The Conquest of Granada* (1670). As Tiffany Potter writes, these "new tragedies that were staged were often derivatives of classical Roman narratives or plays that located themselves in the exoticized Orient" (28). Except for the appropriation of the names of some real historical figures and the loss of their supposed homelands, these plays, with their invented stage costumes, had little referential quality. Sayre writes that in Dryden, "the setting is exotic rather than historical. *The Indian Queen* begins with a battle between the Mexica [*sic*] and the Inca, which of course never took place" (*Tragic Hero* 18).[1] He adds: "Elaborate costumes and sets, including feather headdresses brought from Surinam by Aphra Behn . . . , provided the exotic American interest" (18). What these plays taught their audience about their supposed referential "other" was minimal.[2]

Instead, they would rather focus on the actions determining the fortune of their tragic hero-protagonist, whose fate was usually inspired by a selective appropriation of moral qualities borrowed from classical heroes of antiquity, as in Joseph Addison's smash hit *Cato: A Tragedy* (1713), which set the standard for generations of playwrights to come.[3] Critics have noticed that *Ponteach* plays with the *Cato* heroism, but they have also observed that it fails to live up to all its philosophical values and conventions. Cato stands for the incorruptible politician, whereas Ponteach, though also of superhuman stature, has his shortcomings and private ambitions. If Morsberger claims that Ponteach "sounds like Addison's Cato" (254), Marilyn Anderson notes that "Roger's [sic] noble savages were not noble *enough* [for the contemporary] reviewer [who] expected the literary conventions of the day to be followed" (228, original italics).[4] Tiffany Potter thus explains: "Ponteach is not an exemplary hero, and he is driven as much by his private ambition as by any desire for public good" (29). He is not the selfless public servant of the Roman ideal. Moreover, the fact that Ponteach survives also breaks with the habits of the Roman drama, introducing the emerging American convention of the "vanishing" Indian moving west.[5] Again referentiality stands in the way of literary conventions, because the real Pontiac still lived and went about his business in 1766, whereas the Roman Cato had been long dead and was therefore a much easier object for dramatic appropriation.

Nevertheless, it is striking to see so many classical references interfere with Rogers's ethnography. Thus the Roman slave, who would dog the American stage and screen for centuries to come in endless Spartacus remakes, also lurks in *Ponteach* as an exemplification of oppression.[6] The cautious Chekitan, for example, fearing defeat in battle, expresses himself as follows:

> Our Troops repuls'd, or in th' Encounter slain;
> Where are our conquered Kingdoms then to share,
> Where are our Vict'ries, Trophies, Triumphs, Crowns,
> That dazzle in Thy Eye, and swell thy Heart;
> That nerve thy Arm, and wing thy Feet to War
> With this impetuous Violence and Speed?
> Crest-fallen then, our native Empire lost,
> In captive Chains we drag a wretched Life.[7]
>
> (2.2.230–37)

The language of this statement coincides with the glorious imagery of European warfare, imperial histories, the triumphal arches of Titus and Constantine, and the proverbial slaves dragged in chains that would again haunt American culture in the debates on slavery. The contrastive "win[ged] feet," in turn, go back to the god Mercury.

We find many references to Jupiter as well. Thus the young Murphey likes to swear by the king of the Gods when he praises the profits of business: "By *Jupiter*, it's artfully contriv'd" (1.1.68). He is certainly impressed: "By Jove, you've gain'd more in a single Hour / Than ever I have done in Half a Year" (1.1.100–101). And there is meaning in this reference, after all: *Quod licet Iovi, non licet bovi*—as Indian traders, they see themselves in terms of entitlement above the law. We find the same attitude in the two hunters when they steal the furs from the Indians. Says Honnyman: "By *Jove* we'll ease the Rascals of their Packs" (1.2.48). Throughout the play, a classical sense of order and privilege is being referenced.

More Roman influences are noticeable when Chekitan promises Monelia: "I'll fight, I'll conquer, triumph and return; / Laurels I'll gain and lay them at your Feet" (4.2.135–36). This behavior and the associated paraphernalia hark back to ancient imperialism. The scene in the Indian "Senate-house" (3.3) of course also suggests Roman politics. Finally, we can add a reference to the classical underworld in Chekitan's parting statement before he commits suicide: "And my *Monelia*'s Shade is satisfied" (5.3.148).[8] This notion of afterlife is closer to the Greek Hades than to aboriginal concepts.

A European Bestiary of "Tygers" and "Vipers"

In the wider sense, many references in this play are simply European. Thus we also find English military terms applied to Indian warfare when Chekitan worries that "many *Indian* Chiefs refuse / To join the Lists" (2.2.101–2).[9] But the most fascinating marker of such cultural inconsistency in *Ponteach* is the use of animal imagery. Though the elk in Ponteach's dream certainly smacks of authenticity, the appearance in particular of wild "tygers" and vicious "vipers" seems out of place in the American context. Rogers should have known better. He had written a chapter-long "account of the most remarkable animals in America, and of the manner in which the savages take them" in the *Concise Account* (253), discussing in great detail first and foremost the beaver (253–59), then the muskrat, bear, elk, and panthers: "Their flesh is white like veal, and agreeable to the palate, and their fur is valuable" (262). He also describes fox, skunk, martin, then the "*Opposum* . . . , having under its belly a bag or false belly, in which they breed their young" (263), followed by porcupine and moose. In comparison to such careful observations, the bestiary of the play is curiously limited.

The most jarring reference in the play is the "tyger," mentioned no fewer than eighteen times.[10] Though Tiffany Potter observes that the word "probably refers to the mountain lion or other large cat" (Rogers, *Ponteach* 2010 ed. 68n), Rogers (and here we also have to speculate about one or more possible co-authors) sometimes uses the word *tyger* together with the more proper term *panther*.[11] Thus "the fierce Tyger yell'd the loud Alarm, / When Bears, Cats, Wolves, Panthers, and Porcupines" (2.2.167–68) attacked "the lordly Elk." And in the Senate House scene, the Indian chief called Bear argues: "Does not the ravenous Tyger feed her Young? / And the fierce Panther fawn upon his Mate?" (3.3.147–48). The two names are used side by side in a way that suggests two different animal species. I can only attribute this to the influence of European convention. As Morsberger observes, "like Goldsmith and William Collins," the author "tells of fierce tigers in America" (253).

A similar European use of animal terminology can also be found in the very negative use of "snakes," "serpents" and "vipers." We find no Indian symbolism of snakes and no native rattlesnake in the play.[12] Thus Ponteach claims that the English "hiss and spit their Poison forth" (2.2.45), and proposes to "kill the Serpent ere we feel it sting" (3.3.36). Torax says of his "old Man" (i.e., King Hendrick): "I told him often that he cherish'd Serpents / To bite his Children, and destroy his Friends" (3.1.159, 161–62). And Monelia curses the French priest who wants to rape her: "Base, false Dissembler—Tyger, Snake, a Christian! / I hate the Sight; I fear the very Name" (4.2.61–62).[13] This negative, devilish imagery of the snake as evil, poisonous, and even hypnotizing ("their very Eyes are full of Poison" [4.2.86]) has little to do with the respect that Native Americans accord this animal as a totem.[14] Even James Fenimore Cooper knew about "Le Gros Serpent," but there is no Chingachgook in this play. Its use of snake imagery rather suggests the European influence of Aesop's fable of the farmer who takes pity on a freezing viper, puts it inside his coat, but gets bitten when it warms up: "Their Forts and Settlements I've view'd as Snakes / Of mortal Bite, bound by the Winter Frost," says Ponteach (2.2.42–43). And in the torture scene of Honnyman, one warrior warns of "young Vipers in his Bosom" (4.4.154).

Much of the discussion also concerns mercy toward Honnyman's young children, and this issue is again approached from the angle of the proverbial viper's nest: "Who ever spar'd a Serpent in the Egg? / Or left young Tygers quiet in their Den?" (4.4.151–52). Moreover, in his speech mentioned above, the Bear also talks of the emblematic "poisonous Serpent feed[ing] her hissing Brood" (3.3.150). This language harks back to the imagery of dragons' eggs and the general Judeo-Christian antireptilian propaganda. Philip slaps Mrs. Honnyman: "You Tygress Bitch! You Breeder up of Serpents!" (4.3.77). Note that the raising of the new generation is an issue—even among tigers: thus Ponteach wants to "[f]irst kill the Tygers, then destroy their Whelps" (4.4.122). The genealogical imagination of an evil brood much determines the protagonists' attitudes.

Additional symbolic European animals appear in the play in ways that have nothing to do with their Native American significance. Thus in the Indian assembly the Bear comments on the English king: "What of his Strength and Wisdom? Shall we fear / A Lion chain'd, or in another World?" (3.3.144–45). This clearly alludes to the British lion in the faraway Old World. And when Ponteach describes variety among the Indians, he uses European animal imagery as a means of contrastive characterization: "Some are Insidious as the subtle Snake, / Some innocent and harmless as the Dove; / Some like the Tyger raging; cruel, fierce, / Some like the Lamb, humble, submissive, mild" (1.4.179–82). The case is a bit more intricate when Philip describes the role distribution of the brothers as follows: "Thoul't gain the Prize of Love, and I of Wrath / In favor to our Family and State / Thoul't tame the Turtle, I shall rouse the Tyger" (2.2.323–25). Tiffany Potter suggests in a footnote (and rightly so) that the "turtle" here is not a tortoise but a "turtledove" alluding to Chekitan's love for Monelia in a "European tradition" (Rogers, *Ponteach* 2010 ed. 100n). Torax, moreover, believes that Philip is "crafty as the Fox" (3.1.195), which is closer to Reynard the Fox of European folklore than to the American wily coyote.[15]

Judeo-Christian Images

We find more Old World conventions in the biblical imagery of the play. Certainly the peaceful doves mentioned above originate in the Bible. And when Chekitan sadly calls his dead Monelia "Thou dear cold Clay!" (5.3.71), he exhibits Old Testament knowledge about the origin and the end of humans (Genesis 3:19).

At the beginning of act 2, when Chekitan and Philip first appear, we get the impression that they live in a land of milk and honey. Outside their modest home, the "Indian House," they return from hunting "loaded with Venison" (2.1) in an opening scene reminiscent of the Hebrew scouts showing off the grapes they found in the promised land. Chekitan praises the "unstain'd Fruits of Peace, / Effected by the conqu'ring British Troops. / Now we may hunt the Wilds secure from Foes" (2.1.10–13).[16] It is into this paradise that the culture of the devil enters, not only through the cursing of the English (remember that the innocent Ponteach does not even know what "d—d" means) but also through their "art." This notion of art is more than civilizational superiority. It is also artfulness, artificial, and a sign of unnatural manipulation, generally a sign of devilish agency—and it appears surprisingly often in the play; in fact, there are eleven occurrences of "art" or "artful." Thus the cheating trader M'Dole explains: "But, as you are my Friend, I will inform you / Of all the secret Arts by which we thrive"

(1.1.18–19). He distributes rum "with a lib'ral Hand, / . . . / Which makes them think me generous and just, / And gives full Scope to practice all my Art" (1.1.52–55). The young Murphey calls the manipulated scale "artfully contriv'd" (1.1.68). He is certainly impressed by this deception: "Curse my Honesty! I might have been / *A little King*, and liv'd without Concern, / Had I but known the proper Arts to thrive" (1.1.102–4). And he thanks M'Dole for the "kind Instructions" (1.1.111). Like Faust, they have used *techne* to cheat the naive Indians. The image of the foot measuring weight, moreover, creates a link to the limp of the devil's cloven foot.[17]

An abusive use of Western technology also appears in the governors' already-mentioned reference to their superiority in the cultural skills of reading and mathematics. The theological dimension and abuse of such means are again obvious when the evil French priest interprets the Elk dream. As already mentioned, he "pumps" Ponteach in a popish way that he describes as follows: "I've used the Arts of our most holy Mother" (3.2.19). Not surprisingly, the devilish Indians later also take their revenge "by all the Arts of Torment" (4.4.142). And a desperate Chekitan plans fratricide after the murder of his beloved Monelia: "Teach me the Arts and Cruelty of Wrath" (5.3.146).[18] In the European sense, there is something utterly wrong and devilishly manipulated about this colonial cultural transfer.

Moreover, in addition to such contrived "arts" and savage "desarts," forty-nine "hearts" are also mentioned in this play, many of which, obliquely or less obliquely, allude to Christian notions of identity and even compassion. Hence people's attitudes are expressed with their hearts. It is because the heart is supposed to be the locus of motivation that the artful French priest, who turns out to be a treacherous spy, wants to "know the Secrets of [Ponteach's] Heart" (3.2.23). And Ponteach himself hopes that the English king is "friendly in his Heart" (1.4.15). Philip accuses his brother of being "a very Woman in [his] Heart" (2.2.198). He also knows that "in their Hearts" the English "hate the Name of *Indians*" (2.2.340). Things get more complicated when Chekitan assures Monelia of his love: "Such Baseness dwells not in an *Indian's* Heart, / And I'll convince you that I am no Christian" (3.1.113–14). Although we know from Jesus iconography that according to Christian notions compassion originates in the heart, this Indian bosom uses and at the same time rejects that meaning.

The heart is also an important locus of power in Indian tradition, but in *Ponteach* notably no hearts are cut out of victims, smeared into prisoners' faces, or eaten by the victors.[19] Still, cannibalism is referred to twice in the play: first, when Honnyman asserts that he "cou'd eat an *Indian's* Heart with Pleasure" (1.2.39), and again when Philip wants revenge against the English: "Yes, I could eat their Hearts and drink their Blood" (3.3.100). Yet that cannibalistic imagery associated with Indians eerily connects with the Holy Communion suggested in the second part of the phrase, which muddles its ethnographic significance. All things considered, the meaning of the heart in *Ponteach* seems mainly European.

And if we look at the heart as the site of compassion, moreover, in many ways the Indians in this play are more compassionate than the whites. Chekitan, for example, releases the French priest after his sexual assault of Monelia: "I spar'd his guilty Life, but drove him hence" (4.2.90). And in the torture scene, Honnyman hopes to placate the Indians, addressing his wife and children:

> Who knows but by pathetic Prayers and Tears
> Their savage Bosoms may relent towards you,
> And fix their Vengeance where just Heaven points it?
> I still will hope, and every Motive urge.
> Should I succeed to melt their rocky Hearts,
> I'll take it as a Presage of my Pardon.
>
> (4.4.107–12)

Ponteach has a heart and limits his revenge to the offender Honnyman, freeing the wife and children. Furthermore, at the end of the play, he shows real emotions after the murder of Monelia and Torax: "Thus would I have it; let no Eye be dry, / No Heart unmov'd, let every Bosom swell / With Sighs and Groans" 5.2.15–17). He feels for Chekitan: "His grief is inward and his Heart sheds Tears, / And in his Soul he feels the pointed Woe" (5.2.68–69). The latter in turn, before killing his brother, makes the accusation: "Can *Philip* be so false? / Dwells there such Baseness in a Brother's Heart?" 5.3.118–19). The heart, to be sure, is a major focus of both identification and compassion—also for the Indians.

Familiar Plotlines

Beyond the micro level of imagery, wider European cultural conventions also manifest themselves in the general plotlines of the play's events. If we stay with Christianity in our analysis, it is obvious that the fratricide of Ponteach's sons echoes the story of Cain and Abel. This plot element is certainly imposed and ahistorical.[20] As a powerful European cultural paradigm, it appropriates our understanding of the events, which are drawn into the maelstrom of the Old Testament origins story, and the fall from ignorance to sin. The plotline suggests that the Indians are noble, but at the same time, like the Son of Man, they have lost that Otherly innocence and will now also be punished for their sins. In a curious projection, this suggests that the Great Lakes Indians are subject to some kind of divinely sanctioned narrative—they may be conquered and colonized as an extension of the world corrupted in a theological sense. Moreover, the fact that in this respect they are no better than the European Christians puts the Indians in the same category, inviting future interaction or possibly even new prospective business partnerships—an issue important to Rogers that we shall discuss later.

The historical complexity of the Indian insurrection we have already traced is also expressed in the romantic love story of Chekitan and Monelia, modeled on the trope of incompatible clans, exemplified in another icon of European culture, *Romeo and Juliet*. Thus Castillo finds their love "reminiscent of Shakespeare's *Romeo and Juliet*" (220). It was certainly a popular story to borrow. Analyzing the London theater season of 1765–66, Friedrichs sees a predominance of the genres of pathetic drama, heroic classic and pseudo-classic. The most frequently staged tragedy of the season was *Romeo and Juliet* (146). Being a good German Democratic Republic dialectical materialist, he regrets that the realism of the play's beginning is eclipsed in that love story, which he attributes to stage realism being sacrificed to the genre's requirements.[21] What is more interesting is of course the fact that the story of the star-crossed lovers is projected onto the real historical situation and the rivalry between the Algonquian people (the Ottawa Ponteach) and the Iroquois (the Mohawk Hendrick), and their respective alliances with the French and the English. Though such a clear division of intertribal organization does not apply to the complexity of the situation on the Great Lakes at that time, the sense of important family politics is not as unrealistic as we might assume at first sight. James Axtell observes that parents' consent for marriage was important in Indian societies "because a marriage represented a union of two clans as well as two individuals" (71). As McDonnell writes, "marriages were the real glue of kinship relations" (94).[22] But the village culture of such intermarriages (see White 14–20) was probably more on the scale of Shakespeare's Ravenna than on the level of Habsburg's imperial expansion through marriage (*tu felix Austria nube*). Still the love story of Monelia and

Chekitan does the cultural work of explaining a complicated foreign historical constellation to a European audience in terms of a tale they already know well. We can see this plot element as yet another hybrid didactic strategy to familiarize outsiders with the complexities of the American reality.

Beyond that, Friedrichs notices numerous stylistic inconsistencies,[23] among them the motif of the sons vying for the inheritance of their father's empire (151), and generally much European terminology, such as "King," "Senate-house," or "Generalissimo" (152). He also notes that the Indian notion of marriage in the play is utterly European, including the expectation that a prospective bride be a virgin and that a match-maker, here Philip, would be involved.[24] As Monelia says about the im-pudent "lac'd Coat Captain" with the "Cockaded Hat": he "ask'd to stain my Virtue" (3.1.75–76, 93). And Chekitan accuses the priest of vio-lating "the Rites of Wedlock" (4.2.28). Such attitudes collide with what scholarship tells us about the courtship of Native Americans. As Axtell writes: "Before serious courtship leading to marriage, the young people of most eastern tribes indulged in sexual exploration with the tacit ap-proval of their parents, sometimes even before puberty" (71).[25] Virginity certainly was not a condition for marriage among the Indians.

Royal Lineages

I have already mentioned that the "royalty" of the Ponteach family also reflects European notions rather than Native American practice. Among the Indians in *Ponteach* we find values like Roman virtue (Cato), virginity, and honor. As Monelia tells Chekitan: "Mistake me not, I don't impeach your Honour" (3.1.121). The play is full of references to kings and empires, feudalist dependencies, and royal lines of inheritance or the usurpation of thrones (i.e., Philip) among the Indians. Thus Pon-teach resents that he "became a Vassal of their Power [of the English]" (2.1.36) and doesn't want to "be a Vassal to his [the English king's] low Commanders" (2.2.72). Nor is he pleased that the "imperious haughty *Mohawk* Chief" makes the tribes under his control pay "annual Homage" (2.2.108–9). Instead, as his councilor Tenesco expresses it, Ponteach rather wants the other tribes to "join and own [him] for their Sovereign, / Pay full Submission to [his] scepter'd Arm, / And universal Empire be [his] own!" (2.2.127–29). This is the vocabulary of European political organization, even imperialism—Pontiac was, after all, called an "Em-perour" in the *Concise Account*. Thus the terms *king* and *kingdom* appear eighty-four times in the play, and there are fourteen instances of *prince* or *princess*.

Accordingly, Chekitan self-consciously introduces himself to Monelia as an "Indian Prince" (3.1.103), and she is herself a "*Mohawk* Princess" (3.2.87). But the European notion of monarchy also manifests itself in Philip's usurpational schemes. They ring of the intrigues of Shakespeare's histories; thus before he murders Monelia, he observes:

> There's something awful in the Face of Princes,
> And he that sheds their Blood assaults the Gods:
> But I'm a Prince and 'tis by me they die;
> Each Hand contains the Fate of future Kings,
> And, were they Gods, I would not balk my Purpose.
>
> (5.1.27–31)

At the same time the fact that Philip is so evil also suggests that this "Prince" is rather a prince of darkness. He gives his father false evidence: "O see, my Father! see the Blood of Princes, / A Sight that might provoke the Gods to weep" (5.1.46–47). But this last statement in turn also eerily suggests the blood of the prince of princes, God's son, the blood of the ultimate martyrdom (while at the same time it agrees with European notions of aristocratic blood lines). Such a meaning is certainly not denied by Philip's gesture of demonstrating, like a false Jesus to St. Thomas, his fake stigmata, in a lie about two English murderers: "There I receiv'd this Wound. [*shewing his Wound to* Ponteach" (5.1.51). I would conclude that even when inverted by the Indians, all this imagery powerfully stays in place, paralleling a European tradition of Christianity and blue-blooded royals associated with the gods.

Ponteach certainly is a powerful king, and he complains about his humiliation: "Can this become a King like *Ponteach*, / Whose Empire's measured only by the Sun?" (2.2.75–76).[26] There is royalty galore among the Indians. After the tragic end, the faithful Tenesco mourns the "[u]nhappy Princes" (5.4.67) and the fate of the Indian empire: "When it begins with Kings and with their Sons, / A general Ruin threatens all below" (5.4.74–78). As if Indian tribes also had some kind of royal lineage or even a politics of dynasties, the vanquished Ponteach resumes in the last scene of the play:

> My Sons, my Name is gone;
> My Hopes all blasted, my Delights all fled;

> Nothing remains but an afflicted King;
> That might be pitied by Earth's greatest Wretch.
>   (5.5.8–11)

This is a King Lear moment concerning the loss of heirs. Ponteach now describes himself as a

> piteous wretched King,
> Look on a Father griev'd and curs'd like me;
> Look on a King whose Sons have died like mine!
> Then you'll confess that these are dangerous Names
>   (5.5.28–31)

As often in this mysterious play, the "dangerous Names" seem to impose a conceptual framework of understanding, and they may even imply some uncanny criticism of the workings of European notions of royalty on the Great Lakes. Ponteach then rattles on, elaborating on his own name:

> Yes, I will live, in spite of Fate I'll live;
> Was I not *Ponteach*, was I not a King,
> Such giant Mischiefs would not gather round me,
> And since I am *Ponteach*, since I am King,
> I'll shew myself Superior to them all,
> I'll rise above this Hurricane of Fate;
> And shew my Courage to the Gods themselves.
>   (5.5.64–70)

Ponteach means king, and king means Ponteach. Also note the tautology of the play's final line: "*Ponteach* I am, and shall be *Ponteach* still" (5.5.102). The crucial plot problem that Rogers and his associates had to solve was of course that the tragic hero of this play was still alive—thus the piling up of so much grandiose wording.[27]

But beyond the imposition of European terminology on Indian tribal organization for a simpler intercultural understanding, the use of a European aristocratic title is also used in order to suggest a hierarchical matching with the king of England. Ponteach wants to talk to an equal: "With Pleasure I wou'd call their King my Friend" (2.2.64). His final message to the governors is: "Tell your King from me, / ... / That I have Warriors, am myself a King, / And will be honour'd and obey'd as such" (1.4.207–9). As we shall see, Rogers placed these appeals in the mouth of Ponteach because he had his own personal reasons to prepare another plotline of future Michilimackinac cooperation after the play events, a promising future beckoning from the far west in a negative royal mirror, inviting more colonization by the First British Empire. We note in this context that such notions are also usurped in commercial ways by "little kings" in this play when we hear that the successful trader "old Ogden . . . grew a little King" (1.1.38–39). And Murphey observes, "[I] might have been / *A little King*, and liv'd without Concern, / Had I but known" (1.1.100–104). European royal terminology is thus imposed in order to help play audiences better understand exotic Indian politics, but it is also used to signal that the English conquest of Canada may lead to new figurative business "royalties" in future colonial relations.[28]

7

The Aesthetic Dimension

From an aesthetic point of view, another fascinating contrast to the merely factual realism of *Ponteach* can be found in its internal formalist literary qualities. Because many critics—from Rogers's contemporary reviewers down to our own contemporaries—have ridiculed the aesthetic value of this play, I think it is high time to rescue its low reputation and illustrate that *Ponteach* has a powerful literary quality that goes beyond the mere following of plot conventions and the copying of European imagery. As already mentioned, though Rogers only had a grade-school education and a reputation for creative spelling, many critics appreciate the clarity of his prose style. He certainly knew what he wanted to say—as military commander that trait was essential for his success. At the same time, we notice that Ponteach is a verse play in traditional iambic pentameter, and as a teacher of early American drama (if not the British bards), I find its use of blank verse correct. The lines do not limp, and if they vary, it is usually for a reason. It is clear that Rogers probably procured help—as Sayre states: "Perhaps Rogers . . . came up with an outline or plot and then a ghostwriter with a greater fluency in iambic pentameter penned the speeches of Ponteach and the other characters" (*Tragic Hero* 154). But for an assessment of the text, it is first important to note that this material is as solid as the production of any other rhymester of its time—and some of the lines even remain truly memorable in their dramatic force. It is for this reason that I intend first to look at the use of prosodic rhetorical elements used in the play, at the artful composition of the scenes and the general coherence of the play, and then at its truly innovative elements and its entertaining nature as a formidable stage spectacle.

The Art of Prosody

Once we get used to the rattle of the iambic pentameter, we find that there are many more sophisticated formal poetic elements in the dialogues. To be sure, they constitute enough material to teach an undergraduate class the secrets of prosody. Thus we find many examples of alliteration. When the two white hunters see the Indians, Orsbourn expresses military logic with an alliteration on /p/: "What will you do? Present, and pop one down?" (1.2.45). And when they kill the two Indian hunters to steal their hides (and that in a double sense of scalping as well), we get happy accumulations on /b/: "They're down, old Boy, a Brace of noble Bucks!" (1.2.61). Beyond the cynical comparison to deer hunting, this is an innovative combination of classical rhetoric (i.e., iambic pentameter and alliteration) with, most surprisingly, the use of frontier slang. A similar example that combines these elements is when the officers leave "to crack a Bottle" and Captain Frisk accepts "With all my Heart, and drink D—n to them" (1.4.85–86).

To continue, here is Philip, who gets some good rhetorical lines as well. Thus he first praises Nature's gifts as the "Pleasantness of Plenty" (2.1.2), and later comments on his brother's worries about an impending war with alliterations on /s/ and /k/ that "Such stale Conjectures smell of Cowardice" (2.1.83), hissing sounds that characterize him as the very snake in this paradise. Later he accuses Chekitan: "Thou always wast a Coward and hated War, / And lov'st to loll on the soft Lap of Peace" (2.2.196–97). Here the repetitions of sleepy /w/ develop through /t/ and lolly /l/ to snappy /p/. In parallel, furthermore, note how assonances in the final line rise from an intense repeated low /o/ to /æ/ and a sneering long high /i:/. These are well-crafted, highly motivated poetic sound patterns, handling both consonants and vowels with ease. Philip generally likes alliterations on /p/: "Act but thy Part, and do as I prescribe, / In Peace or War though shalt possess the Prize" (2.2.276–77)—and again, we can't keep from noticing that he hisses like a snake.

Here Ponteach combines alliterations with assonance as well: "Or should we fail, and Fortune prove perverse, / Let it be never known how far we fail'd, / Lest Fools should triumph or our Foes rejoice" (2.2.10–11). We get some hissing /s/ to boot, and an impressive upward vowel development from /uː/ to /œi/ in the last line. Also other Indians use alliteration, and one of them puts a lid on the life of an English murderer, with a rhyming couplet reminiscent of Shakespearean emphasis: "Go tell your Countrymen, whose Blood you shed, / That the great Hunter Honnyman is dead" (4.4.205–6).

Like alliteration, anaphora is a pervasive rhetorical device in this play. Ponteach really piles it on in the following speech:

> Indians a'n't Fools, if White Men think us so;
> We see, we hear, we think as well as you;
> We know there's lies and Mischiefs in the World;
> We don't know whom to trust nor when to fear;
> Men are uncertain, changing as the Wind,
> Inconstant as the Waters of the Lakes,
> Some smooth and fair, and pleasant as the Sun,
> Some rough and boist'rous, like the Winter Storm;
> Some are Insidious as the subtle Snake,
> Some innocent, and harmless as the Dove;
> Some like the Tyger raging, cruel, fierce,
> Some like the Lamb, humble, submissive, mild.
>   (1.4.171–82)

Speaking to the governors, Ponteach directly characterizes the humanity of his own people ("we") and describes humankind more generally with a string of similes. Another example of anaphora comes from Philip, when he contradicts Chekitan with a series of anaphoric "No"s to demonstrate his father's warlike nature: "No Arguments will move him to relent, / No Motives change his Purpose of Revenge, / No Prayers prevail upon him" (2.1.86–88). And Chekitan tries to convince Monelia of his love with an anaphoric list of witnesses: "Witness thou Sun and Moon and Stars above, / Witness ye purling Streams and quivering Lakes, / Witness ye Shades, and the cool Fountain, where / I first espied the Image of her Charms" (3.1.65–68). Shifting his perspective toward these witnesses, he even changes his addressee from second ("thou") to third person ("her Charms").

Anaphora is also exploited in Ponteach's introductory speech in the Senate House, further supported by alliteration and assonance:

> I'll try my Power
> To Punish their Encroachments, Frauds and Pride;
> Yet tho' I die, it is my Country's Cause,
> 'Tis better thus to die than be despis'd;
> Better to die than be a Slave to Cowards,
> Better to die than see my Friends abus'd;
>
> . . .
>
> Better to die than see my Country ruin'd.
>
> (3.3.16–23)

As Laura E. Tanner and James N. Krasner have aptly observed, this kind of speechifying anticipates the future rhetoric of the American Revolution. In *Ponteach* one get the impression of being in the House of Burgesses long before the performances of Patrick Henry.[1] Further on, Ponteach uses anaphora in a variation of alternate lines:

> Who is it don't prefer a Death in War
> To this impending Wretchedness and Shame?
> Who is it loves his Country, Friends and Self,
> And does not feel Resentment in his Soul?
> Who is it sees their growing Strength and Power?
>
> (3.3.29–33)

Still in the Senate House, Chief Astinaco, another master of Indian oratory, creates a series of anaphoric lines with additional parallelism ("must"):

> If we have Wisdom, it must now be used;
> If we have Numbers, they must be united;
> If we have Strength, it must all be exerted;
> If we have Courage, it must be inflamed,
> And every Art and Strategem must be practis'd.
>
> (3.3.114–18)

Then Philip combines simple alliterations with anaphora (and still keeps on hissing): "All fear—all Hope—all Diffidence—all Faith—/

Distrusts the greatest Strength, depends on Straws" (2.2.351–52). Caught in his own scheme like Milton's Satan, who has no place to flee because hell is wherever he is, Philip hesitates twice to kill Monelia and Torax, with anaphoric questions that he answers himself:

> Is it because my Brother's Charmer dies?
> That cannot be, for that is my Revenge.
> Is it because *Monelia* is a Woman?
> I've long been blind and deaf to their Enchantments.
> Is it because I take them thus unguarded?
> No; though I act the Coward, it's a Secret.
>
> (5.1.19–24)

This language has a subtle rhetorical purpose and displays a psychological depth that goes far beyond mechanical blank verse.

An echo of this call-and-response pattern can be found when the brother, Chekitan, finds his love Monelia murdered:

> O! had I never seen thy Beauty bloom,
> I had not now been griev'd to see it pale:
> Had I not known such Excellence had liv'd,
> I shou'd not now be curs'd to see it dead:
> Had not my Heart been melted by thy Charms,
> It would not now have bled to see them lost.
>
> (5.3.12–17)

This time the antiphonal pattern consists of conditional phrases. Chekitan grieves in a powerful monologue that also involves chiasmus in "had I" and "I had," asking his own set of rhetorical questions that provoke fatalist answers, connecting via "had," "shou'd," and "would" to the repetitive negative "not now." The final vowels move from low /u:/ up to /ei/, /i/, /e/, and back to low /a/, ending on a desperate /o:/. There is no end to sound effects in *Ponteach*.

Indians are not the only ones who employ the mirror structure of chiasmus. Even the murderous hunters can do so. When Honnyman claims that Indians have no ghosts, he explains: "But as they live like Beasts, like Beasts they die" (1.2.95). A more complex chiastic logic sounds through Governor Sharp's statement, "Subtraction from these Royal Presents makes / Addition to our Gains without a Fraction" (1.4.45–46). The internal rhyme "Subtraction" and "Fraction" underscores the symbolizing losses that frame the positive "Addition" of "Presents" and "Gains." Again several rhetorical devices are subtly combined to form intricate sound patterns.

A further rhetorical device we find in *Ponteach* is oxymoron, whose exclusionary contrast is repeatedly used to state the inexpressible, for example, in the superlative stress of the torture scene. Thus Mrs. Honnyman expresses her terror in a contradictory paradox: "An Infidel would pray in our Distress: / An Atheist would believe there was some God" (4.4.30–31). Prayer and belief combine with their opposites, and when Mrs. Honnyman looks upon her children, wild animals and mineral substances are found to act against their own natural properties: "Tygers would kindly soothe a Grief like mine; / Unconscious Rocks would melt, and flow in Tears" (4.4.48–49). Also note the Christian imagery in the latter statement. Yet she may have been inspired by the mythological Niobe as well, a grieving mother who was turned into an eternally weeping stone, also cited in Shakespeare,[2] who often combines tigers and weeping parents.[3] Her husband's final experience is equally oxymoronic, when Honnyman is happy that Ponteach has spared his family and he can "die with Comfort when I see you live" (4.4.113). The negative chiasmic development is artfully illustrated in the vowels that connect "die" and "live" from high sounds of /æi/ and /i/ via low sounds on /o/ back to /æi/, /i:/, and across a short dent on /u/ to the final /i/.

Rhyming has a very special function in verse, often adding further emphases within the metric scheme. Thus Governor Catchum's worries are first expressed in a darkening echo: "I do not like old *Ponteach*'s Talk and Air, / He seems suspicious and inclin'd to war" (1.4.223–24). This slant rhyme moves from a high /æ:/ to a low, warning /a:/. But ultimately the administrators are elated by the plan of their new business venture—I am repeating the final lines of the scene by Governor Sharp in order to show that not only is their Brechtian message powerful (as mentioned above) but so too is their rhyming quality:

> We throw the whole into a common Stock,
> And go Copartners in the Loss and Gain.
> Thus most who handle Money for the Crown
> Find means to make the better Half their own;
> And, to your better Judgments with Submission,
> The self Neglecter's a poor Politician.
> These Gifts, you see, will all Expences pay;

> Heav'n send an *Indian* Treaty every Day;
> We dearly love to serve our King this Way.
> (1.4.255-63)

Using the stop of "Stock" as a jumping board, the governor moves through "Gain" and "Crown" to "own," ironizing in another rhyme "Submission" with "Politician," and then extending in an insistent triple rhyme their "Pay" to the repetitive times of "every Day" and the space of "way" as a road to success.

Rhyming often emphasizes a character's plan, formally supporting the mechanical continuation of an idea. This applies to Philip in his solus scene:

> Thus am I fix'd: my Scheme of Goodness laid,
> And I'll effect it, tho' thro' Blood I wade,
> To desperate Wounds apply a desperate Cure,
> And to all Structures lay Foundations sure,
> To Fame and Empire hence my Course I bend,
> And every Step I take shall thither end.
> (2.2.382-87)

These heroic couplets sound like a parody of Dryden's examples of Roman virtue in the mouth of the play's main villain. Obviously, his path is "fix'd" to destruction, and the three couplets emphasize that conceptual framing.

Word repetition is mostly used for emphasis, as in this speech by Mrs. Honnyman: "Ourselves, our Babes, O cruel, cruel Fate! / This, this is Death indeed with all its Terrors" (4.4.137-38). The repetition also announces consonantal echoes that fatefully move from soft /b/ and /d/ into hard sounds of /f/ and a closing /t/. And after Philip blames his murder on the English, Ponteach urges him: "Pursue, pursue, with utmost speed pursue" (5.1.56). This triple eagerness in the wrong direction contrasts with his other son's triple misery, when he learns about the death of Monelia: "Oh wretched, wretched, wretched *Chekitan*!" (5.2.48). He mourns, adding alliteration: "O wherefore, wherefore, wherefore do I live: / *Monelia* is not—What's the World to me?" (5.3.18-19). For Chekitan, it is full of humming *wh*-questions. In happier moments, alliteration may be simply ironic, as when Monelia ridicules Chekitan's emphatic use of anaphora (already quoted): "But save these

Repetitions from the Tongue" (3.1.124). The rhetorically challenged Chekitan characteristically responds with anxious alliterative lisps: "Forgive me, if my Fondness is too pressing, / 'Tis Fear, this anxious Fear, that makes it so" (3.1.125–26).

A further anaphoric extension of such repetition is the use of listing, as when in his speech Ponteach demands action beyond "words alone": "This Hand shall wield the Hatchet in the Cause, / These Feet pursue the frightened running Foe, / This Body rush into the hottest Battle" (3.3.54–56). The Indian chief uses verbal repetition as a means to list the very parts of his physical commitment to a real fight beyond rhetoric alone. A contrasting example of listing can be found in Honnyman's racist characterization of the Indians when he is on the torture stake:

> Their brutal Eyes ne'er shed a pitying Tear;
> Their savage Hearts ne'er had a Thought of Mercy;
> Their Bosoms swell with Rancour and Revenge,
> And, Devil-like, delight in others Plagues.
>
> (4.4.10–13)

These examples of anaphora list concrete physical images that accumulate in a terrible allegorical conclusion, that is, a metaphysical understanding of reality.

To continue our discussion of formal elements: in certain passages, the play uses iambic pentameter with expressive freedom. Thus when Ponteach warns the insolent officers, he thunders: "Colonel, take care; the Wound is very deep, / Consider well, for it is hard to cure" (1.3.68–69). The iambic stress pattern is upset by the trochee of "colonel," which is then immediately followed by the double-stressed, spondaic warning "take care." This line performs caution with a halting, memorable rhythm. One cannot but admire this sophisticated wording.

On a more conceptual level, powerful superlative notions appear both in the positive and the negative sense of hyperbolic statements. Thus when Chekitan is in love, he compares Monelia's beauty in a simile referring to the blinding sun:

> Each time I see you move, or hear you speak,
> It adds fresh Fuel to the growing Flame.
> You're like the rising Sun whose Beams increase
> As he advances upward to our View;

> We gaze with growing Wonder till we're blind,
> And every Beauty fades and dies but his.
>
> (3.1.57–62)

The synesthesia of "see" and "hear" in this example, and the Latinate, male personification of the sun are aesthetic features that suggest training in the classics. Another hyperbolic example, this time of pain beyond limits, is expressed in the oxymoronic torture experiences already presented. But we also find superlative notions associated with the murders at the end of the play, which Philip, that is, the murderer himself, describes as "[a] Sight that might provoke the Gods to weep" (5.1.47)—which makes him later convince his father that "[t]he Gods must be in Council to permit it" (5.1.63). And when Chekitan finally corners the murderer of his love, he resorts to comparative hyperbole improved by alliteration in order to express his anger: "Thou Tyger, Viper, Snake, thou worse than Christian; / Blood thirsty Butcher, more than Murderer!" (5.4.13–14). He suggests a level of evil beyond murder. Also note the inverted iambs in the second line that turn into aggressive trochees. Moreover, his revenge is supposed to exceed counting: "Had you a thousand Lives, they'd be too few" (5.4.32).

On a happier note, I should also add that we find several examples of irony in *Ponteach*. Remember Monelia's witty exposure of Chekitan's lovelorn clichés. I also mentioned the governors who "love to serve our King" (1.4.263). But the best example is certainly when they ask the rhetorical question, "What would the King of *England* do with Wampum? / Or Beaver Skins d'ye think? He's not a Hatter!" (1.4.246–47). The explicit disrespect of this observation creates an irony that powerfully hits home.

The Art of Composition

Formal aesthetic qualities can also be found in the general composition of the play, which is far from flimsy. Thus the scenes are carefully crafted, with subtle transitions to the action that follows, and the plot parts similarly connect to a climactic end. I have already presented the stark logic of the opening act, which has been associated with Brechtian theater, and mentioned some thematic transitions connecting these scenes. Thus M'Dole's remark on the diffusion of vengeance, "Let their Vengeance light / on others' Heads, no matter whose" (1.1.115–16), directly leads to the murder of two innocent Indian hunters by Honnyman and his associate in the next scene, which ends with a blessing of "the first Inventor of a Gun" (1.2.106), leading in turn to following the military scene (1.3) with Ponteach and the officers. The last scene of act 1, again presenting English reasoning and its application, repeats issues of stealing and humiliation, which have systematically moved up the scale of social hierarchy, and at the same time, in the figure of Ponteach and his chiefs, offers a mirror image of resistance to this injustice, preparing the rebellion.

There is a certain logic that the second act opens with an Indian perspective, namely, with Ponteach's sons Philip and Chekitan returning from a successful hunt. We start with a paradisal image of authentic nature and a wilderness of plenty, which is, however, immediately relativized when Chekitan praises these "unstain'd Fruits of Peace, / Effected by the conqu'ring British Troops. / Now we may hunt the Wilds secure from Foes" (2.1.10–13). The structures of human government can simply not be ignored; they are even the cause of this success. Philip immediately notes the trouble with the English and his father's dark visions about a coming conflict. When we enter "Ponteach's Cabbin" in the next scene, the plans for war become more concrete in an intimate discussion that moves from the brothers to the family circle, including the trusted advisor Tenesco. The focus of the scene gets more pointed when the two brothers are alone and Chekitan confides to Philip his predicament in this conflict because of his love for Monelia, and finally, when Philip, solus, confides his murderous ambitions to the audience. As we expect in a good play, we now have the basic exposition and also a reasonably good sense of the *complicatio*, anticipating the subsidiary plotlines of the Romeo and Juliet love story and the fratricide within the context of the rebellion.

The third act again starts in an idyllic landscape, but this time peopled with private conflicts when the unhappy Chekitan meets his love Monelia and her brother, Torax, in the forest. The complexity of private trust and political tensions subtly suggests the important analogy of private and public realms in the play's plotting, and we learn about yet another bad trait of the English, their impetuous courting behavior. This time we find Ponteach's other son, Chekitan, in a balancing solus scene confiding his mission of love to the audience. Ponteach's dream about the "mighty Elk" advances the development of the conflict in a scene introducing us to yet another category of cheaters, the Indian conjurer and the French priest, who take advantage of their attributed power of divination. While the conjurer falls on the ground and pretends to listen to voices—"You are the mighty Elk that none can conquer" (3.2.48)—the priest looks up to heaven: "Your design shall have a prosperous End, / 'Tis by the Gods approv'd and must succeed" (3.2.55–56). Theological posturing harmonizes nadir and zenith.[4] Especially the priest becomes a figure we love to hate. Ending another scene solus on stage, he confides both his ridiculous career ambitions of wanting to become pope and his carnal desire for the beautiful Monelia ("by the holy Virgin, I'll surprise her" [3.2.88]). We now have several strings of possible dramatic development. Thus the last scene of the third act picks up Ponteach's vision about war in the big Indian council scene at the Senate House, finishing the well-crafted move in this middle act from private inception to a public political debate as an occasion to present Indian oratory to the theatergoers. The fact that the French priest also seeks and gets admittance to the council, where he performs with a burning glass that purportedly "brings down Fire from Heaven" (3.3.251), certainly reflects historical French machinations supporting the uprising, and it is also a typical example of European use of bogus wizardry to impress the native peoples. The act culminates in a spectacular war dance with more brandishing of hatchets and flourishing "*scalping Knives*," "*Musick*" playing, and the "*Chorus*" singing a "WAR SONG" to the familiar tune "Over the Hills and Far Away" (3.3.275–318).[5] It becomes a kind of circus performance that embraces the audience—anticipating an important feature of later Indian plays, shows such as Buffalo Bill's Wild West, and Hollywood westerns.

From this loud public scene, we return again to the contrastive intimacy of a grove at the beginning of act 4, where the brothers discuss leadership in the upcoming war—both fittingly influenced by their private goals. The next scene shows another private issue in a comic highlight that treats a revolting issue in a light way, when the priest tries to rape Monelia: "I must, I can, and will enjoy you now" (4.2.7). Its combination of seriousness and laughter represents a benchmark quality of the stage culture Rogers experienced in London, an emphasis on variety that to a large extent dominated the English theater until the arrival of modernism in the twentieth century. Monelia is of course saved by Chekitan, who thus proves worthy of her love. Furthermore, as in any good drama, we have signs of success and signs of failure in the future, and though the lovers worry about each other's safety, the fact that their private affairs could be resolved envisions a happy end for the bigger public events to come.

Thus at the Senate House, the news from the war is all good for the Indians. Three forts have been taken, and in a development that connects with the beginning of the play, the scalps of the cheaters in the first act are presented. Offenses from the beginning of the play are now punished: two scalps of officers, "[t]he mighty Colonel *Cockum* and his Captain" (4.3.38), and then two scalps of traders, "of those two famous Cheats" (4.3.42).[6] The Indians look forward to soon getting the governors' "grey-wig'd Scalps" as well (4.3.50).[7] The evil Philip wants to see them "caper" in "Fire and Flames" (4.3.55), anticipating the upcoming torture scene. The last scalp shown is the hunter Orsbourn's (4.3.65), just before they drag in his partner, the hapless Honnyman, and his family to exemplify the horrors just announced.

Note how the violence has increased. The poetics of the play provides justice, and Honnyman now has to pay for his earlier sins. The captivity-narrative scene unfolding again starts out as an intimate one, presented to the English audience from the perspective of victims with whom they can empathize emotionally—which is useful for the transmission of moral messages. Generally, we can say that the tension in the play here reaches a first climax. We hear of torment, mercy, shock, as Mrs. Honnyman makes her husband recant his evil deeds. And he, in turn, reinvents his earlier savagery and moves from imitating stoic Indian bravery to Christian tears, hoping for forgiveness in the afterlife. Like the war dance, which ended the previous act, this one ends in a big ethnographic theatrical demonstration of "real" Indian torture.

Act 5 again starts in the pristine wilderness, but now there is another evil murder. Clearly the noble paradise has hollowed out and turned savage for many complex reasons. The motif of Honnyman's bad conscience almost rubs off on a guilty Philip, who has become hesitant about the "shocking" prospect (5.1.15) of killing the sleeping Monelia and her brother, Torax. He is so much in character that he even reports on himself like an outsider. The main reason why Philip continues his evil deed is because it is his plan, which he now follows like a puppet. We get a first sense of the causality of a Greek *katastrophe*. Certainly the arc of the tragedy now moves downward, an inevitable development that seems poetically justified after the cruel Indian torture and murder. This time it is Ponteach who ruminates solus about the tragedy of this family crime, which bodes evil for the future of his rebellion. The sense of failure continues in the Senate House, where Chekitan's messages of (public) military success collide with the sad news about the death of his (private) love: "Is this my Triumph after Victory?" (5.2.55). The funeral scene with the dead bodies in a grove is another, third occasion to showcase the theatricality of an exotic Indian ritual.[8] Chekitan's superlative grief and his rueful recantings ("Had I not . . .") echo the pain and insight of the earlier torture scene. His private pain symbolizes cosmic disorder: "The Earth is curs'd, for it hath drunk her Blood" (5.3.26). In a series of "why" questions Chekitan almost goes mad with desire for revenge. Tenesco observes: "His Passion makes him wild" (5.3.51).[9]

This pathos turns possibly unintentionally funny, with the development of Torax's survival and his disclosure of the real murderer, when he names all the protagonists as if in a comedy of errors:

> Yes, you are *Chekitan*, and that's *Monelia*,
> This is *Tenesco*—*Philip* stabb'd my Sister,
>
> . . .
>
> I am myself and what I say is Fact.
> (5.3.93–94, 102)

This new information brings about yet another dizzying change: "May we believe, or is this all a Dream?" says Chekitan (5.3.109)—and off he goes not to take revenge on the English but to kill his brother in the next scene. By this point we've had enough reversal (*peripeteia*—and even its parody), and the tragic catastrophe beyond the control of the protagonists is now confirmed to take its course.

The end of the end starts again in private, with Philip, solus, who does not resist his brother's wrath. Chekitan realizes the scope of his fratricide—"What have I done! This is my Brother's Blood!"—and the destruction of family relations—"A guilty Murderer's Blood! He was no Brother"—which leads to cosmic chaos: "All Nature's Laws and Ties are hence dissov'd" (5.4.45–47). What remains for the mighty Ponteach to do in his final soliloquy in the concluding scene, interspersed with last messages about the failure of the insurrection, is to give in to his fate and yield political power. "I am no more your Owner and your King" (5.5.93), he tells the beautiful land. "Ye fertile Fields and glad'ning Streams, adieu; Ye Fountains . . . , / Ye Shades . . . , / Ye groves . . . ," and so on (5.5.87–90). But—and this is, as already mentioned, the conventional flaws of the play—unlike the heroic role model Cato, he survives, and with an "unconquer'd Mind" (5.5.95) that expresses itself in powerful blank verse interlaced with rhymes:

> Yes, I will hence where there's no *British* Foe,
> And wait a Respite from this Storm of Woe;
> Beget more Sons, fresh Troops collect and arm,
> And other Schemes of future Greatness form;
> *Britons* may boast, the Gods may have their Will,
> *Ponteach* I am, and shall be *Ponteach* still.
>
>   (5.5.97–102)

The message of the tragedy stays open and he ominously ruminates about future things in the mythical West with ambiguous tautological troping, in a verbal statement that chiastically evokes Ponteach's existence in the present mirroring a future existence of Ponteach held up with the rhyming power and double emphasis of "will" and "still." This Indian gets the last word, and he is still standing.

In short, we have a tightly knit and surprisingly coherently composed play, with a clear development from paradise to ruin, which also justifies the many devilish references. As in Shakespeare's *Midsummer Night's Dream*, for example, there is a connection from common people to royals and to gods, and conflicts on the lower echelons have their repercussions above, nay, they even lead to cosmic chaos. Princes are like gods, and when they fail, the gods fail, and the world falls apart. Remember Chekitan's final monologue:

> All Nature's Laws and Ties are hence dissov'd;
> There is no Kindred, Friendship, Faith, or Love
> Among Mankind—Monelia's dead—The World
> Is all unhing'd—There's universal War—
> She was the Tie, the Centre of the Whole;
> And she remov'd, all is one general Jar.
>
>   (5.4.47–52)

Note that, as in many other examples in this play, the climactic events on the macro level are carefully supported by the linguistic soundscapes of the micro level. "Mankind" alliterates with "Monelia." We move from solidly grounded /r/ combinations to whistling /f/ alliterations and a slippery /ʒ/-sound and /v/-s, which lead via the ruminations of labial /m/ and more /ʒ/ to a groaning "World" of "War" (wrapping up the "Whole") that, in turn, rhymes and stops on a shrieking "Jar."[10] This final collapse of the cosmic order is carefully built up, from realism to romance and conventional plotlines, to betrayal, outrageous violence, and grand catastrophe, into the general message that, yes, beyond the fate of mere humans, the overarching order is changing.

Moreover, the emotional tension of this development is paralleled in the building up of a tremendous storm of naturalizing imagery pervasive throughout the play, reminding us of Thomas Jefferson's famous lines in his letter to James Madison that "a *little rebellion* now and then is a *good thing*, and as necessary in the political world as storms in the physical" (n.p.)—but in our case the "little rebellion" grows out of hand. According to Philip, the English takeover of Detroit started the storm, "Like Lightning from the Summer's burning Cloud, / That instant sets whole Forests in a Blaze" (2.1.40–41), which makes Chekitan worry: "Such Hurricanes of Courage often lead / To Shame and Disappointment in the End" (2.1.95–96). Weather change of this kind is also used by Monelia to describe the attitude of her English suitor: "The Scene was changed from Sunshine to a Storm, / O! then he cursed, and swore" (3.1.96–97). Thus in *Ponteach*, tempest imagery is used both for private and for political conflict, for individual high-pitched psychological emotions as well as for societal tensions. For some, like Chekitan, nature itself is out of kilter after Monelia's murder. This also applies to Tenesco's views after the brothers' death:

> For all is Murder, Death, and Blood about us:
> Nothing is safe; it is contagious all:
> The Earth, and Air, and Skies are full of Treason!
> The evil Genius rules the Universe,
> And on Mankind rains Tempests of Destruction.
>
> (5.4.71–75)

A more differentiated view of this storm can be found in Ponteach's opening of his final soliloquy in the last scene of the play: "The Torrent rises, and the Tempest blows; / Where will this rough rude Storm of Ruin end?" (5.5.1–2). The imagery is used to describe his own fight and failure: "'Tis coming on. Thus Wave succeeds to Wave, / Till the Storm's spent, then all subsides again—/ The Chiefs revolted:—My Design betray'd" (5.5.52–54). The subtle caesuras (in addition to the alliterations) are supported by reflective dashes signaling his hesitations—suddenly the units of his planning are cut in half. The Indian king who has caused a storm now finds himself in the middle of it. The image is used for both the failure of his design and his final effort to "rise above this

Hurricane of Fate" (5.5.69). As in the failed conventional closure of the plot, the storm is survived. Unlike Cato, Ponteach lives on; he will "wait a Respite from this Storm of Woe" (5.5.98) and sit it out. His story will continue—almost like Major Roger's previous two books, for which sequels were planned.[11]

The Art of Language Innovation

If so far I have emphasized the realism of the play and many of its carefully composed conventional formal qualities, be it on the level of prosody, imagery or plotting, I should not neglect to emphasize its many innovative aesthetic aspects as well—which have mistakenly been demeaned as flaws by some critical purists. In the way these elements stand out as unconventional, they contribute to the richness of the product. If I have already argued that the realistic elements of topic, historical accuracy, and ethnographic detail are certainly firsts in the development of English stagecraft, I should now also add the more aesthetic innovations offered by this tragedy on "the Savages of America." Generally there is an element of innovation in the way language is used in *Ponteach*. Thus the lofty iambic pentameter is used for earthy North American statements in expressions that simply shocked contemporary reviewers. In the *Gentleman's Magazine* of February 1766, we read: "The dialogue, however adapted to the characters, is so much below the dignity of tragedy, that it cannot be read without disgust; *damning*, and *sinking*, and calling *bitch*, can scarcely be endured in any composition, much less in a composition of this kind" (90, qtd. Rogers, *Ponteach* 2010 ed. 200). Today we may value such new language differently.

Among the more formal innovations, I want to emphasize the first Indian, who speaks pidgin in blank verse, leaving out the copula: "So, what you trade with *Indians* here to-day?" (1.1.74). And later he observes: "No, *English* good. The *Frenchmen* give no Rum" (1.1.87). The other Indians speak a bit more grammatically—thus the third Indians asks: "You, Mr. *Englishman*, have you got Rum?" (1.1.77). And the second Indian says: "Good Way enough; it makes one sharp and cunning" (1.1.83). This kind of diction was certainly new and daring in English drama at that time.[12] Also note Monelia's slangy idiom when she tells the story that she "once was courted by a spruce young Blade" (3.1.74). Tiffany Potter observes that this is the latest slang from Samuel Johnson's *Dictionary* (Rogers, *Ponteach* 2010 ed. 104n). We find here anticipations of an almost romantic modern preference for natural diction. The whole scene of Monelia's first encounter with Chekitan is actually built on her destruction of his ridiculous lofty discourse, as I will argue further on. The Mohawk princess, who comes from the East and has been thoroughly exposed to English culture, cuts the young Ottawa warrior off and gives him some of the language of her English suitor, which changed from swearing how "he lov'd," to "O! then he cursed, and swore, and damn'd and sunk, / Call'd me proud Bitch, pray'd Heaven to blast my Soul" (3.1.97–98). Thus Monelia also distrusts Chekitan's rhetorical constructions and makes him finally use straight talk to explain his dilemma in contrasting alliterations: "[B]ut your Father is a Friend of *Britons*, / And mine a Foe, and now is fix'd on War" (3.1.132–33). Monelia teaches Chekitan to use a more natural language, until he finally also interrupts her brother, Torax: "Are you sincere or do you feign this Speech?" (3.1.149).

Often language itself is exposed in its limitations and analyzed in meta-discourse, for example, when Chekitan lists all the uncertainties that worry him with hesitant pauses marked by dashes, and concludes: "The bare Perhaps is more than Daggers to me—" (I4.1.48). This high consciousness of the nature of language also appears in the constant awareness of names in the sense of conceptual framing. Thus Honnyman describes his racist hate of Indians with "I hate their very Looks and Name" (1.2.33). And when Monelia expresses her revulsion against the lecherous French priest as a "false Dissembler" and "Christian," she adds: "I hate the Sight; I fear the very Name" (4.2.61–62). Her disagreement is with the conceptual identity itself. Real truth, for Monelia, as in Wittgenstein, is beyond words:[13]

> Then do not swear, nor vow, nor promise much,
> An honest Heart needs none of this Parade;
> Its Sense steals softly to the listening Ear,
> And Love, like a rich Jewel we most value,
> When we ourselves by Chance espy its Blaze
> And none proclaims where we may find the Prize.
> . . .
> When our Hands join you may repeat your Love,
> But save these Repetitions from the Tongue.
>
> (3.1.115–24)

Monelia is a linguistic pragmatist.[14] Words come second to "Hands." Compared to deeds, they are mere empty shells.

This strong awareness of language is politicized in the final soliloquy of Ponteach, when he ruminates "My Sons, my Name is gone" (5.5.8). He refers to the destruction of his royal lineage as a conceptual residue of power: "Look on a Father griev'd and curs'd like me; / Look on a King whose Sons have died like mine! / Then you'll confess that these are dangerous Names" (5.5.29–31). As already hinted earlier, it seems that control cannot be grasped by dynastic discourse. A further, almost postmodern, perspective manifests itself in Philip's metaleptic comment, immediately after he has murdered the Mohawk children: "The Play is ended (*looking upon the bodies*) now succeeds the Farce" (5.1.35). Like an author, he comments on his own agency of jealousy and revenge, impersonating the two worst character traits stereotypically attributed to Indians and initiating the failure of the uprising.

Innovative are certainly also the performative opportunities in *Ponteach*, which make it even more deplorable that this play has never been staged. It has all the qualities of the melodrama and the circus, sex and crime—you name it. On the serious side, we find intercultural encounters, antagonistic speeches, lofty oratory, heartbreaking suicides, funeral rites, and memorable soliloquies. The play also offers both deep and witty love talk, spiced with the pain of conflicting tribal predicaments. Most spectacular, we have an opportunity to see entertaining songs, wild war dances, and experience the perverse thrill of witnessing brutality, scalpings, torture, and murder—all in loud and also in quieter scenes. In that sense, Major Robert Rogers's play offers simply . . . the works. Many of its flaws as a heroic tragedy can, in the sense of Raymond Williams's theory about genre development, also be seen as "emerging" practices of the future melodrama, a form Peter Brooks associates with unsteady political times—a situation fitting North America at that time.[15] Brooks asserts: "Melodrama starts from and expresses the anxiety brought by a frightening new world in which the traditional patterns of moral order no longer provide the necessary social glue" (20). Though the play harks back, as many critics have noted, to earlier role models like Shakespeare, Dryden, and Addison, it certainly also looks forward to the melodramatic stage and its anti-purist notions of spectacle that would shamelessly combine comedy and didacticism, *delectare* and *prodesse*, even if they discarded blank verse and often had much less to say than *Ponteach*.

8

Important Issues

As I have demonstrated, one can get lost in the details of this play. This is why at this point I would like to focus on some of the internal argumentations I find in the text, some of the issues addressed, and additional interesting observations and claims. I find among these further issues we have not yet discussed: the constant tension between the private and the public; the role of teaching (or lack of it) and bad role models that influence cultural encounters; the small but interesting role of women in the play; the ambivalent presentation of the French; and the jarring anti-Christian argumentations.

Private over Public

The constant discussion of private versus public ambitions and responsibilities in *Ponteach* has been associated with the same concern in Addison's *Cato* and mostly considered a failure in Rogers's play, where the protagonists do not live up to Roman levels of duty. Though there is a solid exposure of the graft of the English public servants as a negative example, the Indians, and especially the designated hero Ponteach, are not selfless enough to take their place. Let me therefore suggest that this play is not primarily about duty; rather it is more realistically about causality.

Thus a first intimation about the public versus private conflict is made in Chekitan's previously quoted fear that the tribal uprising will create an internal family feud: "Fathers perhaps will fight against their Sons, / And nearest Friends pursue each other's Lives" (2.1.79–80). Significantly, the origin of the uprising is presented as private, pertaining to the village culture of the middle ground. From the perspective of structure, it is carefully developed from Ponteach's private dream to a family discussion in the interior of his "Cabbin," to the public oratory in the Indian "Senate-house," which certainly is the right place to invoke pubic duty.[1] Thus Tenesco responds to the English "high Provocations" (3.3.71) by arguing, "Wrongs like this are national and public, / Concern us all, and call for public Vengeance" (3.3.88–89). He is Ponteach's advisor and stands for an elevated moral position. This is less the case with Philip, who muddles things and merely wants bloody revenge against the English, "Public or private Wrongs, no matter which" (3.3.91).

But overall, many of the conflicts originate in the different solus scenes, where particular characters voice their private ambitions: Philip, Chekitan, the French priest, and finally Ponteach. The agency moves up, from individual inception to open conflict. Only the case of Ponteach is special. His plan manifests itself first in the reported dream vision about the elk, which is duly repeated up the ranks, until the uprising erupts. In his case the private inspiration goes full circle and originates in an unconscious (public) mythical imagery—as in poststructuralist language theory. As a consequence, his solus scene comes only at the pointed end, when the struggle is over and he is lonely, summarizing the tragic events, the limits of Indian agency, but possibly opening up a new vision for the West.

The binary of Ponteach's sons is also used to perform the opposition between private and public, a polarity of inverted motivations deconstructed in the course of events. Thus Chekitan and Philip first see their own interests distributed according to the private-public divide. Philip states: "Thoul't gain the Prize of Love, and I of Wrath / In Favour to our Family and State / Thoul't tame the Turtle, I shall rouse the Tyger" (2.2.323–25). But soon we learn about Philip's private ambitions and villainous murder plan: "I'll serve my Country, and advance myself" (2.2.369). Accordingly, he now proposes to do private diplomacy, negotiate with Monelia's father, Hendrick, and sends Chekitan into battle. The lover thus clearly commits to public duty, delegating his private concerns: "Was not the Public serv'd no private Ends / Would tempt me to detain him from the Field, / Or in his stead propose myself a Leader" (4.1.32–34). This does not mean, however, that his private hopes are irrelevant. He ends his last encounter with the living Monelia with the words, "My Honour calls—and, what is more, my Love" (2.1.54). Thus she is even "more" important than his public reputation.

Challenging the heroic convention of Addison's role model, Rogers's play makes experience larger than the conceptual framework. Rather than a top-down hermeneutic appropriation of understanding by concepts (or "names," as we had it above), this refutation of (or at least non-accordance with) the genre expectations advocates a different view of reality and politics, in which the private and the public have to harmonize in a de-hierarchized sense, as seen in the parallel plotlines of the (public) uprising and the (private) love story. More significant, Chekitan's statements even suggest that the absolute subjugation of the private to the public as we have it in *Cato* is rejected in favor of a bottom-up construction of new concepts based on private relations. The utopia of (Indian) peace and understanding is possible in the private realm, and it can be implemented only as an extension of that. As Chekitan insists, Monelia "was the Tie, the Centre of the Whole" (5.5.52). Without private harmony, public agreement is not possible. In that sense, the very claims of political virtue are reversed, and certainly to some extent democratized, favoring what White would see as a local village culture. The man who has this insight is Chekitan, and in many ways, he may be the real tragic hero of the play, rather than his father, Ponteach of the "unconquer'd mind" (5.5.95), who stands more for an experience of what Gerald Vizenor would call "survivance" and for the historical facts in this conflict.[2] It is Chekitan who does much imaginative reflection on public issues, responsibilities, and causalities. It is he who makes the wrong decision to trust Philip and leave Monelia exposed, and who finally pays for his mistake with his suffering and ultimate (tragic) death.

Bad Teachers

As indicated above, the lack of Roman virtue does not mean that all ethics stay privatized in *Ponteach*. The whole point of this argument is that virtue has to move from the private example to the public realm. A major concern, then, is the responsibility of the people who are knowledgeable and superior for many different reasons, who should know better but who don't teach virtue to their children. Thus in the first act, pairs such as the traders and the hunters are organized as teacher and novice, old and young, and their interaction demonstrates that the transmitted values are corrupted. For example, the bad teacher M'Dole asks Murphey: "Are you experience'd in this kind of Trade? / Know you the Principles by which it prospers, / And how to make it lucrative and safe?" (1.1.7-9). As already illustrated, he then demonstrates to his student how to cheat Indians as "the very Quintessence of Trade" (1.1.34) and of "*Indian* Commerce" (1.1.37). As Castillo writes, young Murphey first has scruples: "Murphey initially is reluctant to emulate this chicanery" (216). He worries: "Are they not Men? hav'nt they a right to Justice / As well as we, though savage in their Manners?" (1.1.31-32). But M'Dole explains: "None who neglect it will grow rich" (1.1.36). His own role model is "old Ogden," who accumulated his wealth "like an honest Man, bought all by Weight, / . . . / And died in Quiet like an honest Dealer" (1.1.40, 44). Murphey quickly learns from this cynicism; he is quite impressed and thanks M'Dole for his "kind Instructions" (1.1.111).

The setup in the second scene is very similar. As an audience, we participate in another true learning moment. The hunter Honnyman first teaches efficiency when he kills two Indians with "a single shot" (1.2.66). Again the younger one, here called Orsbourn, has reservations about these proceedings, especially when they scalp the Indians for cash: "I vow I'm shock'd a little to see them scalp'd" (1.2.90). But Honnyman teaches him that Indians are not human and have no soul. Thus there is no reason to feel guilty: "And think no more of being hang'd or haunted" (1.2.103). The issue is not merely about lofty heroism or abstract duty but also about teaching the practice of actual behavior in a real existential context, one that Rogers knew well.[3]

Such teaching on a personal level then moves up the ranks on the intercultural level, when the English officers refuse to bring the traders to justice—unlike the French, they are unwilling to negotiate a middle ground. Thus Ponteach rightly complains: "If *Indians* are such Fools, I think / White Men like you should stop and teach them better" (1.3.34-35). But Colonel Cockum refuses, retorting: "I'm not a Pedagogue to you curs'd *Indians*" (1.3.36). Instead he proposes: "The Devil teach you; he'll do it without a Fee" (1.3.50). Certainly these English commanders show no interest in carrying any "white man's burden." They merely intend to profit from their superior cultural technology—like the governors in the following scene, when Sharp rejoices that the Indians don't know how "to add / Or calculate" (1.4.36-37) and acknowledges:

"Ay, Want of Learning is a great Misfortune. / How thankful should we be that we have Schools, / And better taught and bred than these poor Heathen" (1.4.38–40). We find different examples of such abuse of European cultural technology: the manipulated scales, the watered-down rum, the blessing of "the first inventor of a gun," literacy, calculation, and later the priest's burning glass. All these technologies are used *against* the Indians, not *for* their interest or shared with them. Sharing know-how is not part of this colonial vision.[4] Worse, this attitude also affects the transmission of values and leads to corruption of the young generation.

Among the characters who are able to learn and who change is Honnyman, who recants in the torture scene. Helped by his wife, he finds his way back to Christian ethics, confessing that he's guilty, "I am indeed, I murdered many of them" (4.4.73). And he regrets his evil teaching:

> I feel the Smart and Anguish,
> The Stings of Conscience, and my Soul on Fire.
> . . .
> How could I think to murder was no Sin?
> Oh my lost Neighbour! I seduc'd him too.
>
> (4.4.91–96)

It is, curiously, the white English character who is forced to learn in the play, because he was mistaken—the message is that the colonizers have to change their views. This is in contrast to the Indians, for whom no such reconciliation is possible. The evil Philip is a truly flat character Fate is too hard; and I'm obliged to yield.

> 'Twas well begun—but has a wretched End—
> You cannot boast to've shed more Blood than I—
> Oh had I—had I—struck but one Blow more! [*dies.*
>
> (5.4.40–41)

Philip yields to his fate without resistance—and also without changing his views. In a similarly hopeless way, Chekitan's suffering drives him mad. Sadly he has learned only violence from his horrifying experience:

> Help me, ye Powers of Vengeance! grant your Aid,
> Ye that delight in Blood and Death, and Pain!

> Teach me the Arts and Cruelty of Wrath,
> Till I have Vengeance equal to my Love,
> And my *Monelia*'s Shade is satisfied.
>
> (5.3.144–48)

Ponteach's stoicism or "survivance" at the play's end may be an asset in comparison and can be reassessed as standing for a willingness to move beyond cynical selfishness or paranoid desperation. As I will discuss below, his staying power signals the option of a dialogue of empires and intercultural negotiation that was still thinkable for Rogers in 1766.

Good and Bad French

Another open issue is the ambivalent description of the French in *Ponteach*. From an ideological point of view, the good French father Onontio is generally mentioned in this play in order to contrast his behavior with that of the evil and rapacious Englishmen who set the tone of the first act. Thus the chiefs second Ponteach's complaints to the English officers: "*Frenchman* would always hear an *Indian* speak, / And answer fair, and make good Promises" (1.3.46–47). And later Ponteach himself tells the English governors, "Your Men make *Indians* drunk, and then they cheat 'em" (1.4.79), adding: "We never thus were treated by the *French*" (1.4.84). It is no wonder that in the great oratory scene with the chiefs, this view is again confirmed when Ponteach wants to convince them to go to war against the English. He has also looked on the French "with a suspicious eye" (3.3.40) for a long time, even "as Snakes / Of mortal Bite" (3.3.42–43), but in a statement of praise that bears repeating, he explains:

> The *French* familiarized themselves with us,
> Studied our Tongue, and Manners, wore our Dress,
> Married our Daughters, and our Sons their Maids,
> Dealt honestly and well supplied out Wants
> Used no one ill, and treated with Respect
> Our Kings, our Captains, and our aged Men;
> Call'd us their Friends, nay, what is more, their Children,
> And seemed like Fathers, anxious for our Welfare.
>
> (2.2.50–57)

We get here a glimpse of the culture of the middle ground, a sense of respect and cooperation that contrasts with English haughtiness. The goodness of Onontio, the former French governor of Canada, is emphasized in order to better expose the villainy of English colonial rule.

Nevertheless, one of the most memorable characters in *Ponteach* is the French priest, who is certainly evil in his private machinations, and who gets some of the best lines in the play. Like others, he uses slang ("pump him" [3.2.68]), and his invocations of the Holy Virgin and St. Peter are ridiculous, especially because he doesn't mind the chastity of the former but follows the imperative of the latter, nominally in his ambition to become pope in Rome, but in truth as a low sexual pun catering to the gallery:

> But stop—Won't this defeat my other Purpose,
> To gain the *Mohawk* Princess to my Wishes?
> No—by the holy Virgin, I'll surprise her,
> And have one heavy Revel in her Charms,
> By now I'll hasten to this *Indian* Council.
> I may do something there that's à-propos.[5]
>   (3.2.86–91)

The contrast of "holy Virgin" and "heavy Revel in her Charms" can even be considered a cynical example of oxymoron. This priest obviously has ambitions not in harmony with his official vocation, which also shows in the unfitting French expression à-propos that sticks out and, unlike the last lines in other scenes, doesn't rhyme on purpose.

When Chekitan saves Monelia from the priest's assault, he points out the priest's sexual hypocrisy: "Have you not told us holy Men like you / Are by the Gods forbid all fleshly Converse?" (4.2.24–25). And further: "That your God's Mother liv'd and died a Virgin, / And thereby set Example to her Sex?" (4.2.29–30). The chiasmic sounds in the "Example to her Sex" move from /ks/ to the plosives /p/ and /t/, and back to /ks/, which chiastically expose the moral reversal and further add to the literary quality of this comedy. The priest becomes rather graphic when he argues: "I have a dispensation from St. *Peter* / To quench the Fire of Love when it grows painful" (4.2.33–34). Again the vowels participate in the message, going from high /i/ to low /o/ ("dispensation") and another /o/ to high /i:/ again ("from St. *Peter*"). His constantly swearing by "St. *Peter*" is certainly ambivalent. The "it" growing here is the penis that is associated with "Peter"—significantly, only "*Peter*" is italicized, not the "St."[6]

The powerful comic force of the French priest in *Ponteach* certainly contrasts and strongly undermines the positive image of the fatherly Onontio. French culture is, furthermore, also associated with wild dancing and singing after the brutal torture and execution scene of Honnyman, which ends on the deft rhyme: "This will be joyful news to Friends from *France*, / We'll join the Chorus then, and have a Dance" (4.4.229–30). Ponteach's metaleptic reference to the stage "Chorus" manifests a stage consciousness that may even suggest a stereotypical framing of decadent French court culture. On a different note, it should be acknowledged that French Catholicism had nothing to do with the Indian uprising. In fact, in contrast to English propaganda, the opposite was true. As Dowd writes: "Catholic Indians were the least likely to ally with Pontiac; the Catholic mission repelled the militants' spirited appeals" (*War* 3). We notice that the text is torn between its own didactic message contrasting bad English colonialism in North America against that of the French, on the one hand, and the general English urge of French-bashing, on the other, especially after the long conflict of the Seven Years War.[7] That latter urge was certainly strong in the theater community in London, and the textual contradictions testify to these tensions.

Good Women

What about other "minority groups" in this play? What is the role of gender? We know about Rogers's loving but failed relationship with his wife, Betsy, yet there is little information about his general attitude toward women. In the play *Ponteach*, we only have two female characters: Monelia and Mrs. Honnyman. The latter is interesting because she is the only character who teaches something good, namely, when she helps her husband recant his earlier behavior and save his soul. She is also able to save her children. Generally, she reasons like a good Puritan Christian woman: "O dreadful Scene! Support me, mighty God, / To pass the Terrors of this dismal Hour" (4.4.23–24). Like Mary Rowlandson in the famous captivity narrative, in a "residual" kind of still-active cultural reference, Mrs. Honnyman sees the Indians as instruments of God's punishment for her husband's sins: "But now we die as guilty Murderers, / Not savage *Indians*, but just Heaven's Vengeance / Pursues our Lives with all these Pains and Tortures" (4.4.84–86).[8] She certainly doesn't learn much about Indian culture beyond confirming her worst prejudices. Also note the powerful spondee on "just Heaven's," which testifies to her pious Christian attitudes.

The case of Monelia is more interesting. Critics have ridiculed her part as weak and obedient, a mere passive object in the hands of the good brother, Chekitan; the bad brother, Philip; and the evil French priest. Tiffany Potter notes: "Monelia is certainly rendered a passive, typically feminized object" (43). Instrumentalization haunts her interpretation as well. Thus Potter observes that the priest's attempt to rape her "replicates symbolically the economic and political relationships that have been set up in Act I," that is, Monelia's gender symbolizes the victimhood of the indigenous colonials because "the action of the French priest is aligned so explicitly to the earlier acts of the English that the scene becomes one of equation, rather than differentiation of two European nations and their relative values" (45). Potter insists on the "central role of women" in the sense that "Monelia's body does function in the play as a fairly straightforward metaphor for the body politic" (48). This means that "the articulation of indigenous identity in the play depends at times upon the conventionalized vulnerability of the feminine, and the idea of an identity eradicable by force is rendered through metaphors of rape" (45). She insists that "in *Ponteach*, the threat of subordination is quite consistently framed in gender terms" (46). Referring to Edward Said's claim of a "long-standing association of femininity and weakness with the racialized Other" (47), Potter furthermore connects Monelia's role with a powerful negative pull of structuralist semiotics: "Women are at the centre of every action" (47). Quoting Chekitan's definition of Monelia as "the Tie, the Centre of the Whole," she also finds confirmation of such negative agency in the fact that the "fair Donata," the slave girl of whom Chekitan had deprived his brother, Philip, triggers the action forward as the motive for the latter's plans of usurpation (47).

Though I certainly share some of these positions, I disagree with Potter's claim that "as a character, Monelia owns no discursive strategies to counter her relegation to dehumanized object and geographical metaphor . . . , and her psychic and physiological resources are presumed available for consumption" (48). Such theoretical appropriation ignores Monelia's powerful anti-Christian views, which she, moreover, teaches her lover, Chekitan, and which become one of the most interesting jarring elements in this text, as I will show below. In my opinion, Potter drifts too much into a poststructuralist reading that puts language and linguistic existence at the center of agency and ignores the fact that the character Monelia is herself a deft user of language.

I have already mentioned that Monelia is a witty and intelligent character. Though the opening of act 2 presents idyllic nature, she remains skeptical. While her brother, Torax, raves, "To view the Beauties of th' extended Lake, / And on its mossy Bank recline at Ease, /While we behold the Sports of Fish and Fowl" (3.1.20–22), Monelia, as if she had just experienced the cheatings of act 1, worries that this beauty is mere facade: "The outside Shew, the Form, the Dress, the Air, / That please at first Acquaintance, oft deceive us, / And prove more Mimickers of true Desert" (3.1.30–32). And when later her suitor Chekitan uses overblown language to declare his love, stating the conventional simile, "And like the Earth, my Love can never move" (3.1.40), she literalizes his metaphor, cleverly retorting with her knowledge about earthquakes:

> The Earth itself is sometimes known to shake,
> And the bright Sun by Clouds is oft conceal'd.
> And gloomy Night succeeds the Smiles of Day;
> So Beauty oft by foulest Faults is veil'd
>
> (3.1.41–44)

She counters his romantic imagery with the knowledge of natural science. But Chekitan rattles on, and it is necessary to interrupt his ardor a second time: "Hoh! now your Talk is so much like a Christian's" (3.1.71). She exposes the shallowness of his notions with the falseness of her English suitor: "And everything was clever but his Tongue; / He swore he lov'd, O! how he swore he lov'd, / Call'd on his God and Stars to witness for him" (3.1.77–79). Monelia then reports on the suitor's advances and the foul language used upon her rejection, concluding: "This was an *Englishman*, a Christian Lover" (3.1.102). Chekitan has no option but to accept her ethnic categorizing: "Would you compare an *Indian* Prince to those / Whose Trade it is to cheat, deceive and flatter?" (3.1.103). More, he is even manipulated into accepting her anti-Christian rhetoric: "Such Baseness dwells not in an *Indian's* Heart, / And I'll convince you that I am no Christian" (3.1.113–14). But it is certainly Monelia, one of the few females in this play, who is the foremost critic of Christianity—a major issue that we will again address below.[9]

To be sure, Monelia's rhetorical self-assertion is limited by her choices of seeking protection, first from her brother, Torax, and then from Chekitan, after he has gallantly saved her from the impudent French priest: "I am your Captive now, your lawful Prize: / You've taken me in War, a dreadful War! / And snatched me from the hungry Tyger's Jaw" (4.2.70–72). She presents herself as some kind of voluntary trophy. As already mentioned, her notions of chastity are European and not as free as those of Lahontan's Indian girls, who are "Master[s] of [their] own bodies." Yet she does choose her own lover— she is certainly not a mere "fair Donata," a female commodity to be given by one man to another.[10] Monelia's perspective is also important because she exposes and questions Chekitan's assimilationist attitudes. Tiffany Potter writes that he "has absorbed other modes of European language" and sees Chekitan as an "example of the slightly distorted way in which the colonized repeat the colonizers' discourse" (47). Pointing out many of these language issues, Monelia makes an important contribution to the ideological complexities of *Ponteach*.

Bad Christians

We are struck by the strikingly negative use of the label "Christian." What are we to do with that? It certainly goes beyond any narratologically justifiable Indian focalization. White Christianity, both English and French, is generally exposed as hypocrisy in this play, in word and action. Thus the two hunters make us associate their murderous racism with Christianity when they complain that the Indians

> infest the World, and plague Mankind.
> Curs'd Heathen Infidels! Mere savage Beasts!
> They don't deserve to breathe in Christian Air,
> And should be hunted down like other Brutes.
>
> (1.2.20–23)

And the greedy governor Gripe justifies his theft: "Ay, Christian charity begins at home" (1.4.7). Such demonstration of Christian misbehavior is exposed by Monelia, as we have seen, who explodes into a fury of Christian bashing when she meets Chekitan for the first time. She is the one who starts what will then be echoed by other Indians' anti-Christian statements. Thus the assimilated Chekitan first, very naively, asked his own brother, Philip, "Plead, promise, swear like any Christian Trader" (2.2.347), but after meeting Monelia, he changes his opinion and starts denying all Christian inclinations (see above). The anti-Christian rhetoric first triggered by Monelia continues in Ponteach's speech to the chiefs: "Our pleasant Lakes and fertile Land usurp'd / By Strangers, Ravagers, rapacious Christians" (3.3.27–28). Later he even applies this negative attitude to Philip's lie about the murderers of the Mohawk children: "But your more savage Murderers were Christians" (5.1.94). This is followed by Chekitan's raving against Christians—and though he knows that Philip is the murderer, he still does not change that attitude when he addresses the latter in hyperbolic language: "Thou Tyger, Viper, Snake, thou worse than Christian; / Blood thirsty Butcher, more than Murderer!" (5.4.13–14). Also at the end of the drama, the vanquished Ponteach blames Christians: "They have no Faith, no Honesty, no God, / And cannot merit Confidence from Men" (5.5.56–57). Turn it any way you want: Christians are bad in this play.

A very negative Christian example is of course also the French priest, who stands for the lowest moral values: greed, lechery, treason, hypocrisy. In the scene where he tries to rape her, Monelia calls him a "cruel barbarous Christian" (4.2.8), and then a "foul Christian" (4.2.16). And later: "Base, false Dissembler—Tyger, Snake, a Christian! / I hate the Sight; I fear the very Name" (4.2.61–62). The language of the bestiary again culminates in Christianity—which turns into its opposite, the value of the antagonist ("Dissembler"). And fearing its very name, Monelia points out that she is concerned about Christianity as nothing less than a conceptual framework of thinking. In the case of the Catholic priest, this negativity may be explained in terms of Puritan propaganda and its association of Rome, the pope, and the French with the Antichrist.[11] But then all the English Christians are negative figures as well, and Christianity simply characterizes all the European actors in this drama. As Monelia explains to her brother, Torax: "[A] Christian lurk'd within the Grove, / And every Christian is a Foe to Virtue; / Insidious, subtle, cruel, base, and false!" (4.2.83–85). Thus Anderson notes: "Rogers's attack is on civilized man, with his pretension to Christian ethics, rather than on the French or on the Catholic Church. The Englishmen in the play are certainly not seen as in any way possessing higher ethical standards than the priest. Through the priest, Rogers demonstrates that those with the opportunity for a scholarly education can use it in a perverted way, by twisting semantics and logic cleverly in order to gain their own selfish ends" (235). She certainly has a point here. Subtle logic and planning is an important part of the traders' strategy as well as the governors' reveling in their cultural superiority in the play, and it is ultimately supported by a materialist base of power ("bless the first Inventor of a Gun"). Remember that the organizational structures of the Christian empires (both English and French) relied much more on coordinated formal hierarchies and procedures than the Algonquian alliances and their village justice, which were based on local, on-the-spot analogies.

The only good Christian we can find in the play is possibly Mrs. Honnyman. But significantly, she doesn't really fit with the other Europeans in *Ponteach*. Her introduction of Rowlandson-like Puritan views of faith somehow clashes with the official religious ideology of the Church of England in London. From another angle, Slotkin criticizes Rogers's use of "the term *Christian* as an insulting epithet throughout the play" as a mere ploy of his appropriating the Indian's role for himself (236). But one would then wonder: to what purpose?

Also Morsberger notes this persistent criticism of Christianity: "One might expect the Indians to have anti-Christian sentiments, but the plot of the polluted priest and the pervasive indictment of Christianity have the intensity of Thomas Paine and seem to express the convictions of the author of these scenes, probably Nathaniel Potter, an unfrocked clergyman" (253). As I shall argue below, Mr. Potter may certainly have had a hand in this, especially in the Puritan argumentations of Mrs. Honnyman. Rogers's own religious alienation as an Irish Protestant growing up in Puritan New England may further explain some of the theological irritation. He had already expressed generally negative attitudes towards religion in his *Concise Account*: "Religious impostures are not less frequent among the Indians of America, than among the Christians of Europe; and some of them are very successful in persuading the multitude that they are filled with a divine enthusiasm, and a kind of inspiration, few knowing better how to act their part in this sacred juggle than they" (217). Superstitious priests are pumping the people on both sides of the colonial encounter, contributing little to better intercultural relations. Rogers's view of reality was certainly based less on metaphysical values, which he consistently exposes as falsities, than on direct human interaction—his sense of respect was the existential respect of the battlefield.

9

Open Questions

The many issues posed in this text lead us in circles to more centrifugal questions. If *Ponteach* was not appreciated by the critics, for whom was it written? Thus we are going to raise the question of the targeted audience and find a mismatch responsible for the negative reception of the play. This endeavor leads us to the important question about the possible coauthor and to a closer look at the writing skills of Nathaniel Potter and, finally, to a new suggestion to explain the strange name of our protagonist "Ponteach."

No Audience
(or the Wrong Audience?)

Especially in view of the play's commercial and critical failure, audience reception is an important issue to discuss. *Ponteach* criticizes Christians and stages explicit violence. Thus Castillo writes that the "giddy mélange of stirring rhetoric and lurid episodes involving priest-rapists, axe murders and tragic thwarted lovers, and its oscillation between the representation of Pontiac as statesman and Pontiac as bloodthirsty killer would have left most readers blinking in bewilderment" (221). Tiffany Potter offers a good selection of excerpts from the *Gentleman's Magazine*, the *Monthly Review*, and the *Critical Review*—important London publications that had previously reported on the major's adventurous life and his military exploits as a successful Ranger. They had been very supportive of the first two books of "this brave, active, judicious officer . . . to whom the public [was] obliged for the most satisfactory account [they had] ever yet been favoured with, of the interior parts of that immense continent which victory ha[d] so lately added to the British empire" (*Monthly Review* [January 1766]: 9; qtd. Rogers, *Ponteach* 2010 ed. 203). This article even helped advertise Rogers's planned subscription sequels and calls the author, "Happily for our country, the better qualified not only for the task he hath new enjoined his pen, but also for the achievement in which his sword hath been employed" (10; qtd. 203). This extensive review copied eight pages from the *Concise Account* (see Rogers, *Ponteach* 2010 ed. 204), finding in the description of Rogers's Indians what Tanner and Krasner would certainly consider the values of "Whig revolutionary rhetoric" (4). Thus it continues:

> Here we cannot help observing what a noble and consistent spirit of liberty prevails among these Indians, with respect to the method used by their chiefs of *inviting*, not *impressing* the people to accompany them to the wars. What a striking contrast does this afford to our tyrannical practice of *seizing* our fellow subjects by brutal force, *imprisoning* and *transporting* them like felons and Newgate convicts; and after such base treatment, compelling them to go forth with our fleets and armies, to fight in defence of the RIGHTS and LIBERTIES of their country! (18–19; qtd. Rogers, *Ponteach* 2010 ed. 204, original italics and capitals)

The review then quotes a further seven paragraphs form the *Concise Account* and compares it to another author, "Mr. Colden,"[1] who wrote about the Five Nations, praising the Indians' "noble virtues," sullied only by their "cruel passion" for revenge. Colden is extensively quoted: "But what, alas! have we *Christians* done, to make them *better*? We have, indeed, reason to be ashamed that these infidels, by our conversation and neighborhood, are become *worse* than they were before they knew us. Instead of virtues, we have only taught them vices, which they were entirely free from before that time" (21–22; qtd. 204–5). This is a reference to the classical version of the noble savage: "None of the Roman heroes have discovered a greater love to their country, or a greater contempt of death, than these people called *barbarians* have done, when liberty came in competition" (21; qtd. 204). We find in the arguments of this reviewer another fascinating possible influence on the play, or at least we realize that some of the issues in *Ponteach* were being discussed within an already-existing historical discourse.

Above all, the reviews emphasize the experience and authenticity in Robert Rogers's texts. Hence the reviewer in the *Gentleman's Magazine* notes that the *Concise Account* is "very different from the compilations which [were] undertaken for booksellers, by persons wholly unacquainted with the subject" (584; qtd. Rogers, *Ponteach* 2010 ed. 201). The author is especially interested in the reporting on "the interiour part of *America*": "This is a very entertaining as well as useful part of the work, for which the Major was particularly qualified, by a long and experimental acquaintance with their several tribes and nations, both in peace and war" (585; qtd. 202). And he also looks forward to a continuation by subscription. Ditto the *Critical Review: or, Annals of Literature*: "The credibility of his [i.e., Rogers's] accounts . . . rest upon the moral character of the author, of whose person we know nothing; tho' we are rather pre-possessed in his favour, by the air of openness with which he writes, unmixed with the marvelous (387; qtd. 202). This reviewer went on to suggest: "The picture which Mr. Rogers has exhibited of the emperor Ponteack, is new and curious, and his character would appear to vast advantage in the hands of a great dramatic genius" (387; qtd. 203). Obviously, late 1765 was a good time for Rogers in London. This is the statement that probably motivated the whole project of the play.[2]

The same *Gentleman's Magazine*, however, only three months later, wrote a very negative review of the play, summarizing its plot and listing its characters, but noting that the "indignation which the reader feels at the villainies of [England's] traders, hunters, officers, and governors" creates interest in the play but was "immediately destroyed, by representing *Ponteach* as equally cruel and perfidious" (90; qtd. Rogers, *Ponteach* 2010 ed. 199–200). Especially the character of Philip shocked this reviewer: "We are struck with horror at the project so diabolically cruel, but we abhor the projector yet more, when we find that *Monelia* is beloved by his brother *Chekitan*, with the utmost tenderness and ardour" (90; qtd. 200). He summarizes: "All the personages of the play may be considered as devils incarnate, mutually employed in tormenting one another; as their character excite [*sic*] no kindness, their distress moves no pity." The reviewer is especially appalled by "a scene in which *Indian* savages are represented as tossing the scalps of murdered *Englishman* from one to another" (90; qtd. 200). Obviously the enthusiasm for Rogers's work founders in the face of polite audiences' expectations about tragedy and its conventional values.

The assessment of *Ponteach* by the *Critical Review: or, Annals of Literature* was negative as well: "Though we very readily embraced the opportunity of doing justice of the character of major Rogers, as an officer [with reference to their review November last], and an itinerant geographer, yet we can bestow no encomiums upon him as a poet. The performance before us is the most insipid and flat of any we have ever reviewed, belonging to the province of the drama" (150). The most negative review was possibly printed in the *Monthly Review, or Literary Journal*, which had welcomed the *Concise Account* with empathy and enthusiasm, but sarcastically trashed the play:

> [It is] one of the most absurd productions of the kind that we have seen. It is great pity that so great and judicious an officer should thus run the hazard of exposing himself to ridicule, by an unsuccessful attempt to entwine the poet's bays with the soldier's laurel. His journal, and account of our western acquisitions, were not foreign to his profession and opportunities; but in turning bard, and writing a tragedy, he makes just as good a figure as would a Grubstreet rhymester at the head of our Author's corps of North American Rangers. (242; qtd. Rogers, *Ponteach* 2010 ed. 200–201)

This very negative appraisal has been repeated by critics over the centuries. Here is Anderson's assessment from 1977: "Why the British and American public . . . failed to respond to *Ponteach* is not immediately clear. Certainly, the play is weak from an artistic point of view" (227). According to Nevins, *Ponteach* "closed disastrously Rogers' brief career as an author" (*Ranger* 79).

As already mentioned, critics after Parkman have accepted only the factual realism of the play and discarded the rest. Thus Rogers's biographer Cuneo states: "The first act and the first part of the second—while they share with the remainder of the play its remarkable lack of artistic qualities—display familiarity with frontier conditions which must have been based on first-hand information. . . . the remainder of the play lacks even a historical interest" (181). And Nevins, who was an eminent historian but not a literary critic, in his introduction to the Caxton Club edition, as already cited, even compares *Ponteach* unfavorably with Godfrey's *Prince of Parthia* (15). These laymen judges of theater aesthetics consistently follow Rogers's old critics in London, who, for the very same reasons, had first been supportive of Rogers but then simply panned his play.

To be sure, the brutality portrayed in many scenes of the play alienated many contemporary readers. Cuneo writes that they were "repelled by the cruelty shown by the characters" (181), explaining that the "eighteenth-century sense of elegance was badly upset by the scalpings and gore" (182).[3] I have already quoted the disgusted reviews. As we have seen, the low language also upset the critics. These are elements that no longer disturb us today—I have even described them as innovative. But the main cause for the critical rejection of *Ponteach* was, in my opinion, that the play did not offer any identification figure to a European audience. All the white characters, English or French (except in reports on Onontio or the English king), are negatively charged, and the Indians cannot compensate for this. The only exception may be Mrs. Honnyman, but as a pious Puritan woman in a subplot, she cannot fill the void. Moreover, Castillo finds that her husband's confession and repentance "strains credibility" (221). Furthermore, though the hunter gets more stage time, he is also a minor character. And as already mentioned, the protagonist Ponteach remains alive—which slighted contemporary expectations of a Cato-like flawless hero that were raised but not satisfied. Hence I see this issue of the positive hero as the main reason for audience irritation. Though Rogers's Indian is vanquished, he doesn't vanish; he is not yet dead and gone like the last of the Mohicans and therefore does not provide a sufficiently clean slate of projection for savage nobility.[4] As a result, *Ponteach* remains disturbing. Yet from our perspective today, that is, of course, exciting. Rogers, in a sense, had a direct message for the king that overruled the expectations of contemporary London audiences, one that involved his personal view of politics in the Great Lakes and his own ambitions, as I shall argue in the conclusion.

The Other Voice; or: Who Was Rogers's Collaborator?

Critics with an interest in postcolonial issues and the new voices of hybridity, mestizos, and border identity have approached *Ponteach* from that particular angle. Thus for Castillo, "Rogers is in many ways the embodiment of the English Creole in America" (223). She suggests that he "is ventriloquizing the character of Ponteach in order to enact some of the dilemmas of Creole subjectivity that he himself had encountered" (222). The texts by Creole settlers, she explains, exemplify the dilemma of "attempting to reconcile a sense of loyalty to, and nostalgia for, a 'home' where he or she no longer lives or perhaps has never lived, and the need to survive in a new and often radically different reality" (213). A similar perspective can be found in Tiffany Potter's Canadian approach, when she cites authorities like Edward Said and Homi Bhabha. Potter emphasizes that Rogers's perspective "originates from shifting affiliative ground, his own voice hybridized by a lifetime spent in sites where no single discourse was entirely dominant, at the fringes of empire, but firmly surrounded by Indian cultures and modes of authority" (34). As in Chekitan (see above), Potter also finds in Monelia "an ambivalent colonial mimickry" (34). Nodding in the direction of postcolonial criticism (as Canadian scholars are supposed to), she shows us that, like many other texts of its time, *Ponteach* manifest a hybridity that has possibly caused critical rejection but makes its study interesting, rich, and exciting for the contemporary generation of readers.

At the same time, as we have observed above, this heteroglot quality in the play, which even manifests itself in some of the characters, often reflects two specifically different modes—one dominated by an ethnographically correct quality of North American know-how and realism and the other dominated by European values and aesthetic conventions. There is a sense of two different discourses at odds, and many critics simply explain this by the fact that the Ranger Rogers could not have written a play in blank verse, and that all these inconsistencies are explained by the existence of a coauthor. Hence much of the postcolonial hybridity may simply be the result of these two "different" voices in the literal sense. Cuneo surmises that "Robert [Rogers] himself never claimed its authorship; he never disclosed any inclination to write blank verse. It is possible, however, that Rogers played a role in its composition. . . . [He] would have been the most likely person in London to have been consulted by an ambitious playwright" (181). Also Nevins in his introduction to the Caxton edition sees a cooperation in which Major Rogers is mainly responsible for the realist elements in *Ponteach*: "Indeed, Rogers' informing historical accuracy is—beyond the many definite parallels between the language of the play and that of the *Concise Account*—one of the surest establishments of the authorship which he never formally claimed" (12). Many critics have suggested that Rogers had help with the playwriting, but the exact division of labor will probably forever remain a mystery.

Nathaniel Potter

The most likely candidate for coauthorship is Nathaniel Potter, first suggested by Nevins, who calls him "an educated and rather clever, but disreputable Englishman" (*Ranger* 79). Also called his "literary facto-tum" by the editors of the *Adams Papers*, Potter became Rogers' secretary and probably traveled to London with him. Cuneo writes: "Undoubt-edly he was assisted by his secretary, Nathaniel Potter, a Princeton graduate and former minister, who had been hired in Boston during 1764" (174). Kenneth Roberts also suggests Potter's hand in writing the play,[5] and he even has major role for a fictional daughter, Ann Potter, in his novel.

We know little about Nathaniel Potter. Who was he? A young gossip from Boston, who would later play a major role in the new nation of the United States, confided to his diary of "1760 Decr. 18th. Thursday": "There is every Year, some new and astonishing scene of Vice, laid open to the Consideration of the Public. Parson Potters Affair, with Mrs. Winchester, and other Women, is hardly forgotten. A Minister, fa-mous for Learning, oratory, orthodoxy, Piety and Gravity, discovered to have the most debauched and polluted of Minds, to have pursued a series of wanton Intrigues, with one Woman and another, to have got his Maid with Child and all that" (Adams n.p.). A footnote from the editors of the *Adams Papers* is about as much as we get when it comes to the biography of this interesting clergyman:

> Nathaniel Potter, College of New Jersey 1753, and honorary A.M., Harvard 1758, was minister at Brookline from 1755 until dismissed in June 1759. Little is said of him in the local histories of Brookline, but the Plymouth church, which seriously con-sidered calling him, heard in July 1759 "some melancholy things opened with Respect to Mr. Potters moral Charecter." This was just in time to save "this poor Church . . . from Ruine." In 1765 Potter took up with another adventurer, Maj. Robert Rogers, accompanied him to England, and probably had an important hand in Rogers' several literary productions published at that time. With the promise of a good salary as secretary, Potter went

with Rogers to Fort Michilimackinac, but quarreled with him in
1767, and died in the English Channel later that year while
bringing his charges against Rogers to the British government.
(n.p.)

On "Dec. 27th 1765. Fryday," we find another entry from our diarist:

> At Home all day. Mr. Shute call'd in the Evening, and gave us a
> Number of Anecdotes, about Governor Rogers and Secretary
> Potter, their Persecution in Boston, their flight to Rhode Island,
> their sufferings there; their Deliverance from Goal, and Voyage
> to Antigua, and Ireland without Money, their Reception in Ire-
> land, and Voyage to England, their Distresses in England till
> they borrowed Money to get Rogers's Journal printed, and pres-
> ent it to his Majesty; which procured Each of them his Appoint-
> ment at Michilimachana. (n.p.)

John Adams seems not to have known about the play, but he was interested in Rogers's career, and he suggests a possible literary cooperation
as well.

We have only a few traces of Nathaniel Potter's writing before he
met Rogers. Fortunately, one of his sermons was printed in 1758, and
though much of it reads like many other Puritan sermons of the past, he
mentions a few things in his *Discourse on Jeremiah* that suggest compati-
bility with Rogers's values. In this classical jeremiad,[6] Potter compares
"the Zeal of our Fore-fathers" to the "Vices" and "Degeneracy of their
Sons, neglecting those Virtues" (8). He wants his congregation to be
"truly sensible of our Sin" (9) and deplores the weakness of the English
in the French and Indian War, asking for more manliness and vigor, of
both the moral and the military kind, for "truly martial Genius or Spirit
of Soldiery" (12). Potter certainly would have admired a hero like Rogers
and maybe even had him in mind in a footnote stating, "We have many
brave Soldiers among us, some have proved themselves so, and perhaps more would, had Opportunity been given them" (24n). In an earlier
note, he makes clear that the "Enemy" he is talking about are the
French: "Both by the Provisions and Arms at *Braddock's* Defeat, at *Oswego*
and *Fort-William-Henry*; the latter of which was actually reduced by the
Arms and Ammunition taken at the two former; at least, these were
used, and were of great Service to the Enemy" (5n). Note Potter's interest
in military matters and his sarcastic irony.

Moreover, we also find rhetorical elements that correlate with *Ponteach*. Thus Potter lists savage animals in order to compare the situation of the Jews of yore to the contemporary New Englanders. Both were surrounded by enemy neighbors "compared to Lyons, Wolves and Leopards" (5). Potter certainly knew how to use alliterations: "Behold trouble; our Circumstances wax worse and worse" (6). He observes that "Preservation or Punishment" are sometimes "crowned with Peace, Health and Plenty, at others distress with War, Pestilence and Famine" (10–11). Though the capitalization of nouns may have been a standard printing practice of the day, we note that in this sermon it is the same as in *Ponteach*, which was produced on the other side of the Atlantic—at least there is no divergence. Like the author of *Ponteach*, Potter also likes to play with sounds and chiasmic sounds effects: "The Causes of our Misery, and Means of our Recovery, remain a Secret" (7). We go from /c/ to /r/ and /m/, and back to /r/ and /c/ again, both times mediated by /s/. Also consider the following mirroring of /r/ and /p/, interlaced with /s/ and /c/: "Whatever Reformation in these Respects, may be proposed and recommended" (7). There is no lack of words in this sermon, but much of the argumentation remains shallow. One gets the impression that Potter is a sweet talker who repeats his strongest phrases, a man who likes the sound of his own words.

Thus again, "the martial Genius of a People, or the true Spirit of Soldiery, is no less in Danger from the inside [?] Luxury, Drunkenness, Debauchery and all Kinds of Excess" (17). As in *Ponteach*, there is criticism of public officials, of "Men who wallow in Luxuries and sensual Delights . . . attend to the public *Business*, and manage the weighty *Affairs* of State" (16), and the moral vigor required connects, again as in *Ponteach*, the private to the public domain: "Men may prove Friends to the Public, from a Principle of Self, and the Views of present and personal Benefit" (15). Potter certainly likes alliterations on /p/—I cannot list all of them here. But the public and the private are important: "Is it not the bad Principles and Practices of particular Persons, that denominates a Nation corrupt and vicious? And is it not the Follies and Disorders of single Members, that render the whole Body Politic, weak and contemptible?" (26).

Moreover, Potter knows his classics and quotes role models, from Hannibal to Scipio and Caesar, to the British Marlborough, who were "careful to inculcate and preserve these Virtues in their Armies" (18). We also find reference to Indian captivity, to "Captives, the abject Slaves of Barbarians and Infidels, of the Subjects of studied Cruelties and Torture" (21). This "Tryal" is spelt with *y*, like the "Tygers" in *Ponteach*. Potter then rattles on, enumerating atrocities:

> The Captivity and Bondage of Friends, Relatives and Neighbors—Men, Women and Children, widowed, deprived and orphaned, by *Pagan* Barbarity, by *Gallic* Cruelty,—there are Parents who have seen their own dear Children, their sucking Infants, murdered and dashed, in Pieces before their Eyes—Children who have seen their tender Parents abused and tortured—Friends and Neighbors, who have been mutual Spectators of each others Captivity, Torment and Chains. (22)

Again, note all the alliterations, the sound play, and the subtle chiastic argument connecting parents' "dear Children" and children's "tender Parents." Potter ends on a conventional note of spiritual causality, that their "present Sufferings and Virtue be rewarded with Crowns of Glory that fade not away" (27). What we learn from this sermon is that he was interested in soldierly virtue, that he hated corrupt officials and saw a correlation between the private and the public, that he knew his theology and his classics, but also that he had a facility with words, and liked to use alliterative sounds, chiasms, and so on. Thus many of the topics of the play and many of the rhetorical tropes in it coincide. This sermon certainly does not exclude Nathaniel Potter as a possible coauthor of *Ponteach*.

But can we find further evidence of Potter's influence in *Ponteach*? Is he responsible for the iambic pentameters and the heroic drama conventions? Nevins writes: "If he were actually with the major at this time, he may be partially deserving of credit for the *Concise Account* and *Ponteach*, which represent a greater literary facility than do the *Journals* or Rogers' ordinary letters and reports; although the content of both is by internal evidence largely Rogers'" (*Ranger* 80). The situation is far from clear. I also see a possible influence of Potter in all the clever theological observations in *Ponteach*. Some of the sophisticated argumentation smacks of professional knowledge. Thus we have constant remarks about artificial manipulation and devilish "arts" or nonsensical "noise" attributed to the Indians' discourse, as I have observed above. And in addition to that, we have very direct references to the Bible by the three governors. Thus when Gripe justifies his graft with, "Ay, Christian charity begins at home" (1.4.7), Catchum immediately adds: "I join with *Paul*, that he's an Infidel / Who does not for himself and Friends provide" (1.4.9–10). To which the third governor, Sharp, adds: "Yes, *Paul* in fact was no bad Politician" (1.4.11). This very pointed attack on an abuse of Pauline theology hints at a theological interest that may go beyond Rogers. Furthermore, as if they were students of divinity, these royal politicians seem to know exactly how sermons are structured, and they apply this to their own behavior. Says Gripe: "We've heard the Doctrine; what's the Application?" (1.4.18). Their theory-to-practice mode even makes us have second thoughts about our earlier, Brechtian didactic understanding of these opening scenes of the play. The systematic composition of theory leading to demonstration may also reflect religious formation. Theology, after all, has its own subtle forms of dialectic logic.[7]

The exposure of the French priest's hypocrisy, for example, certainly doesn't deny a conscientiously Protestant hand. Though the American universities had become centers of the Enlightenment by the mid-eighteenth century, and breeding grounds of a new generation that would become the Founding Fathers (see Ferguson 403), the old Puritan views that framed the pope as the Antichrist were still strongly present when Potter attended the College of New Jersey and when he worked as a minister in Brookline, Massachusetts. This is evident in the jeremiad of his published sermon. That his own clerical career was aborted for adultery also suggests his hand in all the bawdy preoccupations of the priest. The latter's far-fetched excuses (of which we have already heard some) are twisted and forced. After elaborating his "dispensation from St. *Peter*," he goes into the technical details: "For, being holy, there is no Pollution" (4.2.38). Sexual activity is rather a means of purification: "Nay, Maids are holy after we've enjoy'd them, / And, should the Seed take Root, the Fruit is pure" (4.2.40–41). Note another sonic highlight here in the logic building up from /u/ to /iː/ to /uː/ to /u/, and finally to the diphthongish /iu/. These lines are true acoustic treasures. The fact, moreover, that this is one of the most memorable scenes of the play, with some of the most successful versifying, also signals a strong emotional involvement. Certainly both Rogers and Potter had reasons to be critical of religion, but the sophism of all these argumentations points to a specialist. References to Christian imagery in general, which I mentioned earlier, to dissemblers and serpents, hearts like rock that should melt, and so on may also signal Potter's influence. This is, however, not enough evidence to prove that he is the coauthor. Because we don't have access to an archive of John Millan, we cannot determine if he employed other writers to help with the

Ponteach project. But in any case, the play text remains as it was printed. As one eminent Shakespearean told me: proven authorship is of secondary importance when we have a good text.

A Highlander Called /pon'tiax/?

An interesting element that may be responsible for the exotic spelling of "Ponteach" can be seen in the rising influence of things Scottish in the British Empire. Chris Gibbs writes that

> with the demise of Jacobitism and the advent of the Union thousands of Scots, mainly Lowlanders, poured into England and took up numerous positions in politics, civil service, the army and navy, trade, economics, colonial enterprises and other areas. . . . In 1762 the Scot John Stuart, the 3rd Earl of Bute was appointed as first lord of the treasury, basically the role of prime minister and the first Scotsman to be appointed to the position. Bute was only the tip of the iceberg, as Scots took up important positions all over the empire. (n.p.)

This ascendancy is also invoked by Ross, who finds a Scottish tradition in J. Millan's book shop: "Millan may have recognized the same raw talent [in Rogers] that he had seen earlier in his friend the Scottish poet and playwright James Thomson. After all, Millan had made his name at 25 by publishing Thomson's poem *Winter*, whose blank verse broke with the arch, artificial style of the poets of the day" (358). Millan knew, of course, that Robert Rogers was Scots-Irish; he was a virile hero with Scottish ancestry. Hence the strange transformation from the French "Pondiac" to Rogers's "Ponteack" in the *Concise Account*, and to "Ponteach" in the play may well reflect a literary exploitation of the powerful wave of Scottish nationalism after the unification of Britain in the Acts of Union of 1707.

As an important cultural event shortly before the composition of *Ponteach*, we should also take into consideration the Ossian craze that had taken London by storm. Gibbs writes:

> In 1760 [James Macpherson] published *Fragments of Ancient Poetry, collected in the Highlands of Scotland, and translated from the Gaelic or Erse Language*. This was followed in 1762 by *Fingal* and then *Temora* in 1763, both of which were complete epic poems.

> Macpherson claimed that they had all been written by a Celtic
> bard named Ossian in the 3rd Cen. AD. Here were Scottish epics
> to rival the *Iliad* which proved that the ancient Celtic culture had
> been culturally sophisticated and colourful. However their true
> nature and authenticity has been debated ever since. (n.p.)

According to Gibbs, the poems "picture a Gaelic world in which the old
order of the warriors and heroes, the spirit, romanticism and traditions
of the people, of a pre-modern life without corruption, are all falling,
never to rise again—a romantic world" (n.p.). And this suits colonial
attitudes perfectly: "The analogies with the current times, less than
twenty years after the final fall of the Jacobite cause and the Highlands
were subtle yet clear to those who knew their history and politics. Yet
it was an assertion of the spirit only—the legacy of the 'noble savage'
ancestors, and not one that impacted on the contemporary world or
Britishness" (n.p.).[8]

In Major Rogers's North American world, Scotsmen were represented by the many Highlander soldiers brought there to fight the imperial war. Dixon writes, "From the time they first landed in America in
1756, the Highlanders had been regarded with awe" (158). He quotes
"one observer" stating that "the Indians flocked from all quarters to
see the strangers who, they believed, were of the same extraction as
themselves," and notes that others "saw the similarity between the
Woodland Indians and the Scots, including General Forbes, who once
jokingly referred to the Highlanders as 'cousins' of the Cherokees"
(159). According to Dixon, the "French labeled them *les sauvages sans
culottes.*" He explains: "The Highlanders and Indians had more in common . . . than the fact that neither wore pants: they also shared an in-
domitable warrior spirit" (159). And Brumwell writes: "Because of their
rugged homeland, Highlanders were viewed as particularly suited to
the rigours of campaigning in North America" (271). He adds: "It was
widely believed that the Highlanders enjoyed some form of mysterious
kinship with the woodland Indians of north-eastern America" (272).[9]
Todish and Harburn's illustrated history, *The British Military and the
Pontiac Indian Uprising*, shows Robert Griffing's painting *Warriors*,
which depicts a Highlander soldier and an Indian (99).[10] Robert Rogers
himself trained officers from the Forty-Second Regiment and provided
them with his famous Twenty-Eight Rules of Ranging. Following the
Earl of Loudon's orders, he "took these men under his wing and provided them with a set of written rules specifically designed to govern

their conduct in wilderness combat," for example, he taught them "firing at particular targets rather than delivering mass volleys, which seldom found their marks in the dense forest" (Dixon 160).

Hence Rogers was familiar with Highlanders and probably also with their association with Native Americans. It is therefore entirely possible that the pronunciation of our dramatic hero's name should not so much rhyme with *teacher* but rather reflects an earthy Caledonian tonality ending on /x/. Ponteach's name would then be pronounced /pon'tiax/.[11] Associating the "Savages of America" in the West with wildly independent Scots in the North was probably a way for Rogers's publisher to translate the unknown foreignness of American Indians into a more familiar British one.

Conclusions

The Original
American Backwoodsman?

10

Centrifugal Insights

After such a long contextualization and discussion of the "what" of *Ponteach*, we may also want to reach a few conclusions to take home from our analysis, starting with the question "why," and look at the play as a part of Major Rogers's rocky career planning and his economic ambitions at a very specific time in history. The play reflects the Ranger's own imperial ambitions, which were possible only in the short historical time slot between the patriotic pride of conquering Canada and dreams of western expansion of the First British Empire, and the rise of a nationalist American independence movement that aborted these plans within a bit more than a decade. A further point to discuss is our judgment of Rogers's attitude toward Native Americans. His depiction of Indians in *Ponteach* is closer to French attitudes and defined by a military sense of respect that manifests a certain sharing of perspective rather than racist prejudices. Rogers showed much interest in the experience of the Other. Furthermore, the very failure of his career also suggests a class issue in America that reflects the values of the new republic as a country run by elites, in which the dreams of a Scotch-Irish country boy were cut short. I will finally suggest that in many ways Robert Rogers should be seen as the "real" Natty Bumppo. He represents a contradictory and unsanitized version of the French and

Indian War and the later backwoods hero, standing at the beginning of an American prototype later appropriated by James Fenimore Cooper.

Imperial Ambitions

Many colonial texts are propaganda to invite new immigrants to a better place, and they are full of economic incentives. This started with Sir Walter Raleigh, Thomas Harriot,[1] and John Smith, continuing over the years all the way to Benjamin Franklin, who likewise gave advice to prospective immigrants. As we shall see, Major Rogers certainly also had such ambitions. Slotkin writes that as "leader of the guerilla-type ranger companies of the last French and Indian War, [Rogers] attempted in the 1760s to dramatize himself to the British Court and public as the American hero par excellence" (187). And Sayre notes: "Like John Smith's literary output, Rogers' two volumes of colonial history and one of drama made a similar bid to raise his stature into the genteel trinity of courtier, soldier, and poet and to win him appointment to a position of prominence in a subsequent colonial venture" (*Tragic Hero* 155). In that sense, *Ponteach* can be seen as a product of Rogers's career planning.

In short, behind the story of the tragic Indian hero we have the economic ambitions of a military hero who is trying to advance his civilian career. Rogers's most recent biographer, John Ross, traces some of these involvements very carefully. Already on his first trip west to Detroit, after arriving in Niagara in 1760, the enterprising Rogers formed a partnership with the traders Edward Cole and Nicolas Stevens, called Rogers & Company, "eager to take advantage of the trade opportunities opening for the King's enterprising subjects in the moment of victory" (296). And Widder offers the facsimile copy (*Beyond* 259) and transcript of a deed "granting him [i.e., Rogers] a 20,000 acre tract of land between the Ontonagon and Copper rivers along the southern shore of Lake Superior, . . . to have and to hold" (66). Later, in 1761, Rogers also created another "partnership of Askin & Rogers, primed to take advantage of the western trade" and "put in a bid for a tract on the western shore of Lake George" (Ross 311). Rogers had recently married, he was in debt, and he needed to sort out his financial situation.

Ross even speculates that after the Indian uprising, the major had intentions to do business with his former opponent Pontiac: "The war would not last forever. He may have imagined the development of a powerful and lucrative partnership. In the paragraph following his account of the gift of brandy [in the *Concise Account*], he noted that

Pontiac had devised a rudimentary monetary system; he had designated a commissary to create bark money or bills of credit bearing his symbol, the otter" (344).[2] This idea of cooperation with Pontiac is elaborated in Kenneth Robert's *Northwest Passage*, which features a long scene of their meeting at Oswego in chapter 62. Pontiac gives advice: "But Michilimackinac, Brother, is different from all the other posts! We question that the mind of Sir William Johnson is wise when he says he wants Michilimackinac treated like all the rest" (501). The novelist obviously had read Rogers's *Concise Account* and put many of its ideas in the chief's mouth.

Not surprisingly, much prospecting is mentioned in Rogers's books, especially the *Concise Account*. Nevins observes: "Again and again he repeats, in effect, the declaration which follows the account in his *Journals* of the surrender of Montreal—that the wealth of the Incas and Aztecs was as nothing to that of the northern continent, and that the Anglo-Saxon peoples could not fail to find in it a home of wonderful scope and resource" (*Ranger* 77–78). This attitude also influences the paradisal descriptions in the play *Ponteach*. The Northwest is a place of milk and honey. Rogers describes his first trip home from Detroit in the *Journals* as follows: "I have a very good opinion of the soil from Detroit to this place; it is timbered principally with white and black oaks, hickorie, locusts, and maple. We found wild apples along the west-end of Lake Erie, some rich savannahs of several miles extent, without a tree, but cloathed with jointed grass near six feet high, which, rotting there every year, adds to the fertility of the soil" (231). Later he notes: "This day killed several deer and other game, and encamped" (225). And on the next day: "I went a-hunting with ten of the Rangers, and by ten o'clock got more venison than we had occasion for" (234). Similarly, after describing the old French and English colonies and their history on the first 150 pages of the *Concise Account*, Rogers becomes effusive when he reaches the Great Lakes. He writes about Lake Superior:

> The Indians in this territory certainly enjoy in the greatest plenty what they look upon to be the necessaries, and even the luxuries of life. Here are fish, fowl, and beasts of every size and kind, common to the climate, in the greatest abundance; nor do I see any reason why this should not become a rich and valuable country, should it ever be inhabited by a civilised people. It has rivers, it has a sea of its own, which make great amends for its inland situation, by facilitating trade and commerce from one

> part of the country to another, by a cheap and easy conveyance;
> nor do the Indians entirely neglect this advantage, but make
> great use of canoes on the rivers and lakes. (159)

Note that this is the very place where he had earlier invested in land
speculation. The way to explore this new territory was mainly the French
strategy based on the natural waterways. Rogers continues: "The land
adjacent to the river between the two lakes is broken and hilly; but
much of it is capable of being improved to good advantage. The timber
is thick and lofty; and iron ore is here found in the greatest plenty, and
is said to be the best in America; and here are streams sufficient for any
kind of water-works" (160). Beyond the traditional riches of waterways, the animals, the timber, the rich soil, we even learn about what is
below the soil ("iron ore") and about waterpower for industrialization
("water-works"). This is truly the time-honored American business of
prospecting.

There are pages and pages of such idyllic description. Here is his
portrait of Green Bay:

> The timber is tall, but not so thick as to prevent the growth of
> grass, which is here very luxuriant, it being generally five or six
> feet high, which sufficiently indicates the goodness of the soil.
> This invites hither the greatest plenty of deer, elks, buffaloes,
> wild cows, bears, beavers, &c. add to these the fish with which
> the waters teem, and it certainly appears a most desirable region,
> for the air is not less agreeable than the soil.
>
> The winters are never severe, and great part of the year the
> country wears a verdure.
>
> Here likewise grow spontaneously a great variety of grapes,
> which are agreeable enough to the palate, and doubtless might
> be manufactured to advantage. (164)

Why grapes? Is this another message from Canaan? As in "The Gift
Outright," the land is beckoning, calling out for its settlers. "The land
was ours before we were the land's / She was our land more than a
hundred years / Before we were her people," Robert Frost opens his
infamous inauguration poem for John Kennedy. Rogers even anticipates
Pittsburgh steel mills: "There is a good coal-mine near Fort Pitt, made
use of by the garrison for fuel" (200). He again hammers home his point
at the conclusion of his book:

> It hath been sufficiently remarked, as we have travelled through
> this extensive country, that it every where abounds with fish,
> fowl, and variety of game, that in its forests are most kinds of
> useful timber, and a variety of wild fruit; and, no doubt, every
> kind of European fruit might be cultivated and raised here in
> great perfection. In a word, this country wants nothing but that
> culture and improvement, which can only be the effect of time
> and industry, to render it equal, if not superior, to any in the
> world. FINIS. (264)

Ross writes about this vision: "Rogers, product of the thin, glaciated
soils of New Hampshire, knew that gold and all the world's precious
elements counted little as compared to the rich earth of the North
American heartland . . . Richness was right at their very fingertips, there
for the taking. These were in deepest essence the words of an imperial
thinker, a man striking to live in and grasp the many natures of a world
that was beyond the ability of most to even imagine" (366). The play
Ponteach, written immediately afterward, certainly must be seen as part
of this advertising campaign.

   As we know from his biography, Rogers procured a governorship
in Michilimackinac, which he wanted to use to put all his ideas into
practice. Here was this big, new part of the British Empire in the American Northwest. And Rogers knew more about it than most other people.
He had Indian friends, and he wanted to profit from this association,
like all the other big players in North American politics. Thus in his
Michillimackinac Journal he would later write:

> It need not surely be repeated that the Case of Michilimakanac
> is very different—This is the outside or Frontier British Post in
> America—It is or ought to be a Barier to all may come Westerly
> Northwesterly or Southwesterly to the Pacific Ocean—It is or
> ought to be a Beacon from which a most Extensive and as yet
> unknown Territory is watched and Observed—It is or ought to
> be a Store House fraught with all manner of necessaries, for
> the Constant Supply of almost innumerable Bands Tribes, and
> nations of Savages . . . removed from it five, Six, & eight Hundred
> and some a thousand Leagues who cannot Annually nor ever in
> their Lives visit it as a Market—They must lose one years Hunt to
> make sale of another—They must leave their Families distressed
> and Starving—Their Country and Substance naked & exposed

It need not surely be repeated that the Case of Michilimakanac is very different. N. This is the outside or Frontier British Posts in America—It is or ought to be a Barrier to all that may come Westerly or Northwesterly or Southwesterly to the Pacific Ocean—It is or ought to be a Beacon from which a most Extensive and as yet unknown Territory is Watched and observed—It is or ought to be a Store House fraught with all manner of necessaries for the Constant Supply of almost innumerable Bands Tribes and nations of Savages—Savages removed from it five, Six & eight Hundred and some a thousand Leagues, who cannot Annually nor ever in their Lives visit it as a Market—They must loose one years Hunt to make Sale of another—They must leave their Families distressed and Starving—Their Country and Substance naked & exposed to Enemies and perhaps perish themselves with Hunger & want on their way—Savages long accustomed to expect Traders Annually with Supplies in their respective Countries—

Page 21 from Robert Rogers's original *Michillimackinac Journal* of 1766–67, later transcribed and published by William Clements. Note the telling "beacon" statement about Michilimackinac. (Courtesy of American Antiquarian Society)

If ye above Queries be answered in ye affirmative, as they surely must, the following Plan, seems absolutely necessary to gain the great, & Valuable Ends, hinted at & proposed by them. Viz:

———— Which is humbly submitted, to the better Judgement, of his Majesty, & the Government of Great Brittain who at all times, have consulted the Interest of his Majesty's Subjects, but more especially at this Glorious period, of the Brittish Annals. Viz:

———— That Michillimackinac & its dependencies, should be erected into a Civil Government, with a Governor, Lieutenant Governor, & a Council of twelve, chose out of the Principal Merchants, that carry on this valuable branch of Trade with Power to enact, such Laws, as may be necessary & those to be transmitted to the King: & for his Approbation. That the Governor, should be Agent for the Indians, & Command of the troops, that may be ordered to Garrison the Fort

Page 28 from Robert Rogers's original *Michillimackinac Journal* of 1766–67, later transcribed and published by William Clements. Note the beautiful hand—what a contrast to holding a scalping knife! (Courtesy of American Antiquarian Society)

to Enemies, and perhaps perish themselves with Hunger and
want on their way. (47–48)[3]

This is why the major proposed the founding of a fourteenth English
colony on the Great Lakes, with himself at the helm to negotiate with
the Indians. On Rogers's famous Michilimackinac memorandum and
his plans "to erect Michilimackinac into a Civil Government independent of any other Post,"[4] Sayre comments: "In his frontier fantasy, Rogers
would outflank the Hudson's Bay Company to control the interior of
North America, and he did not forget his plan for an expedition to the
Northwest Passage, for he wrote that his influence would extend all the
way to the Pacific" (*Tragic Hero* 156). Widder presents a 1767 map of
Major Robert Rogers in which the "district of Michilimackinac" encom-
passes "parts of the present Canadian provinces of Ontario, Manitoba,
and Saskatchewan, and the states of Michigan, Wisconsin, Minnesota,
and North and South Dakota, and parts of Indiana and Illinois" (*Beyond*
xix–xxi). He writes that "Robert Rogers' most important goal at Michilimackinac in 1766 and 1767 was to convince the British government to
create a new colony out of the 'District of Michilimackinac' and name
him its governor" ("Maps" 36). Ross asserts that the post at Fort Michilimackinac "would make Rogers the de facto viceroy of the west and offer
him an ideal location from which to seek the Northwest Passage" (364).
Hence Rogers's economic ambitions also inscribe him in the long tradition of New World discoverers. But he met opposition from the established eastern competitors for the Indian trade (mainly Sir William Johnson) and General Thomas Gage, who refused to reimburse him for his
old Rangers' debts and for his new investments as governor at Michilimackinac.[5] Though some authors claim that Rogers's northwestern expenses were not larger than other governors' in better favor with their
superiors and that by keeping peace he had actually saved the Crown
large sums,[6] the major's vision about his own role in the northwestern
empire ended, as already mentioned, in terrible quarrels and his arrest,
trial, and general downfall.

Soft Power

Interesting for our endeavor to understand *Ponteach* is Rogers treatment of the Indians as a governor: he was more respectful and understanding of their habits than other English officers in the west. Morsberger writes: "During the two years that he was governor, Rogers

drew to Michilimackinac the largest congregation of Indians that history records" (241). According to his biographer Nevins, one of the
main reasons for Rogers's big Indian conference at Michilimackinac
was his aim to avoid a war between the Chippewa and the Sioux—
which would have been disastrous for business prospects at a trading
post catering to both (*Ranger* 99). He explains: "This conflict Rogers
labored anxiously to prevent, fearing that it would disrupt the whole
western trade" (100). Rogers's own report on the Grand Council in
Michilimackinac, the speeches and the smoking, the gifts, and so on
(*Michillimackinac Journal* 36), has already been quoted. According to
Ross, Rogers

> began to preach cooperation, in an attempt to reorganize the
> relationship between the cultures, based on an expansive, gen-
> erous, and largely constructive vision of the Indians. Supply the
> Indians heavily, he implied, and they would return the favor
> with a heavy flow of furs. Rogers here exercised a trait later evi-
> dent in the great industrialists who would not settle for small
> returns. He would apply ranger tactics to trade, expanding by
> dynamic penetration, just as Bridger, Astor, and others would
> forty to fifty years thence. (382–83)

Rogers's approach to intercultural relations seems more that of an enterprising Onontio than that of a stern English commander.

    The attitude toward the Indians that we find in the *Michillmackinac
Journal* is one of compassion for all the Indian visitors. Thus Rogers
listens to their questions about "bad birds" from the West, namely,
rumors that the French will return (11). It may be interesting to consider McDonnell's observation that the local Indians "kept on pressure
on Rogers by warning of great unrest in the west" and that he "caved
in" (261), that is, they also fabricated information to manipulate him.
Roger lists all the presents that he gives away. The fourteen chiefs of the
Ottawas, for example, get "Eight stroud Blankets, eight pair of Leggins,
eight breech Clouts, twelve ratteen Coats, twelve Callimanco Gowns,
fourteen Shirts, sixty pounds of Powder, one hundred and fifty pounds
of Shott, four hundred Gun flints, seventy eight pounds of Tobacco,
three pounds of Vermillion, twenty-four Gallons of Rum, & fourteen
lac'd Hats" (*Michillimackinac Journal* 16). The spelling, by the way, according to William L. Clements, at this point is Potter's. We also find
many Indians begging for charity. Thus on 15 October 1766, two chiefs

of the Chippewa visit and declare: "We are come this day to smoke a pipe with you . . . give us a little Milk, to drink . . . have pity on us & give Charity, eight of our Young people have lately died, & we hope you will give us something to wipe away our Tears from our Eyes" (17). The "milk" is, of course, an image for rum. Rogers knows their culture and gives them presents "to bury [their] dead & wipe away the tears" (18), and they answer that they are "greatly oblig'd" to him "for covering the dead bodies of [their] relations" (18). These are the habits of the middle ground. The power of chiefs depends on their ability to distribute goods to their tribe. Thus on 23 May 1767 Minetawaba arrives with his "young men" (30). He wants more rum than offered by Rogers: "I expected rum enough to make them merry." And he shows medals from Sir William Johnson in the expectation that none of his wishes shall be denied: "I ask for a Cannoe load of Rum" (31). He mainly has social obligations: "I told my young men to come here & speak to thier father, . . . don't make us asham'd" (31). This shows that Rogers had to negotiate within a framework of such Indian social habits.

Rogers's politics are also well illustrated in these journals. When on 25 October 1766 Ottawas from Island of Beaver in Lake Michigan complain about bad hunting grounds and want (Catholic?) "compassion" (18), Rogers tells them that they are "not a good sett of *people*" because they have stolen "Goods from the traders at the expence of every Indian on the Islands. . . . I am a Man that come out of the middle of the Ground, & if you do the least hurt either of the french or English, [I will surround your] Cabbins with a Bloody Hatchet" (18). Note the *Ponteach* spelling of "Cabbins" and, most impressive, Rogers's definition of himself as a man of the "middle of the Ground." His temperate jurisdiction also reminds us of Richard White's earlier examples; he threatens that he will give gifts only under strict conditions: "If you will bring me in those frenchmen to this Fort in the Spring that told you to plunder the Boats that went from there, unhurt with out taking anything from them to this Place: I then will think of your miserable Situation which your own folly has brought upon yourselves" (19). Rogers wants peace in the West, and he tries to educate the Indians in a positive way. On 10 November he gives presents to a chief of the Misisagas, "although, you have done wrong & acted like fools by fighting against your Brothers the Seoux" (21). He gives him wampum: "Look at the BELT, when you strike the Seoux you strike the English also, for [we] have given them our hands & trade with us, therefore for the future, You must never go to war against those people without letting Sr. William Johnson know . . . as I'm order'd to make all reports to him" (21). In his encounters with the Indians, Rogers constantly mentions that the king and Johnson want peace among the Indians. There is, at least on the surface, no trace of disloyal behavior in these notes.

According to Widder, Rogers appropriated French trading strategies for himself, "working closely with the French-Canadian traders (who were now British subjects), Indians, and Metis as he put the French system of trade back into practice for the benefit of Great Britain and himself" ("Maps" 37).[7] He also used the French for spying. Thus he writes on 13 April 1767 that he "Sent Mrs. Cardin a frenchwoman to Abacroach [Arbre Croche] to find out what the Indians were about. . . . [He] gave her three gallons of rum to talk privately with them, & find out thier designs" (*Michillimackinac Journal* 24). He wanted to know if they had any "intention of going to war against the Seoux," and "persuade them from it" (25).[8] Widder asserts that the "Indians in the West welcomed the attention Rogers—who understood their world view—gave to them at their traditional gathering place at the Straits of Mackinac," and notes that it is "striking how closely Rogers's way of relating to Native leaders and their people fulfilled the Chevalier de Raymond's account of the prerequisites for successful diplomacy by French officers when treating with their Indian counterparts" ("Maps" 52). As Cuneo observes: "Some Indians could not believe the word that there was an English post commander who welcomed Indians" (205). Like the French governors before him, Rogers honored the Indian tradition of gift giving. Gelb writes in his introduction to Jonathan Carver's *Travels*: "They wanted to persuade [the Indians] to look upon Fort Michilimackinac as a major trading center" and "lavishly distributed gifts . . . infuriating the white traders at Prairie du Chien" (25). Nevins explains: "Most of the goods for his lavish gifts he had secured on credit from the favorably impressed and over-confident traders" (*Ranger* 100).

The figures didn't add up, of course, but Rogers was trying to do business in the Indian fashion. The fact that he gave gifts, organized big conferences, and smoked the calumet with them does of course not mean that Rogers met them on eye level, but it signals that he was certainly aware of issues of cultural diplomacy. Thus William Clements emphasizes in his introduction to Rogers's *Michillimackinac Journal* that "no event in Rogers's career shows him to greater advantage than his tactful negotiations with Pontiac and his people near Detroit, the peaceful occupation of the fort, and the peaceful submission of the Indian tribes thereabouts" (6). Nowadays his strategy would probably be called one of using soft power.[9] In this respect, Rogers was like Sir William Johnson, who was also of Irish descent but had a better understanding of British colonial administration.[10]

Rogers and Race

It is interesting that although Rogers was a military man who killed many Indians and even scalped them, he was not a racist in our contemporary sense of the word. Thus Fulford asserts that Rogers's representation of Pontiac in *Ponteach* "was one of the very first of a person of colour—Indian or African—to move beyond crude stereotyping" (78). Also military historians mention that Rogers was "hardly an Indian hater" (Ross 360). And Todish claims: "Many people have made the assumption that because Rogers was so good at fighting Indians, he hated them. Nothing could be further from the truth" (16). Anderson notes: "Apparently all of his battles with the Indians did not make him despise them, but rather inspired him to respect their courage and to understand the terrible effects that the loss of their land entailed" (229). Nevins writes about the *Concise Account* in a language that betrays his early twentieth-century sensibility about race:

> A real sympathy, if not triteness, is brought by Rogers to this exposition of savage life. He recognizes the errors and weaknesses of the race, but he does ample honor to their virtues. In their domestic institutions he finds much that is admirable: their rigid if somewhat oblique ethics; the respect in which the aged are held; the fine appreciation of personal dignity which restrains the parent from chastising his child; their universal equanimity under the assaults of every passion (except revenge), "surpassing all but the most Christian philosophers;" their respectful unselfishness toward friends and allies. (*Ranger* 76–77)

He summarizes: "In short, Rogers attitude toward the savage race bespeaks a liberality almost anomalous in one whose earliest lesson was to fear and hate the redskin" (77). The point that Ross, Todish, Anderson, and Nevins make is rather that *because* he had fought so hard against Native Americans, Rogers knew them well and did not underestimate their abilities. You respect your opponent because he knows your qualities, and you know his. Knowledge fosters realism and, in competition, respect.

I find this truism well illustrated in Rogers's anti-Semitism. Though he liked Indians, he didn't like Jews. The farmer's son writes about Rhode Island: "This province is infested with a rascally set of Jews, who fail not to take advantage of the great liberty here given to men of all professions and religions, and are a pest not only to this, but the neighbouring provinces" (*Concise Account* 59).[11] He identifies same problem in the province of New York, where Jews "have been tolerated to settle . . . , having a synagogue in the city, who sustain no very good character, being many of them selfish and knavish (and where they have an opportunity) an oppressive and cruel people" (65–66).[12] I would thus suggest that Rogers was prejudiced against Jews precisely *because*, as opposed to the Indians, he knew so little about them. Yet he must have met with some of the Jewish traders in Michilimackinac, among whom Widder mentions Ezekiel Solomon (*Beyond* 129–32).[13]

Rogers also respected Indians because he fought *with* them against the French. As Todish explains:

> One of Rogers' greatest strengths was his ability to accept and work with all kinds of people. His Ranger corps was very diverse, and his men were judged on their abilities and dedication to the ranging service. Rogers enlisted several companies of Stockbridge Mohican Indians into his Rangers, and gave their Indian officers the same status as white Ranger officers. He repeatedly defended them against criticism, at times justified, that they received from officers. (15)[14]

We read that at some point near Fort Carillion, 300 of Rogers's Rangers were "joined by 100 Stockbridge Indians in two companies" (Ross 189). Caleb Stark reports that in 1759 Amherst wanted Rogers "to engage Lieutenant Solomon (Indian) to raise a company of Indians for the ensuing campaign" (456). He also mentions a Rogers letter of 1759 on "the necessity of augmenting the rangers, and the desire of the Stockbridge Indians to reenter the service" (438), and that some letters by General Amherst were "delivered by Captain Jacob Nannawapateonks, who during the last campaign commanded the Stockbridge Indians" (443). Rogers certainly had prestige among these Indian fighters: "The captain of one of the Stockbridge companies, Jacob Maunauphtaunk, had indeed heard about Rogers' interest in signing up the Stockbridges and had come to Albany, refusing to negotiate terms with anyone else" (Ross 221). I would assume that Rogers's intimate knowledge of Indians is also responsible for his realism, for example, the fact that his *Ponteach* failed as the portrayal of a noble Indian. Experience made it impossible for Rogers to reduce his hero to literary expectations only.

Empathy, Dialogue . . . Respect?

Rogers's attitudes toward Indian social organization can be discerned in his description of the "Soutis or Attawas":

> Altho' there is such a thing as private property among them, which they transfer to one another, by way of bargain and exchange, and if taken out of the compass of fair dealing, the aggressor is stigmatised, and punished with disdain: yet no individual or family is allowed to suffer by poverty, sickness, or any misfortunes, while their neighbours can supply their wants; and all this from the simple natural consideration, that they and their families are liable to the same unhappy circumstances they see their friends in. (*Concise Account* 157)

There is a certain humanity, a direct involvement with the people, in Rogers's observations. This attitude is also shown in the great speeches characterizing the figure of Ponteach, who does not limit human variety to racial traits. I have already quoted the example of the theater chief's anaphoric characterization of human traits ("We see," "We know," "Some are"). Significantly, this long catalog connects qualities of difference with rhetorical sameness. And it is introduced by Ponteach's observation that "*Indians* a'n't Fools, if White Men think us so; / We see, we hear, we think as well as you; / We know there're Lies, and Mischiefs in the World; . . . Men are uncertain, changing as the Wind" (1.4.171–75), which ends on the statement: "But I call no Man bad, till such he's found, / Then I condemn him and cast him from my Sight; / And no more trust him as a Friend and Brother. / I hope to find you honest Men and true" (1.4.184–87). Though we know that "Christians" are bad, the emphasis in these statements is that both Indians and whites are "Men," that is, primarily human beings. On the negative side, we find Chekitan, who extrapolates from his brother's murder of Monelia a loss of belief in all humanity, Indian and white, asking rhetorical questions: "So much Dissimulation in the Earth? / Is there such Perfidy among Mankind?" (5.3.120–21). Though pessimistic, his view refers again to "Mankind," beyond any narrow ethnic framing. In any case, both of these Indian heroes are foregrounding generally human rather than ethnic qualities.

As Ross writes: "Rogers had carefully noted in the journal that he looked upon the Indians neither as besotted idiots nor as vicious terrorists but as men and women not unlike the English, if less organized and less civilized" (392). The Indians in turn respected him as well—Todish emphasizes Rogers's role as a peace broker in Michilimackinac: "As a result of Rogers' fairness towards Indians, he was well liked and respected among them" (16). David Armour writes that he "listened attentively and provided presents to show his affection. Chief La Fourche and the L'Arbre Croche Odawa established a warm personal relationship with Rogers" (*Colonial Michilimackinac* 74). According to Armour, the Indians objected to his arrest in Michilimackinac: "When la Fourche and his band returned in the spring from their winter hunting, they were very upset. The Odawa expressed their displeasure by throwing the British flag in the lake" (74). There had been a positive rapport between Rogers and the Indians.

Even Rogers's very prose style reveals a sense of empathy, an ability to change perspective in order to understand the other person. Thus Fulford insists on the sensibility in *Ponteach*: "Rogers clearly knew in detail about the motivating force of spiritual revival for Pontiac and his followers. Needless to say it was rare for white authors to present Indian beliefs sympathetically, and rarer still to get the details right" (89). One of Rogers's important economic arguments had always been that the control and restriction of trade to the East would limit the market because of the long travel distances. He talks about this trip to get to the English forts, sometimes lasting half a year, of the families left behind, and the dangers of starvation or attacks by wild animals or enemy Indians. The entire argumentation of Rogers's Michilimackinac project is based on extending the reach of English trade and the virtues of its civilization further west, beyond the Algonquians of the Great Lakes to the Sioux in what is now the Dakotas. In his formulation it is the Indians who crave these services and whose lives are supposed to be made better. Thus Rogers writes in his *Michillimackinac Journal*, in a draft of his proposal to set up a new colony in the Northwest (and make himself governor thereof), that the Indians need reliable trading partners for the following reasons:

> In case of any emergency or Accident they must often suffer great inconveniences if traders are not among them or near at

Hand to Supply them afresh, for Instance the Loosing or or [*sic*] of a Hatchet or two or three Knives & the like may lay a Whole Family under great inconveniences for six or eight Months together, the Spoiling of a Small quantity of Gunpowder, the breaking a Spring of a gunLock &c may be the means of destroying a whole Seasons Hunt and of distressing and Starving a numerous Family. (42–43)[15]

This predicament is also described by the historian Richard White in another geographical context: "Hunting beaver for exchange and undertaking the long and arduous journey to transport the beaver to Montreal could be justified only in years free from the threat of Iroquois attack, when ample food supplies were available" (24).[16] No wonder Widder reports that Rogers was much appreciated by the Indians: "When Rogers was relieved of his command at Michilimackinac on December 6, 1767, he had allowed the traders to winter in the interior and had brought a relative peace to the region" ("Maps" 37). The Indians felt that he had made efforts to understand their needs.

In our assessment of his personality and his way of interacting with the Other, we can also consider Rogers's attitude toward animals in the *Concise Account*. Again, I sense a certain element of fundamental respect. Memorable is his seven-page description of the beaver: "The industry, foresight, and good management among these animals is very surprizing, and scarcely credible to those who never saw them. When they want to make a settlement, three, four or more assemble together, and first agree, or pitch upon a place where they may have provisions (which is the bark of trees, lilly-roots, or grass) and every thing necessary for erecting their edifices, which must be surrounded with water" (255). Note that Rogers presents the beavers from their own point of view. They act, plan, build, have intentions. Though he explains how they can be trapped, beavers are much more than commodified objects to be hunted for gain. Rogers shows admiration for their intelligence: "The construction of their houses is no less artful and ingenious" (256). It is this attitude and narrative perspective that suggest extraordinary qualities of understanding in Rogers, and most of all, an attitude of empathy. Rogers experienced a culture that was sometimes brutal but certainly interactive in the sense of action and response, and this dialogic sense of reality also influenced his attitude toward culturally other people or even different species. This sense of mutuality in experience can also be seen in his writing, which leaves room for the perspectives of others and does not merely operate in a projective field of conceptual negativity. This "respect" in the sense of equal positive value can also be discerned in the naming of nations and ethnic groups in *Ponteach*, which are all in italics, be it the *English* or *Britons*, the *French*, the *Mohawks*, the *Indians*, or individual characters, whose names are in italics as well.

In this context, I want to return to another interesting statement from the very end of the play, when Ponteach suggest that in order to defend themselves, Indians have to "learn to conquer with [their] very Looks" (5.5.44). If Shakespeare's Caliban has profited from the master's language by learning "how to curse," Roger's Ponteach is more of a Medusa, or at least an insistent "other" who looks back and wants to impose a dialogue in the pragmatic dimensions of interaction, reminiscent of the gesture James Clifford finds in the "Igorot Man" exhibited at the St. Louis Fair of 1904 (164), who unabashedly looks back into the ethnographer's camera: "If we look intimately into his face, what disturbances appear behind?" (163). Rogers's vision of the world was open to respect, empathy, and dialogue.

A Lesson about Class

It is entirely possible that Rogers received more recognition for his bravery and his middle-ground diplomacy from Indian chiefs than from his English superiors. In that sense, the fate of his visions laid out in his books, his memoranda, his proposals, and in *Ponteach* reflect Rogers's career, the failure of which is an interesting lesson about class and political power in the American colonies and the emergent independence movement. Rogers could not buy a "harpsichord" for his wife, Betsy, as he had hoped in his letter addressed to her "on Board the Ship" on his first trip to London. Though appreciated when doing the dirty work of gruesome fighting in the field for his superiors, his own bourgeois ambitions were stunted, and he could not send his "Dearest Betsy" any "pretty things from England first from Ladeys" (Letter of 27th [??] 1765).

The best way to understand this issue is the encounter between Rogers and the leader of the revolutionary American forces, George Washington, who rejected the returning Ranger's offer to join the Patriots in 1776 and had him arrested. Nevins already notes their contrasting profiles in his MA thesis of 1913, when he observes that Rogers was born "scarce three months before one of the richest and most patrician

My only Life   on Board the Ship 27th 1765.

By this opportunity I enclose you some notes of
hand — not knowing But that you may get some thing thereby
and hope they will arrive safe to your Dear hands — its all I
have in my power to do at present but hope soon to make you
some Remitances there is some Effects I have left in the hands of mr
James Nyonen who will deliver you an account of and when he
Gits the money will give it to you his obligations I enclose
but it will be near twelve months Before he can Recover the
money from South Carolina

                    Blanchard did me no manor of service
But has Brother Been a doing how ever I will let these
Disagreable Subjects Drop and tell you what I am now
about I am going to England as fast as I posibly can begin
what ever may offer if any thing valuable so much the better
if not its my Intentions to take Even a Company and Dispose
of it together with my Books and Return to my own
and Dear Betsy as soon as ever I can — therfor do not grieve your
Self to Death I will lose no time posable to avoid in Returning to my
Dear Betsy — you may Direct your letters to me by every posage
at the New England Coffee house London till I arrive ther when
I shall give you a full account of my Voyge and letters
by the first opportunity — I shall take One to omit none
thats any Likely for a tollorable Conveyance — I spose I
shall see mrs s to as the Vessel I go in is bound for Dub
lin and from

Above and right: Letter by Robert Rogers written to his wife, Betsy, on the boat to Europe, promising to settle his affairs in London, 27th [month unknown] 1765. (Courtesy of William L. Clements Library, University of Michigan)

from thence I shall cross in ye Rachel Boate for London, I
have but little money or would send you some you must
my Dear excuse me at present for I cannot spare any
yet I shall should I stay any time remit as much
as possible Dear — pray be contented I could not pay
for a horseload or would a hove sent you one but
hope soon for Better times — I have good incouragem[t]
and shall take the first opportunity to inform you my
Betsy what success I have — pray my Dear let me hear
how your helth is I fear your Will not set on enough
of flesh — devert your self in wrighting youl find
th' agreat amousement I will send you some pretty
things from England fit for ladeys — the news papers
shall likewise be sent you I hope youl find my
arivel by them, its nedless to say more than this
that you are the only Joy of my heart and the
pleasent thoughts I have of seeing you again when
in a better scituation Preserve me and believe
me my Dearest your ever faithfull and
Loving Husband while life Remains

Rob't Rogers

My Dutyfull Regards to Dr and Madam Browne
Love to polley and peter

this not in Dr Blanchards name be locke from Brair for
a note of myne and Brair will charge with you gives you
a new note and takes up this one in Blanchards name

of Virginia [i.e., Augustine Washington] witnessed the birth of the father of the republic" (3). The juxtaposition of the careers of these two famous military leaders is strongly emphasized by Ross: "These two charismatic, boldly ambitious alpha males, both more than six feet tall, both well proportioned and physically commanding, each a presence to the other for nearly two decades, now stood eying each other" (430). He explains: "No better example exists in eighteenth-century America to illustrate the importance of family standing, good luck, and the ability to win friends in high places than the contrast between the unfolding fortunes of Washington and Rogers" (430). And the reason for this difference is definitely class: "One was Scots-Irish, rough-hewn, and of little formal education, his life forged in the rugged New England wilderness; the other was a princely magnate in tidewater Virginia" (431). While the young Washington couldn't lie when he proverbially cut down his father's cherry tree, Nevins reports in his MA thesis that the Indians who plundered and burned the old Rogers homestead "spread such devastation through their orchard that but a single apple-tree remained standing" (12). Young Robert and the Founding Father certainly began their lives on different ends of colonial American society.

The two figures thus stand for a wider class division in colonial America, one that seems to eerily parallel the contemporary political culture of the Donald Trump era: "The seeds of mutual distrust lay deep: the coastal elites had never accepted the ever-prickly Scots-Irish, often changing the rules and laws right under Rogers' feet. Washington was involved in a revolution largely controlled by people of his own background [from the] self-satisfied landed class" (Ross 431). This contrast is mentioned not only by Nevins and Ross but also by Cuneo, when he discusses the counterfeiting episode of Rogers's life: "Poverty rampant on the frontier produced a society cynical of tidewater wealth, ready to dare anything for financial return, and hungry for land as a means not of sustaining life but of producing the ever-illusive fortune" (3). Being a lawyer, Cuneo goes into the details of these resentments by the immigrant have-nots against a "new foe: the tidewater proprietors, who always seemed to have the law's assistance in ousting pioneer settlers from hard earned homes. James Rogers [the Ranger's father] and Joseph Pudney [his friend and partner] were caught in the toils of a long-standing dispute over the territorial limits of Massachusetts Bay, which colony had set up a claim to lands west of the Merrimack River" (9). Rogers's career is in many ways an example that exposes some of the hollow promises of the revolutionary American rhetoric that claimed republican equality but not only denied participation in its success to black slaves but also created a glass ceiling for the lower-class white population. In Rogers's grand failure one almost gets a sense of Faulkner's Scots-Irish Sutpen from the mountains and his ambitions stemming from the humiliation of being sent to the backdoor at the big plantation house. Still, where the Faulkner character copies the hierarchical ways of southern slavery and becomes an evil racist, the northern Indian fighter kept a sense of egalitarian human relations.

Rogers and Washington had also been in competition in the business of land speculation. Thus Ohio History Central states about Washington: "He became a skilled surveyor and used this knowledge to assist the Ohio Company during the 1750s to prepare the Ohio Country for white settlement. Washington also invested in the Ohio Company, having come into a sizable fortune with his father's death in 1752" (n.p.). It explains: "The Ohio Company's desire to acquire land in the Ohio Country partly resulted in the French and Indian War."[17] Thus Washington's construction of Fort Necessity and the French taking of it on 3 July 1754 "is considered by many historians to be the start of the French and Indian War in the New World." Danny Sjurson describes the Ohio Company as "a land speculation outfit at heart, the company's investors hoped to claim land in the Ohio Country, buy it cheaply from the Crown and sell at a profit to westward-bound settlers [in order to] enrich the already wealthy plantation families of Virginia" ("Whose Empire?" n.p.). Southern aristocrats like Washington certainly had a head start and more reliable legal support. In his chapter titled "Land Speculation: Individual Purchases, 1746–1770," Albert T. Volwiler calls Washington "a leading land speculator" (233). He "was interested in Ohio lands. In 1767, he instructed [Captain William] Crawford while ostensibly engaged on a hunting trip to spy out the choicest lands near Fort Pitt" (291).[18] Volwiler explains: "Most of the public men of the east were interested in this movement. Washington, Franklin, Johnson, and Patrick Henry all held shares in such companies" (234).[19] When he reports on the "great struggle going on in London over the proposed establishment of Vandalia" in Western Pennsylvania and West Virginia (294), we realize that Robert Rogers was not the only American dreaming of yet another English colony beyond the East Coast.[20]

A case comparable with that of Rogers is the Western acquisitions of the Indian trader George Croghan, whose influence with the Indians was second only to Sir William Johnson. Volwiler writes that Croghan's "early life was spent in Dublin, Ireland. The education which he there received was so meager that he was pronounced illiterate by Bouquet. . . . He migrated to America in 1741" (23). Like Rogers (and Johnson), he was Irish and had no formal schooling. An interesting aspect of his case is the connection with James Fenimore Cooper's ancestors. Thus in Cooper's *Chronicles*, the whole first chapter is basically about the debts of George Croghan and how he had to sell the land that would become Cooperstown. We read that "the grounds of the 'Hall,' [i.e., the Cooper family's later Otsego Hall] was erected by Col. Croghan, as a place in which he might hold his negotiations with the Indians, as well as for a commencement of a settlement" (11). Volwiler offers a long discussion and a map of the "patents granted in the region around Cherry Valley and Lake Otsego" (245–46). Thus when Croghan "decided to settle in New York, he selected as the site for his future home, a delightful location at the foot of Lake Otsego. Here was the source of the Susquehanna which at this place was a swift little stream twelve yards wide. In the lake near its source lay 'Council Rock,' later made famous by James Fenimore Cooper" (252). Again Washington was involved: "When Washington, who had a keen eye for good lands, visited Lake Otsego on his western tour in 1783, he was impressed with their excellent location" (252). Croghan first wanted to do business with him and had Washington dine "at Croghan Hall" (293) but at one point "felt bitterly disappointed [and] put forth every effort to hold his lands and to prevent Washington from winning them. Squatter rights would be certain to be an important factor in the final outcome" (293). Volwiler then discusses the "questionable methods" by which grandfather William Cooper and his partner Andrew Craig "purchased the Otsego lands for only £2,700. An attempt was made by other creditors of the Croghan estate to pay their claims and take over the lands, but this attempt was unsuccessful" (330). Like Rogers, Croghan was an Irish immigrant of little education but great talent, who could make deals with Indians but was cheated out of his legacy by the eastern patriot elites. At one point he even owned Glimmerglass Lake of *Deerslayer* fame.[21]

These examples illustrate that Robert Rogers was instrumentalized by the class in power, used and supported by General Amherst in war, when he was needed, but brutally cut short in peace, when he wanted a piece of the cake for himself, by more established personages like Sir William Johnson and Amherst's successor, Thomas Gage, who did everything to keep him out of the colonial trade business. If Johnson himself had also been an Irish immigrant at one time, and worked his way up in similar ways, also fraternizing with the Indians (the Mohawks in his case), he may have had better diplomatic skills or simply been lucky—while Rogers was unwilling to play according to the social power structures, or simply in the wrong place at the wrong time to implement a new English "middle ground" of cooperation. Yet all these facts shed new light on the values and practices of the honored founding fathers and the lofty values of the American revolutionaries. If the question of identity in America has for a long time been mainly seen as one of race (and the "problem of the color-line," as W. E. B. Du Bois once claimed), America has certainly also been haunted from the very beginning by intricate issues of class conflict, triggered by a sense of elitist *aristoi*, as Jefferson would famously call them in his letters to our diarist John Adams (see Costopoulos)—an issue that American democracy continues to struggle with today.

The "Real" Natty Bumppo?

In many ways, Robert Rogers can be seen as the role model for James Fenimore Cooper's *Leatherstocking* hero Natty Bumppo. We find many parallels between Rogers's career and events in Cooper's tales, especially *The Last of the Mohicans*. Like the literary hero, Rogers fights but also understands Indians. Rogers and his Rangers roamed exactly the same territory of the French and Indian War as Cooper's heroes. They had the same problems with English regulars (or worse), and introduced the very fighting tactics learned from the Indians that are celebrated in Cooper's books. If Rogers's own powder horn, on exhibit in Fort Ticonderoga and depicted in Ross (262), is the only personal object of his that we still have, Natty Bumppo also shows much concern about the "last bullet in [his] pouch" and the "big horn [with] all the powder [they had] left" (*Mohicans* 1:165). And the stern humiliation of the English whipping post that led to the mutiny on Rogers' Island in December 1757 is in Cooper visited on an Indian, the evil Magua, also known as Le Renard Subtil, by Colonel Munro, who has him whipped in public for being drunk: "Magua was not himself; it was the fire-water that spoke and acted for him, but Munro did not believe it. The Huron chief was tied up before all the pale-faced warriors, and whipped with sticks like a dog" (*Mohicans* 1:235). Furthermore, when we read in Caleb Stark that "on the 26th of August, 1755, [Rogers] was employed in escorting provision wagons from Albany to the Carrying Place, since called Fort

Edward" (390),[22] we realize that this is roughly the same landscape and trip that Cooper later used in *The Last of the Mohicans*, when the protagonists ride from Fort Edward to Fort William Henry.

Rogers's conflict with commandant Haviland at Ford Edward on the issue of shooting practice and the cost of powder (see Ross 163) and the episode at the ruins of Fort Anne, when he responds to a challenge and shoots "at marks against an old tree" (Ross 209) may also anticipate the many shooting competitions in Cooper, such as the shooting match in *The Pathfinder*, famously lampooned by Mark Twain: "The bullet of the first marksman chipped an edge of the nail-head; the next man's but drove the nail a little way into the target—and removed all the paint. Haven't the miracles gone far enough now? Not to suit Cooper; for the purpose of this whole scheme is to show off his prodigy, Deerslayer-Hawkeye-Long-Rifle-Leatherstocking-Pathfinder-Bumppo before the ladies" (n.p.). Also in *The Last of the Mohicans*, we have an incident of shooting practice, again in a competitive context, this time between Natty and his challenger Heyward: "You see the gourd hanging against yonder tree, major; if you are a marksman, fit for the borders, let me find that you can break its shell!" (3:167). Mark Twain would have liked this performance of the "Longue Carabine."

Furthermore, like Natty Bumppo, Rogers was a footprint specialist, as exemplified in the legend of Rogers's Slide, when, "by backtracking in his own snowshoe prints—or else reversing his snowshoes . . . , he fooled the Indians into thinking he had actually slid down the rock face" (Zaboly in Rogers, *Annotated and Illustrated Journals* 98). For comparison, here is Cooper using a subtle backtracking ruse to make Natty and his friends confuse their enemies:

> The canoe was lifted from the water, and born on the shoulders of the party. They proceeded into the wood, making as broad and obvious a trail as possible. They soon reached a water-course, which they crossed, and continued onward, until they came to an extensive and naked rock. At this point, where their footsteps might be expected to be no longer visible, they retraced their route to the brook, walking backwards, with the utmost care. They now followed the bed of the little stream to the lake, into which they immediately launched their canoe again. (2:224–25)

In Cooper they also find the big foot steps of the singer David Gamut: "Others have trod in his [the singer's] steps, imitating their formation," which makes the search party hope to soon see the captive girls' "pretty little feet again" (2:238–39).[23] Of course our backtracking legend may have gone full circle, from Cooper to Gary Zaboly's understanding of Major Rogers's slide, but there is certainly an overlap of stories.[24]

Another parallel is the scene near Fort William Henry already quoted, of the French "centinel" asking, "Qui etes vous?" and being overpowered by the polyglot Rogers: "I answered in French, signifying that we were friends; the centinel was thereby deceived" (*Journals* 35). The main difference is that the American writer Cooper makes the gallant English officer Heyward parlay in French for almost two pages, not the lower-class Natty Bumppo (2:33–34), and has the Indian Chingachgook kill the sentinel: "While they yet hesitated in an uncertainty, that each moment served to render more painful, the form of the Indian was seen gliding out of the thicket, and rejoined them while with one hand he attached the reeking scalp of the unfortunate young Frenchman to his girdle, and with the other he replaced the knife and tomahawk that had drank his blood" (2:36). Comparisons are telling, and they are not necessarily in Cooper's favor as far as intercultural sensibility is concerned.

Moreover, Rogers's ties to Fort William Henry, which lies at the center of *The Last of the Mohicans*, are of course very close. His brother Richard had died of smallpox there during the siege by the French, and in 1758 we find Rogers encamping "at the place where Fort William-Henry stood" (*Journals* 109)—like the fictional Natty Bumppo. Cooper writes a whole chapter on the "massacre of William Henry" and has his hero on the third day return to the "smouldering ruin" and a "scene of wilderness and desolation," presided over by "a few hungry ravens" (2:148–49). Certainly, that Cooper territory is also Rogers territory.

The Ranger writes that in 1755 he had joined "the troops put under the command of Major General (since Sir William) Johnson," noting, "I had the honour of commanding a company in the troops furnished by the province of New Hampshire, with which I made several excursions" (*Journals* vii–viii). He had participated in the campaign against the Swiss mercenary Baron Dieskau, whom they took prisoner, a conflict in which Rogers possibly even met the old Mohawk chief Hendrick, who appears as Monelia's father in *Ponteach*.[25] Rogers only mentions the baron once in his *Journals*: "I was recommended as a person well acquainted with the haunts and passes of the enemy, and the Indian method of fighting, and was by him [Johnson] dispatched with small parties on several tours towards the French posts, and was on one of these up Hudson's River on the 8th of September, when Baron Dieskau was made prisoner, and the French and Indians under his command defeated, at the south-end of Lake George" (viii). Although he doesn't mention "the bloody pond" in his *Journals*, it was in this conflict, that Rogers's stellar military career began. Again, the direction of intertextual influences is murky, and Parkman's dark ruminations about that colonial bloodbath may actually go back to Cooper's earlier novel: "This memorable conflict has cast its dark associations over one of the most beautiful spots in America. Near the scene of the evening fight, a pool, half overgrown by weeds and water lilies, and darkened by the surrounding forest, is pointed out to the tourist, and he is told that beneath its stagnant waters lie the bones of three hundred French men, deep buried in mud and slime" (Parkman, 1994 ed. 120). This "bloody pond" is exactly the pond where the fictional Natty and his cohorts would camp in the novel: "Ha! that sheet of dull and dreary water, then, is the sepulchre of the brave men who fell in the contest!" (*Mohicans* 2:29). Natty remembers fighting in this campaign: "Then we rallied behind our fallen trees, and made head against him, under Sir William—who was made Sir William for that very deed—and well did we pay him for the disgrace of the morning! Hundreds of Frenchman saw the sun that day for the last time; and even their leader, Dieskau himself, fell into our hands" (2:30). Note that both Rogers and Natty fought as rangers in this battle and comment on Johnson's knightly title. The intertextual influences are complex here and often go in circles.

Let me finally also mention the parallels between the funeral scene in *Ponteach* and Cooper's long elaborations in his exotically orientalizing chapter on Uncas's funeral (*Mohicans* 3:266–89). In short, we find in Cooper a military prehistory of Natty Bumppo's life that overlaps in many points with the activities of Major Robert Rogers, who can therefore justifiably be seen as a historical type foreshadowing Cooper's fictional antitype.

Scalping scenes, torture, exotic Indian oratory, war dances, and even funeral obsequies—all elements that we find in Rogers. And as *Ponteach* demonstrates, we even already find them in literary form. In short, Robert Rogers is certainly a great influence on, and possibly the early historical role model of, the white woodsman later appropriated by American nationalism. For that reason he is the typical target of Slotkin's line of argumentation in his chapter about backwoods heroes like John Mason, Davy Crockett, or even Andrew Jackson.[26] Slotkin maintains that Rogers "offered himself to the British public as a white man acculturated to the Indian's world," but "emphasized the 'English' half of his nature by publishing a tragedy in verse" (235). He assimilates Rogers (unjustifiably, I think) to his own genealogy of violent white backwoodsmen who appropriated Indian forest-fighting skills, noting at least that, as opposed to Daniel Boone's story, Rogers's adventures "were not published for American consumption" (296). What I have argued in this study is, however, that Rogers's attitudes cannot be limited to "personal contempt for the savages as a race, mingled with admiration of their ability as warriors," as Slotkin claims (235). In reducing Rogers's depiction of Indians in *Ponteach* to an appropriation as noble savages, Slotkin is doing justice neither to the complexity of Rogers the man nor to his play, which is certainly more than the employment of "Rousseauistic imagery in an unsystematic way" (245). Rather it reflects, as I hope to have demonstrated, the centrifugal contradictory pull of Rogers's own cultural origins, his ambitions, and his egalitarian personal experience within the American colonial environment of the First British Empire.

Notes

ACKNOWLEDGMENTS

1. Legendary is the melancholy *Guggisberglied*, about a young lad who became a soldier of fortune in order to escape charges of having killed a rival. This popular song, "S'Vreneli vom Guggisbärg," made Swiss mercenaries so homesick they were not allowed to sing it on pain of death, because it would make them deserters. See www.gemeinde-guggisberg.ch/Vreneliseite.html.

INTRODUCTION

1. There are no Native Americans in George Cockings's *The Conquest of Canada; or The Siege of Quebec. An Historical Tragedy of Five Acts*, also published in London in 1766; in the *dramatis personae* there are only two exotic "Caledonian Chiefs." Walter Meserve lists Nelson Barker and John Bray's "operatic melo-drame" *The Indian Princess* of 1808 as "the first American play on an Indian theme to be performed" (*Emerging Entertainment* 181).

2. This neglect may have resulted from the particular historical context and the short window of British imperial expansion in the American West. After its original publication, the play was forgotten, except by historians.

3. In the *Cambridge History of American Theatre*, vol. 1, *Beginnings to 1870*, edited by Don Wilmeth and Christopher Bigsby, *Ponteach* is mentioned only by Bruce McConachie as "the first play by a colonist on a native topic" (125) and by Gary A. Richardson as "unperformed" (273). There is no discussion of the play itself.

4. A benchmark example of this approach is Christopher Bigsby's influential trilogy on twentieth-century American drama.

5. Generally, the only token example of pre-O'Neill drama in the multi-volume anthologies is Royall Tyler's *The Contrast* (1787). An exception is Montrose Moses's old and more specialized three-volume collection *Representative Plays by American Dramatists* (1918–1921)—some of these hardcover books are still available on the internet for less than ten dollars.

6. As Susan Castillo writes: "No record exists of the play ever being performed" (223). Of my sources, only Gregory Evans Dowd states that Rogers "had already seen [*Ponteach*] staged in London" (*War* 250), and Moses mentions in his introduction to the play an amateur production on Lake George (113).

7. According to the theater historian Walter Meserve, *Ponteach* "would not suffer by comparison" if viewed with the "scores of other Indian plays that appeared on American stages before the mid-nineteenth century" (55).

8. I am not so certain about the case of violence. Though Americans opt for trigger warnings in academic contexts nowadays, Europeans like me tend to associate contemporary American film culture, for example, with an unreasonably high tolerance of violence.

9. One curious organizational reason may be the fact that traditional American "English" departments officially don't do "theater"—though I did attend a guest lecture on hip-hop Shakespeare in Ann Arbor. The categories obviously seem to be fairly arbitrary.

10. On Pontiac's real descendants, see Howard Peckham, *Indian Uprising*, chap. 22.

11. Bakhtin explains: "When we view language and discourse as an activity motivated by the centrifugal forces and when we understand discourse as practice inhabited by heteroglossia, it is not difficult to see how selves are realized in association with varied and shifting voices" (71).

CHAPTER 1. WHO WAS PONTIAC?

1. The strange spelling of "Ponteach" will be discussed later in this study. Various English and French spellings exist. Celia Bland writes that the "name— *Bwondiac* or *Obwandiyag*, as it was pronounced in his native tongue—meant 'Stopping It' in the Ottawa language" (23). Wolfgang Hochbruck from Freiburg (Germany) tells me that in Algonquian, "Pontiac" would have been stressed on the second syllable—which may be in tune with Bland's second option. Unless otherwise noted, quotations from Rogers's *Concise Account* and the

accompanying pagination refer to the 1765 edition, available at the Internet Archive, https://archive.org/details/aconciseaccountoorogeuoft/page/n6.

2. The expression also appears six times in the play *Ponteach*.

3. I capitalize "Other" when I am referring to mainly representational, conceptual Otherness (a projection), in contrast to the experiential, living "other" human being.

4. The Parkman quotations are taken from the 1994 Nebraska edition.

5. Also see Parkman's detailed description of the Indian attackers of Detroit: "Their bold yet crafty features, their cheeks besmeared with ochre and vermillion, white lead and soot, their keen, deep-set eyes gleaming in their sockets, like those of rattlesnakes, gave them an aspect grim, uncouth, and horrible" (225). Parkman clearly fictionalizes his history—we even find an element of the Pocahontas story in the female love interest of his very fictionalized rendering of the Ojibwe girl called Catherine, who "revealed her momentous secret" to Commandant Gladwyn: "There was something unusual in her look and manner. Her face was sad and downcast" (219).

6. His source is probably Carver: "In the year 1762, in the month of July, it rained on this town and the parts adjacent a sulphureous water of the color and consistence of ink. . . . Soon after, the Indian wars broke out in these parts" (106).

7. Still today historians are inspired by Rogers's play. Thus Timothy Todish and Todd Harburn's "Epigraph" to their book *A "Most Troublesome Situation"* presents an excerpt from *Ponteach*: "Our Empire now is large and our Forces strong" (6).

8. Also Michael Friedrichs, citing Rogers's *Concise Account*, sees the Indian commander as a general without any real authority (154).

9. For a blank example of the certificates given to medal chiefs by Sir William Johnson, see Bland (48).

10. David Dixon writes: "Men who were experienced in Indian affairs, such as Sir William Johnson and George Croghan, believed that the Ottawa chief's influence was still absolute among [the Great Lakes tribes]. . . . The attention that George Croghan showered on the chief disturbed many of the other Indians and may have created considerable jealousy among tribal leaders at Detroit" (264).

11. Here is Jennings's original language: "Parkman's work is fiction rather than history. . . . Parkman was a liar. He fabricated documents, misquoted others, pretended to use his great collection of sources when really he relied almost entirely on a small set of nastily biased secondary works, and did it all in order to support an ideology of divisiveness and hate based on racism, bigotry, misogyny, authoritarianism, chauvinism, and upper-class arrogance" (480).

12. On the role of Pontiac, see also Middleton's "Pontiac: Local Warrior or Pan-Indian Leader?"

13. Noting that "the first shots fired in anger against British soldiers took

place at Fort Loudon, on the Pennsylvania frontier, in 1675—not at Lexington Green in 1775" (ix), Dixon explains that this "conflict, later known as Pontiac's Uprising, convinced the frontier settlers that their government could not manage Indian affairs and cared little for their welfare" (x). Patrick Spero's recent discussion in *Frontier Rebels* of the "largely unknown" (xxiv) inland activities of James Smith and the Black Boys in the American Revolution makes a similar point.

14. A different angle can be found in Thomas R. Church's recent study *Operational Art in Pontiac's War*, published by the Department of Defense. Possibly inspired by the recent threat of the Global War on Terror, Major Church finds in "Pontiac's Rebellion . . . an opportunity for military planners to better understand the utility of the current US Army doctrinal concept of operational art" (5), defined as "the pursuit of strategic objectives, in whole or in part, through the arrangement of tactical actions in time, space and purpose" (7). He explains: "Looking at Pontiac's War through the lens of the current doctrinal concept of operational art provides utility in understanding how to combine tactical actions in time, space, and purpose to achieve strategic goals in a complex environment. Today's operational environment for US or western forces is similar to that faced by the British army in 1763 and 1764" (23). Today the U.S. Army is studying the old history in order to improve success in "complex" military environments. The study is followed by a record of "Worldwide Threat Assessment of the U.S. Intelligence Community," listing hotspots of current or possible future U.S. military intervention (33–63).

15. Unless otherwise noted, quotations from Rogers's *Journals* and the accompanying pagination refer to the 1765 edition, available at the Internet Archive, https://archive.org/details/cihm_40213/page/n7.

16. See https://www.kallistimusic.com/LAHblurbs.html, accessed May 14, 2019.

17. But then, Peckham himself also wrote the volume in the series on a famous Indian fighter, William Henry Harrison.

18. On Pontiac and other Indians in Ferrero chocolate eggs (i.e., *Kinderüberraschung*), see http://www.eierwiki.de/index.php?title=Ber%C3%BChmte_Indianer-H%C3%A4uptlinge_2.

CHAPTER 2. THE ADVENTUROUS LIFE OF MAJOR ROBERT ROGERS

1. The information about the conventions of letter writing in the eighteenth century is not always clear, but it is certain that the many variations of epistolary style were an art form. Grace Egan writes: "Letters enact relations of unequal condition by offering addresses that name the respective social positions of sender and recipient" (8). At the same time, hierarchies were often ironically undermined, as in Samuel Johnson's famous letter to Chesterfield. Thus Clare Brant, for example, warns that "politeness breeds its antonym, a discourse of

rudeness deploying irony, satire and abuse" (4). Also see Egan on letter-writing manuals (40).

2. The reference for the Franklin quote is his missive, signed "A New Englandman," to the *London Chronicle*, printed in its May 12, 1759, issue (449).

3. An ample but fairly selective collection of (only positive) contemporary reviews of Rogers's work is reprinted in the little volume by Mary Cochrane Rogers, a "Great-Great-Granddaughter of Major Robert Rogers" (title page).

4. In the Leonaur edition of Nevins's *Ranger*, we read that the Caxton Club was "founded in 1895 by fifteen Chicago bibliophiles who desired to support the publication of fine books in the spirit of the prevailing Arts and Crafts Movement. They named the new organization the 'Caxton Club' in honor of the first English printer, William Caxton."

5. The offerings of this series are quite telling about the cultural framing of Major Rogers these days. Other books advertised are, for example, *Soldiers of Napoleon*, by A. J. Doisy De Villargennes and Arthur Chuquet; *At Them with the Bayonet*, by Donald F. Featherstone, on "The first Anglo-Sikh War 1845–1846; or *With the Imperial Camel Corps in the Great War*, by Geoffrey Inchbald, "The story of a serving officer with the British 2nd battalion against the Senussi and during the Palestine campaign." This confirms the general impression that by far most attention to Rogers's life has come from militaria enthusiasts.

6. Ross also writes about the Ranger legacy in his epilogue: "Remarkably, the tone and spirit of Rogers's 250-year-old journals resonate—sometimes eerily—with the written accounts of SOG [Special Operations Group] operations in Laos in the early 1970s and more recent SEAL [Sea, Air, Land] actions in the central Asian mountains" (452). See also Hubbard.

7. Colin Calloway gives the Indian perspective: "After the war, Abenakis filtered back to their homelands as usual, but now they encountered English families farming their lands, not English soldiers leaving them. The newcomers were here to stay, and they kept coming. They occupied the best land, claimed ownership according to English notions of property, felled trees and inflicted extensive environmental degradation" (51). Middleton confirms that the Abenakis were victims as well, "driven from their homes on the Merrimac, Connecticut, and Kennebec rivers" (*Colonial America* 432).

8. The lawyer Cuneo writes that "acts curtailing legal tender caused people to claim counterfeiting was 'No Sin, for it would make Money plentier among Poor People.' The outraged sputterings of the 'honest' wealthy about the enormous crimes of villainous counterfeiters fell on cynical ears. Sullivan [the counterfeiter with whom Rogers associated and who later was executed] and his accomplices never lacked a sympathetic public among the masses" (12). Ross writes: "Counterfeiters, especially in the backcountry, often emerged as folk heroes who sometimes enlisted whole communities in their illegal business" (66). He explains that on the frontier "there was never enough cash to move trade" (67).

9. The most detailed history of Rogers Rangers is probably provided in the work of the dedicated amateur historian Burt Garfield Loescher.

10. Nester describes it as follows: "Each man was armed with a musket, sixty rounds, and hatchet, was dressed in green wool jacket, waistcoat, and breeches, and during winter wore a wool cap, mittens, and blanket-coat" (*Struggle* 24).

11. See the Wikipedia entry for the "Rules" and, as an example of their popularity, a clip on YouTube that curiously goes back to the fictional adaptation in Kenneth Roberts's novel, presented to the military enthusiast as "Good stuff!" https://www.youtube.com/watch?v=beetThq_sZY. The original "Rules" are reprinted in Ross (appendix 1).

12. See also Rogers Island Visitors Center and its extensive newsletter and gift shop selling many books about colonial history and Robert Rogers.

13. For Zaboly's illustration of this scene, see Rogers, *Annotated and Illustrated Journals* (91).

14. Thomas Mante's six-hundred-page study of twelve books full of cited letters and documents mentions Rogers's heroic fighting exploits many times, for example: "Whilst preparations were making [made?] on both sides for the next campaign, Captain Rogers, on that of the English, was constantly employed in patroling the woods about the Forts Edward and William-Henry, and observing the motions of the French at Ticonderoga and Crown-Point; and this service he performed with so much alertness, that he made a great number of prisoners, and thereby procured very good intelligence of the enemy" (78).

15. See also Cochrane on Rogers and snowshoes, or Lucier's collection of newspaper clippings about the Pontiac Uprising (*French and Indian War Notices*).

16. As an indication of his fame, we note that Rogers appears as many times as the legendary General Wolfe in the index of Lucier's *French and Indian War Notices Abstracted from Colonial Newspapers*.

17. Jennings adds in a footnote: "Perhaps it would be better to say that Rogers *tried* to massacre, though there seems no doubt that he killed indiscriminately. He gave the figure of 200 Indians killed, but French sources allowed only 20" (200n).

18. See also Ross (262).

19. The whole encounter is also reprinted in Tiffany Potter's 2010 edition of *Ponteach* (180–82).

20. Dowd writes that Rogers "later embellished the encounter in his *Concise Account of North-America*, placing Pontiac at the center of the meeting; but this is unreliable" (*War* 56). Nevertheless, this meeting has been immortalized in C. Y. Turner's 1913 mural in the Cuyahoga County Courthouse of Cleveland, Ohio: "It is a large panel 28 feet long by 13 feet high and fills a space at the end of the court room 20 feet above the floor" (1150). At the opposite end of the same hall is an identical space with a painting titled *The Trial of Captain John Smith*—which

marks the historical significance attributed to the encounter of Rogers and Pontiac. For a tentative evaluation of this kind of art, consult Charles Moore's "Memorials of the Great War," which includes a representation of Turner's mural: "Must we suffer not only war but also the commemoration of war?" (233). In 1919 Moore concluded that "wealth has increased very fast—much faster than taste" (233–34).

21. For a beautiful reproduction of Great Lakes maps in Rogers's time, see the lavishly illustrated *Beyond Pontiac's Shadow* by Keith Widder.

22. See Bland for a photograph of the "Pontiac Tree," which "looms over the spot where Pontiac and his warriors attacked Captain James Dalyell's forces on the morning of July 31, 1763. When it fell more than a century later, the huge whitewood tree still carried bullet holes from the conflict" (80).

23. Significantly, all four letters by Robert Rogers available at the William L. Clements Library discuss, among other things, Rogers's financial issues.

24. Millan's name appears in neither Harlan's nor Hernlund's research on William Strathan, the most influential printer in London in the eighteenth century.

25. Among the Millan books advertised in the original edition of *Ponteach*, we find thirty-four entries under "JUST PUBLISHED," among them "2. MILLAN's UNIVERSAL REGISTER of Lords and Commons," "3. JOURNALS of Major R. Rogers" [6 lines], "4. Major ROGERS's Account of NORTH AMERICA" [12 lines], many military books, such as "5. Lieut. Henry Timberlake's Memoirs," "8. Regimental and Recruiting Books," or books about science, such as "24. Hill's History of the Royal Society, 10s. 5d.," "33. Capt. Bontein's large Map of Jamaica, corrected to 1865, 7s. 5d.," or "38. Orthopaedia, or Deformities of Children, 2 Vol. 6s." (111–12).

26. The advertisement in the *Journals* reads as follows: "It is proposed to continue this journal, in a second volume, containing the account of my travels into the country of the Cherokees, and the southern Indians; of my second tour into the interior country, upon the great lakes; and of the Indian wars since the year 1760; together with correct plans of all the British forts on the continent. To be published by subscription. / Subscriptions are taken in by JOHN MILLAN" (237). A tentative beginning of this second volume of the *Journals* may be the apocryphal *Journal of the Siege of Detroit*, signed 8 August 1763 and attributed to Rogers (see Hough 124). And in the *Concise Account* we find this note:

> It is proposed to continue this CONCISE ACCOUNT of NORTH AMERICA in a second volume, containing maps of the several colonies, and of the Interior Country of North America, more correct, and easier to be understood than any yet published. To be printed by Subscription.
>
> Subscriptions to be taken in by J. MILLAN, Bookseller, near *Whitehall*, and by such others as he shall appoint, he being empowered by me for that purpose, and will give proper receipts to deliver the said volume, or return the subscription-money, in a limited time.

Price to Subscribers will be one *English* Guinea, one half to be paid at
subscribing, and the other on the delivery of the books.

Robt. Rogers. (viii)

Judging from the slight changes in wording, it is also possible that after the
great success of the *Journals*, Rogers decided to invest in his literary career
himself.

27. On Rogers's fame also see Gustavson.

28. Ross writes: "On October 16 [1765] Rogers gained an audience with
27-year-old George III at St. James's Palace, an honor most Americans, including
Franklin, never attained. 'Yesterday,' reported *The New-Hampshire Gazette*
some months later, 'Major Rogers, who commanded his Majesty's Rangers in
North America during the last War, had the Honour to kiss His Majesty's hand,
on his being appointed to a Command in the Interior Country of America'"
(364).

29. At this conference, Rogers also met Benjamin Roberts, who would later
make his life miserable in Michilimackinac. In his letter to Sir William Johnson
of 4 September 1767, Rogers writes, "Mr. Roberts the Commissary of Indian
affairs was Pleased to give me Very Abusive Language, and the Reason of my
not sending him down the Country was wholly on your account, I hope you
will be pleased to Remove him from this Garrison. which I don't in the least
doubt you will be Pleasd to do after Perusing those Affidavits." This is how
Nevins describes Roberts: "His zeal in ingratiating himself with the Indians
had first recommended him to Johnson's notice. He early learned the Mohawk
language, and because of this, and a very curious incident, the savages of New
York took a violent fancy to him. While at garrison at Schenectady in 1759, the
gentlemen and ladies acted *Othello*, before an audience room crowded with
chiefs and braves, most of whom were wrought up in an extraordinary pitch of
curiosity. The gallantly attired Roberts strutted upon the stage as Ludovico,
saluted by fanfare and trumpets, and responding to a general burst of acclama-
tions by repeatedly doffing a hat of truly Venetian courtliness. The Indians
were so much struck by his general appearance, especially by his plumed head-
piece, that they concluded him to be a personage of exalted importance"
(*Ranger* 88). Obviously, the theater was in fashion among Indian agents, whose
intercultural skills much depended on explicit gestures.

30. Dowd is probably overly optimistic when he talks about a "staging" of
the play in London.

31. As Orians observes: "Pontiac appeared in Roberts' book, not as a war
chief, but as a skilled commercial advisor" (part 2 32). The words the novelist
put in Pontiac's mouth were probably inspired by Rogers's *Michillimackinac
Journal*, which he had read at the Clements Library, i.e., when Rogers himself
writes of "a Beacon from which a most Extensive and as yet unknown Territory
is watched and Observed" (47).

32. The original manuscript of the American Antiquarian Society has been
transcribed by William Clements.

33. Rogers's original proposal for the financing of an expedition to find the Northwest Passage is reprinted in Elliott. .

34. Note that Rogers's is the first usage in print of the name "Oregon" in an English-language context. See Elliott: "Recent research establishes the fact that the name Oregon is a corruption or variation by Jonathan Carver of the name Ouragon or Ourigan, which was communicated to him by Major Robert Rogers, the English commandant of the frontier military and trading post at Mackinac" (91).

35. Morsberger writes: "Gage and Johnson continued to undermine his authority and sabotage his [Rogers's] projects" (242).

36. McCulloch comments: "His old friend and ally, General Jeffrey Amherst, was replaced by an old rival and bitter enemy, Major-General Thomas Gage. . . . One of Gage's first acts of revenge and malice was to have Amherst's recommendations for Rogers' payment for services at Detroit deferred" (23). As Armour writes in his introduction to *Treason?*: "When Gage replaced Jeffrey Amherst as Supreme Commander in 1764 Rogers lost a close friend and gained a bitter enemy" (3).

37. Unfortunately, the fragile paper of the original has never been scanned and digitalized online.

38. The proceedings of the trial have been published by Armour; see *Treason?* The Johnson papers contain several letters on Rogers's trial in Montreal by General Gage and Benjamin Roberts. Here is Benjamin Robert's letter to Sir William Johnson, dated 11 May 1769, which gives a striking characterization of Rogers's emotional state after that trial: "He Overtook me [about] 200 yards from the House he asked me how I did & then told me [he wa]nted to Speake to me. he had in his right hand a Stick with a Dart in [it, and a] long Spike in the feril, with which he Opposed my going farther [and aske]d me if I would give him Satisfaction for bribing Potter to Swear [his life] Away. I told him when he was at Liberty I would make him [give me] Satisfaction for the ill usuage I had received from him a Mackinak. [He said] he had a Case of pistols in his pocket under his Coat & catched hold to [them,—said] I must immediately take one & fire it in the Street with him" (753).

39. Actually already in "1762, [his father-in-law had] forced Rogers to part with his 500 acres of land at Rumford, with his three negro slaves, and 'one Indian boy named Billy, aged thirteen,' which Browne at once transferred to a brother to hold in trust for Elizabeth Rogers" (Nevins, *Ranger* 61). Note that Rogers accepted slavery as a part of the culture in which he lived. He played by the rules of a colonial society that would ultimately reject him.

40. William Clements speculates: "Had there been any harmony between Johnson and Rogers, and had both continued in the service, a different history might be written of the Indians of the Northwest" (9).

41. See Rogers, "Second Proposal": "To cross a twenty Mile Portage into a Branch of the Misouri, and to stem that North-westerly to the Source: To cross thence a Portage of about thirty Miles, into the great river Ourigan" (108).

42. See also Walter Rogers, who states that in 1772 Rogers "was assigned to service in the East Indies, when the outbreak of hostilities in America recalled him to the scene of his earlier activities" (53).

43. This observation comes from my friend Wolfgang Hochbruck, who knows much more about military uniforms than I do.

44. See also Morsberger's historical comment that "Rogers . . . led his Rangers through a swamp for nine days, . . . ordered his men into a human chain to ford the St. Francis River, and . . . nearly died of starvation in the wilderness" (252).

45. The scene can be found on YouTube, https://www.youtube.com/watch ?v=S1988l3Nmig.

46. I owe most of these references to my old friend Cuno "Comix" Affolter, *curateur* of the extraordinary collection of *bandes dessinées* at the town library in Lausanne.

47. The Italian Wikipedia article states: "Capitan Rogers (alias Geremy Reginald Rogers) è un personaggio umoristico dei fumetti western, creato da Giorgio Pezzin per i testi, con la collaborazione di François Corteggiani, e da Giorgio Cavazzano per i disegni ed edito da il Giornalino delle Edizioni San Paolo. È stato pubblicato fra il 1981 e il 1989 e la sua figura appare sul nono volume della collana 100 anni di fumetto italiano."

48. For contemporary weekend Rangers, see https://www.facebook.com /RogersRangers.org/. For reenacting, see https://www.facebook.com/Rogers Rangers.org/?ref=py_c. For Jaeger's Battalion, see http://www.rogersrangers .com/. This group cooperates with the Maryland Company of Rogers's Rangers (http://www.rogersrangers.com/MDCompany/).

49. See https://www.facebook.com/RogersRangers.org/?ref=py_c.

50. For a German weekend Rangers organization, see Rogers-Rangers -Germany, http://www.rogers-rangers-germany.com/uniform.html. For a German translation of Rogers's twenty-eight *Rules of Ranging* (*Ausbildungsplan*), see https://revwarboard.iphpbb3.com/forum/27582870nx56266/ranger-f61 /rrs-ausbildungsplan-t884.html.

51. See "Zinnfigurenfreunde Leipzig e.V." at http://www.zinnfiguren freunde-leipzig.de/her/ag/ag12.htm.

CHAPTER 3. THE HISTORICAL BACKGROUND OF *PONTEACH*

1. In the context of Jesuits, White's wording is eerily reminiscent of European Inquisition terminology and the infamous *Malleus Maleficarum*. On the conflict between Algonquians and Iroquois at Ste. Marie des Hurons, also see Eccles (53–56).

2. As White writes: "Never again in North America would Indians fight each other on this scale or with this ferocity" (2).

3. White observes that "children of intermarried fathers belonged to the

clan of their mother," which "linked the children of intermarried men to their mother's village despite patrilineal descent" (18).

4. The term roughly means "the land up the river" from Quebec, as the French were using the waterways and accessed the Great Lakes through the Saint Lawrence River.

5. White writes that the Algonquians also "lacked a state with coercive institutions" and that "obedience to authority was usually neither a social fact nor a social virtue" (56).

6. Both of these historical figures have survived in Detroit in the names of cars: the Cadillac and the Chrysler Le Baron, respectively.

7. In her chapter "Sex and Conquest: Domination and Desire on Ethnosexual Frontiers," Joanne Nagel clarifies that much of this permissiveness of course also had to do with a colonial power differential (63–90). She notes: "Romanticized, sexualized natives still inhabit the imaginations of Americans and continue to haunt Americans' images of themselves" (82).

8. This logic is reminiscent of Walter Ong's definition of the "psychodynamics of orality" as "situational rather than abstract" (49). A "judge in an oral culture is often called on to articulate sets of relevant proverbs out of which he can pronounce equitable decisions in the cases under formal litigation before him" (35).

9. White's formulation suggests that beyond Marxist "use value" or "exchange value," we have to consider a category of "relational value."

10. White explains: "Like a chief, a commander ideally gave more than he received. At each post the commander saw to it that Indians regularly received small gifts of powder, ball, tobacco, and sometimes brandy. He had the post blacksmith repair their tools and weapons" (177). White even claims that the "Detroit tribes had by the 1730s achieved what seems a virtual veto over the appointment of the commander at Detroit" (178).

11. See Peckham: "Prices were quoted in terms of beavers or buckskins, from which latter we derive our slang expression of 'bucks' for dollars" (*Indian Uprising* 85). See also White on this kind of currency (484).

12. Michael N. McConnell writes in his introduction to Parkman that it was "one of the biggest and costliest wars in colonial America" (vii).

13. Peckham quotes a 1758 legal treatise of "the eminent Swiss jurist" Emer De Vattel and his "principle that the uncertain occupancy by wandering tribes of the vast regions of the New World 'cannot be held as real and lawful taking possession; and when the Nations of Europe, which are too confined at home, come upon land which the savages have no special need of and making no present or continuous use of, they may lawfully take possession of them and establish colonies in them'" (*Indian Uprising* 104).

14. McDonnell tells us that the situation concerning international law was no better after the Revolutionary War some twenty years later: "Native Americans were not even mentioned in the peace treaty. In their haste to put an end to

another costly and bloody war, both the British and Americans had simply ignored Native Americans" (309).

15. The "Royal Proclamation" included the following provision: "The several Nations or Tribes of Indians with whom We are connected, and who live under our Protection, should not be molested or disturbed in the Possession of such Parts of Our Dominions and Territories as, not having been ceded to or purchased by Us, are reserved to them, or any of them, as their Hunting Grounds" (n.p.). On the politics of the Royal Proclamation Line, also see McDonnell (230–32).

16. See Henry, chaps. 9 and 10.

17. Widder notes: "It is estimated that as many as 450 British regulars and provincial troops died, and when civilian casualties suffered throughout the Appalachian frontier and the Great Lakes are considered, as many as 2,000 Europeans may have lost their lives during this war" (*Beyond* 170).

18. White writes: "In recruiting, Bouquet found that although Pennsylvania offered a scalp bounty to spur enlistments, the settlers of Western Pennsylvania were more eager to slaughter the peaceful Indians than to go to war. Bouquet sneered that they 'found it easier to kill Indian [*sic*] in a goal [jail] than to fight them fairly in the woods'" (293n).

19. Note the historian's use of new-journalist stream of consciousness and free indirect discourse. Later Peckham continues in the same vein: "In New York City, General Amherst, whom we left in a frenzy at the end of June, continued to receive a stream of bad news from the West. His rage and inhumanity increased as each Indian victory or depredation emphasized his seeming helplessness" (226). Parkman's fictional style certainly has made its mark.

20. See also Jennings on "germ warfare at Fort Pitt" and Captain Simeon Ecuyer's presenting Delaware chiefs "with tokens of his personal esteem: blankets infected with smallpox from the fort's hospital" (447–48). On the question of the infected blankets, see also Joseph D. Gasparro (esp. 41–42), who finds Captain Ecuyer at the origins of this strategy (59) but claims that the blankets were not the source of the ravaging epidemic (60). On the international context of germ warfare, see Harold B. Gill Jr., who also discusses the events at Fort Pitt.

21. Smith reports that "some of the Indians solicited and obtained leave to accompany their former captives all the way to Fort-Pitt, and employed themselves in hunting and bringing provisions for them on the road. A young Mingo carried this still further, and gave an instance of love which would make a figure even in romance. A young woman of Virginia was among the captives, to whom he had formed so strong an attachment, as to call her his wife" (34).

22. Morris Bishop writes that in the winter of 1709–10, Peter Schuyler, who was very much aware "of the uses of picturesque publicity, . . . went to England with five Mohawk sachems. The dominant one was Thoyanoguen, commonly known as King Hendrick. He was tall and handsome; his complexion displayed

'the shadowed livery of the burnished sun.' He was about thirty, a man of power among his people, an orator and diplomat, and a faithful friend of the English. King Hendrick was accompanied by his brother (or other close relation), John; by one 'Brant,' grandfather of the famous Joseph Brant of the Revolutionary War; and by an inconspicuous figure known only by his Indian name, Etowa Caume or E-Tow-Oh-Koam. The fifth sachem died on the voyage and has left no mark on history" (n.p.). We learn that "Queen Anne was charmed by the sachems and referred their petition to her Ministry. She engaged them in conversation, through their interpreter, Peter Schuyler's brother John."

23. O'Toole's book has a beautiful portrait of Hendrick (Tee Yee Neen Ho Ga Row) commissioned from John Verelst (210).

24. In the German translation, Johann Tobias Köhler attributes the title "Kayser" to Pontiac (297).

25. Like the Indians, many blacks also fought on the losing side in North America. Jennifer Schuessler writes: "Blacks fought in greater numbers for the Royal cause than for the Patriots" (n.p.).

26. In this context, White writes that "Pontiac's predictable Algonquian evolution from war leader to chief connected with the British creation of what at times seemed an Indian emperor of the *pay d'en haut*, and in this intersection lay Pontiac's downfall. Robert Rogers in his *Ponteach* created a literary Indian who was a great and commanding chief, but great and commanding chiefs did not exist in the *pay d'en haut*" (300).

27. See Cooper as the most prominent example, who writes in the preface of *The Last of the Mohicans*: "There is a well authenticated and disgraceful history of the means by which the Dutch on one side, and the Mengwe on the other, succeeded in persuading the Lenape to lay aside their arms, trusting their defence entirely to the latter, and becoming, in short, in the figurative language of the natives, 'women'" (1:ix). A story character later states: "I have heard that the Delawares have laid aside the hatchet, and are content to be called women" (101).

28. On Indian hating also see Howells's chapter on "Indian Fighters" (112–23) and the example of Lewis Wetzel: "Wetzel was the hero and darling of the border where the notion of punishing a man for shooting an Indian was laughed at" (116). Howells writes on the Gnadenhutten massacre in "The Wickedest Deed in Our History" (74–81) and asserts that the later "torture of Colonel Crawford was the effect of the butchery of the Christian Indians" (88).

29. White writes that John Filson's book *The Discovery, Settlement, and Present State of Kentucky* "described a Boone who adopted Indian virtues in order to kill actual Indians. He had transmuted Indian hating into something more appealing and fine. Lacking Indian vices, embodying only their virtues, Boone rose above the Indians whom he conquered" (422).

30. White adds an interesting ethnographic observation: "Precisely because hunting was a holy occupation, a demonstration of spiritual power in which animals delivered themselves to the hunter with the consent of the spiritual

masters of the game, refusing to kill an animal made no sense to many Algonquians" (492). He puts a limit to our romantic notions of Indian preservationism.

31. William Dean Howells quotes his cry, "Charge the rascals with the
bayonets!" He adds: "Wayne got his nickname of Mad Anthony in the Revolution from his habit of swearing furiously in battle, and now he called the Indians
something more than simply rascals" (108).

CHAPTER 4. AN ARTISTIC FAILURE?

1. Friedrichs: "widersprüchliche dramaturgische Mittel zu einer verun-
glückten Mischung" (145).

2. Of the four letters by Rogers available at the Clements Library, three (the
ones written after his marriage) either mention Betsy or were written to her. In
a letter from New York of 19 July 1761, he begs a Mr. Henry Apthorp to supply
his wife with money, if she "should stand in need of any Cash before [his] return." Another letter in 1765, addressed to "My only Life," was written "on
Board the Ship" to London; in it he promises to lose no time "in Returning to
[his] Dearest Betsy," dreams of buying her a harpsichord, and promises to
"send [her] some pretty things from England first from Ladeys." Also in the
1767 letter to Sir William Johnson, written only three months before his arrest,
Mrs. Rogers "presents her Respects ~ I beg you. Interest your self in giting my
accounts Past." Not surprisingly, all four letters (the first one is from Fort
Edward, 1758) are concerned with questions of money.

3. Rogers writes in the introduction to his *Journals*: "I received my early
education [in] a frontier town in the province of New Hampshire, where I could
hardly avoid obtaining some knowledge of the manners, customs, and language of the Indians, as many of them resided in the neighbourhood, and daily
conversed and dealt with the English" (vi).

4. The episode with the French sentinel is also quoted in Caleb Stark (407).

5. In fact, Ross opens the introduction of his biography with a London episode of "The Bet," in which the old Rogers wins a storytelling contest that we
already find mentioned in Stark (388).

6. The mysterious third river mentioned in the long title of the *Concise Ac-
count*, the "Christino," must be the Cree River, named after the Indian Tribe,
and today mainly famous for competitive fishing. I owe this information to my
Canadian friend Buff Parry. See also Hodge: "Cree (contracted from Kristiaux,
French form of *Kenistenoag*, given as one of their own names). An important
Algonquian tribe of British America whose former habitat was in Manitoba and
Assiniboia, between Red and Saskatchewan rivers" (359).

7. As Nevins writes in his introduction to the 1914 edition of *Ponteach*:
"From the point of view of American literary history the influence of Rogers'
production upon the development of the stage was nil; for at the time, and until
long after, there was no native American stage" (14).

8.   Parkman's omissions concern only two lines in 1.1.: first, Honnyman's fairly innocent "Silence; conceal yourself, and mind your Eye" (line 57) before they kill the Indian hunters, and then his, certainly cruder, scalping comment: "A damn'd tough Hide, or my Knife's devilish dull—" (line 81). Curiously, Parkman thought rather highly of the romantic parts of the play, commenting in the appendix: "The rest of the play is written in better taste, and contains several vigorous passages" (1991 ed. 859).

9.   Nevins's reviewer Milo M. Quaife trashes the respected Columbia University historian's biography of Rogers: "Words are exchanged, phrases and sentences are recast, and combinations and excisions are made, with no indication that such liberties have been taken with the originals" (148). Though he regrets that Nevins "did not devote some time to the criticism of the play itself" (149), Quaife endorses Nevins's dismissal of its literary quality and adds that "judged as literature the work has been regarded from the time of its first publication as a flat failure" (146).

10.   Friedrichs: "kein anerkannter Gegenstand der Literaturwissenschaft" (145).

CHAPTER 5. THE REALISTIC DIMENSION

1.   The historian Nevins was possibly influenced in his aesthetic judgment by the assessment of his senior colleague Parkman, extending the factuality of the play to the "two first and expository acts of the drama" (introduction to 1914 ed. 12).

2.   That is, when Hewitt claims that, in the end, Ponteach "dies bravely" (107).

3.   Dedicating a bare two pages to *Ponteach*, Hewitt then moves on to a lengthy discussion of *Metamora* and the actor Edwin Forrest.

4.   All italics are in the original, if not otherwise noted.

5.   The realistic possibility of such a murder is confirmed in O'Toole, who reports on the commandant of Detroit, Thomas Gage, "reflecting on an incident near Fort Pitt in which two white men were rescued from distress by an Indian hunting party, which they then robbed and murdered" (270).

6.   Ponteach also adds the French perspective in this conflict: "*Frenchmen* would always hear an *Indian* speak, / And answer fair, and make good Promises" (1.3.46–47).

7.   On this cultural attitude, see the famous description of Puritan attitudes by William Carlos Williams: "The jargon of God, which they used, was their dialect by which they kept themselves surrounded as with a palisade" (64).

8.   Here is the manipulated list:

> The British King, of his great Bounty sends.
> To *Ponteach*, King upon the Lakes, and his Chiefs,
> Two hundred, No [*aside*] a Number of fine Blankets,

Six hundred [*aside*] Yes, and several Dozen Hatchets,
Twenty thousand [*aside*] and a Bag of Wampum,
A Parcel too of Pans, and Knives and Kettles.

(1.4.140–45)

9. This is an attitude we find already expressed by the "Ponteack" of Rogers's *Concise Account*: He "expressed a great desire to see England, and offered me a part of his country if I would conduct him there. He assured me, that he was inclined to live peaceably with the English while they used him as he deserved" (242–43).

10. Tiffany Potter writes in a footnote about "Ostenaco's" historical visit, who was one of the famous "four Indian chiefs" (Rogers, *Ponteach*, 2010 ed. 81n).

11. Peckham writes that when the Indians found Dalyell's body in "a barbaric orgy of celebration they cut out his heart and wiped it on the faces of their prisoners. They also cut off his head and mounted it on a pole" (*Indian Uprising* 208).

12. See also Dowd: "The play, the commercial failure it deserved to be, nonetheless is important as a thinly veiled attack on Gladwin, a fellow officer under whom Rogers had served in 1763" (*War* 64).

13. On an intercultural note, James Thomas Flexner writes about this encounter that because Johnson didn't speak French and Curie didn't speak English, "they flirted in Iroquois, which he spoke with a Mohawk intonation, she with a provincial Huron twang" (242).

14. According to Calloway, "Johnson was both friend and exploiter of the Iroquois, an agent of empire and an independent entrepreneur pursuing his own goals. He built himself a personal empire as marcher lord on Indian lands. By the time of his death in 1774, he was the largest land owner in the Mohawk valley" (64).

15. Sayre quotes from John McCullough's captivity narrative, where he copied the illustration: "It would appear, by the above recital, as if they had some idea of the Popish tenet of purgatory" (*Tragic Hero* 148). See also the "rendition of Neolin's map to heaven" in Dixon, who comments: "Neolin insisted that all the sinners living in the left-hand side of the square were those who had accepted the ways of the white man. The Delaware prophet sold maps for one deer hide apiece" (94). He writes that "Pontiac and the others who followed the Delaware prophet Neolin sincerely believed that the Master of Life and the Catholic God were one and the same" (116).

16. Here is White's interpretation of Neolin's Christian theology: "Neolin might denounce white practices, but what he really preached was white guilt. Indians were guilty because they had accepted from the whites things that were unsuitable for an Indian way. The great advantage of accepting guilt in this way is that it restores power to the guilty party. To take the blame is, in a way, to take control. In the 1760s, amid the widespread drunkenness and violence that accompanied the reopening of British trade at Pittsburgh, the fear of British

attempts to settle the Ohio country, pressures from the British to return white prisoners, the occurrence of a devastating epidemic among the Shawnees, and the prophecies that the whites would once again drive the Delawares from their home, Neolin assigned guilt and promised power and well-being to those who reformed. Many Indians already accepted the reality of God's anger at them; Neolin assured them that they could allay this anger and regain control of events" (283).

17. Calloway writes that after the death of his wife, Johnson "promptly took up with Molly Brant, a Mohawk, and used his relations with Indian women to build connections in matrilineal Iroquois society" (26). Parkman is of course more Puritanical about this: "Johnson supplied the place of his former love by a Dutch damsel, who bore him several children" and whom he married "upon her death-bed" (1994 ed. 91). He continues: "Soon afterwards he found another favorite in the person of Molly Brant, sister of the celebrated Mohawk war-chief, whose black eyes and laughing face caught his fancy."

18. Navarre's editors add in a footnote: "Wolf: 'Loups' in French, who called themselves Lenni Lenape, meaning original men, but also called by the English, the Delawares" (22n).

19. Also see Chekitan's earlier argument:

> 'This plain, if they proceed, nor you nor I
> Shall rule an Empire, or possess a Crown,
> Our Countries all will soon become a Prey
> To Strangers; we perhaps shall be their Slaves.
> (3.1.154–57)

20. These images of raising and burying the hatchet are repeated in the scene: "And raise the Hatchet only in your Cause" (1.4.100). And later: "He would not have the Hatchet ever raised, / But buried deep, stamp'd down and cover'd o'er" (1.4.104–5).

21. See, for example, W. C. Vanderwerth's collection of famous speeches, which includes Pontiac's "You Must Lift the Hatchet against Them" of 1763 (26–29).

22. Already when the rebellion is first discussed in private by the brothers Philip and Chekitan, we learn that Ponteach has invited other chiefs, such as "The Fox, the Bear, the Eagle, Otter, Wolf" (2.1.66). These are the names of clans and indicate Indian tribal organization.

23. This episode actually reflects views that Rogers shared earlier in his *Concise Account*, writing that the conjurer "exercises his legerdemain over the patient; and whether the patient lives or dies, the worthy doctor is sure to save his credit" (248). My favorite example of an Indian dream is the anecdote in O'Toole, about a "fine laced coat" Hendrick had dreamed about. Yielding to his friend's desire, Sir William Johnson "pulled off his coat and gave it to Hendrick, who left the council well pleased" (281). The next time they met, Johnson "told him he dreamed that he [Hendrick] had given him a tract of land on the Mohawk River to build a house on, and make a settlement, extending

about nine miles in length along the banks" (281). The anecdote goes on to note that the "sachem smiled and told Johnson that if he really had dreamed it he must have it, 'but that he would never dream with him again, for he had only got a laced coat, whereas Sir William was now entitled to a large bed, on which his ancestors had frequently slept'" (281).

24. Many of these ethnographic elements would later also be described in Carver's *Travels*, such as the animal clans (131), the power of dreams (155), the "hatchet painted red" (157), scalping (160–61), the "Pipe of Peace" (175–77), wampum belts (176, 179), or the sweating "stoves" (197).

25. T. Potter finds this behavior recorded in Rogers's *Concise Account* (in Rogers, *Ponteach*, 2010 ed. 143n). There Rogers describes how they "run from cabin to cabin, and strike with small twigs their furniture, the walls and roofs of their cabins, to prevent his spirit from remaining there to take vengeance for the evils committed on his body" (235).

26. An interesting example of the use of this terminology is McDonnell's quotation of General Bradstreet, significantly the new commandant of Detroit after the conflict with Pontiac, who sent a message to the Indians that the English king "now wishes to adopt you for his *children* instead of Brothers as you have hitherto been" (240–41, original italics). McDonnell comments: "The British inherited not the peaceful middle ground of the French empire, but a complex set of Indian-French relations based on uncertainty, realpolitik, and expense. It was the true cost of empire" (241). Whereas a father's responsibilities are clear—he is a provider of *besoins*—a brother's role may be more competitive. As an example of the complex family terminology among the Indians and its adoptive symbolism, see Steckley, "Huron Kinship Terminology."

CHAPTER 6. THE POWER OF EUROPEAN CONVENTIONS

1. Richard Slotkin also notes that "Dryden's Indian tragedies of a century earlier" simply employed Indian settings "to lend an exotic air to the proceedings" (239).

2. The most successful of these exotic performances was of course the stage adaptation of Aphra Behn's *Oroonoko* by Thomas Southerne (1696).

3. James Stockdale writes about the influence of *Cato* in America: "George Washington was so taken with the character of Cato the younger in Joseph Addison's 1713 play *Cato* that he made the Roman republican his role model. He went to see *Cato* numerous times from early manhood into maturity and even had it performed for his troops at Valley Forge despite a congressional resolution that plays were inimical to republican virtue. Washington included lines from the play in his private correspondence and even in his farewell address" (75).

4. Also note Anderson's astute comment on contemporary impositions— which may explain why *Ponteach* isn't performed today either: "Today the

criticism of Rogers' play would be based on almost the opposite criterion—that is, he tends to too great an extent to follow the literary conventions of his day, stereotyping his characters and dividing them unnaturally into 'good' and 'bad'" (228).

5.   I am intentionally using Raymond Williams's term *emerging* here, which we will again encounter later in the discussion. Werner Sollors writes that the "theme of the dying Indian was also connected to Republicanism, and it conveyed to American culture a touch of Roman antiquity, as the portraiture of Indian chieftains resembled that of the Latin Stoics" (117–18). He sees *Ponteach* as the "historical starting point" of the popular motif of the "vanishing" Indian (119), noting that the "title hero . . . delivers a farewell speech, although he is not dying" (125).

6.   Also the yoke, which is associated with European oxen, appears in Ponteach's speech: "For long their galled Necks have felt the Yoke" (2.2.134).

7.   There seems to be a tradition of such imagery that continues all to way to Ezra Pound's Modernist "making new" in "The Return" of 1917.

8.   Tiffany Potter even finds a reference to Homer's Odyssey (Rogers, *Ponteach*, 2010 ed. 99n) in Chekitan's statement on "the vain Phantoms of a Midnight Dream" (2.2.300).

9.   This image of written registration is repeated in Philip's wish "to bring king *Hendrick* / To join the Lists and fight against our Foes" (2.2.287–88), and later again by Chekitan, when he pleads with Torax, "To be our Friend and join the Lists with mine" (3.1.143).

10.   Plus one "tygress." One of the advantages of the Internet Archive is that the digital versions of the texts provided can be electronically searched.

11.   Rogers's cartographer Jonathan Carver also lists "Tiger" and "Panther" separately (131), yet I suspect he is describing an American puma: "The Tyger of America resembles in shape those of African and Asia, but is considerably smaller. Nor does it appear to be so fierce and ravenous as they are" (215). As also American bears are "somewhat smaller" and the wolves "much less" (216), we can speculate on a possible influence of the French Comte de Buffon's degeneration hypothesis on Carver.

12.   There is no reference to rattlesnakes in the *Concise Account* either. Carver, however, mentions rattlesnakes several times in his *Travels* (73–74, 106).

13.   Chekitan mirrors this language when he corners Monelia's murderer, Philip: "Thou Tyger, Viper, Snake, thou worse than Christian; / Blood thirsty Butcher, more than Murderer!" (5.4.13–14). We count eight "snakes," seven "serpents," and three "vipers" in the digital Internet Archive version of *Ponteach*.

14.   Also see Howells on the "serpent worship" of the prehistoric Mound Builder culture in Ohio, who mentions "the great Serpent Mound near Loudon, in Adams County" (15).

15.   Unlike Tiffany Potter, I don't see an "Iroquois trickster" here (Rogers, *Ponteach*, 2010 ed. 108n). Or maybe this fox stands for an already-existing

European influence on Native American culture, as seen, for example, in Cooper's famous evildoer "Le Renard Subtil" of *The Last of the Mohicans*. Such intercultural references are complex and truly fascinating.

16. Tiffany Potter finds in these lines also a reference to the Royal Proclamation Line of 1763 (Rogers, *Ponteach*, 2010 ed. 85n).

17. In fact, the devil is often very directly referenced. Thus Captain Frisk observes: "Your Honour's right, to wish the Devil his Due. / I'll send the noisy Helhounds packing hence" (1.3.5–6). And Colonel Cockum wants to "give the Devil a Hundred [insolent Indians] for his Supper" (1.3.19).

18. Significantly, Chekitan wishes that the "Powers . . . after Death" may "pursue [Philip] with their Flames of Wrath" (5.4.35–37), when he kills his brother—an obvious reference to purgatory.

19. Remember that Rogers participated in the Battle of Bloody Run, where "John Rutherford remembered seeing Captain Dalyell's heart roasting over an Ottawa fire" (Dixon 180).

20. According to Peckham, Pontiac had two adult sons, who were with him at the time of his assassination in Cahokia in 1769 (*Indian Uprising* 309), but neither was called Philip or Chekitan or committed murder. He mentions Pontiac's widow Kan-tuck-ee-gun and her son Otussa (316) and adds: "The two sons Pontiac definitely had in 1769 are not named. One of them probably was Shegenaba" (317). This is as closely as Peckham can trace the two sons: "The names of two alleged sons of Pontiac were supplied by Jim Pontiac, elderly resident of Northern Michigan. This man claimed to be the great-grandson of Pontiac. He mentioned Kasahda, a son of Pontiac who died childless, and Nebahkohum, younger brother of Kasahda, from whom Jim Pontiac was descended" (317).

21. Friedrichs: "den Anforderungen der Gattung wird der Realismus der Darstellung geopfert" (153). He makes essentially the same statement on the following page: "werden in *Ponteach* die Tatsachen den Gesetzen der Form geopfert" (154).

22. McDonnell states that "women played an enormously important part in creating bridges between lineages and clans, and even between villages and nations" (94). He explains: "A thick web of relations now [in the 1760s] stretched out from Waganawkezee [L'Arbre Croche] as far west as the Mississippi, and down to St. Josephs in the southeast corner of Lake Michigan. Secondary webs knitted these communities together with those in Detroit and farther southeast into Ohio, and also down into the southwestern corner of Lake Michigan and into Illinois country" (244). Also see Carver's encounter with a Winnebago "queen" (69–70).

23. Friedrichs: "zahlreiche Stilbrüche" (151).

24. Friedrichs: "vollständig europäisch, einschliesslich der erforderlichen Jungfräulichkeit und des Brautwerbers Philip" (152).

25. See examples in Axtell's chapter 3, "Love and Marriage" (71–102). Rogers should have known that, as his own cartographer, Jonathan Carver,

presents a lurid anecdote about a young Naudowessie (Sioux) woman who "invited forty of the principal warriors to her tent where . . . she by turn regaled each of them with a private dessert," and yet "in a very short time one of the principle chiefs took her to wife, over whom she acquired great sway and from whom she received ever after incessant tokens of respect and love" (126). Also see John D'Emilio and Estelle B. Freedman, who write in *Intimate Matters: A History of Sexuality in America* that "sexual intercourse and reproductive functions rarely evoked shame or guilt for Indian men or women. Many native American tribes accepted premarital intercourse, polygamy, or institutionalized homosexuality, all practices proscribed by European church and state. In certain tribes, women, like men, could exercise considerable choice in their selection of sexual partners, and children grew up with few restrictions on sexual experimentation, which might range from masturbation to sexual play between same-sex or opposite-sex partners" (7). Also see Steckley's example of the Wyandot in "For Native Americans, Sex Didn't Come with Guilt," or Eccles: "Women were the masters of their own bodies and from puberty until pregnancy they gave themselves to any male who pleased them. To the Jesuits this was carnal sin" (52). A good synopsis of interethnic sexual relations in colonial America can be found in Solomon. Today the existence of multiple genders among North American Indians and the berdache or "two-spirit" people in particular are being researched (see Serena Nanda's *Gender Diversity*, 11–26, and in particular Walter L. Williams's major study *The Spirit and the Flesh*). The best-known example of a berdache in American literature is probably the "creature" Yellow Head in John Tanner's captivity narrative (105–6).

26. Note this slanted allusion to Charles V and the Habsburg Empire, on which the sun never set. Honnyman's comment on his own torture invites another Spanish comparison to the Inquisition: "O dreadful Racks! When will this Torment end?" (4.4.197).

27. On a different note, Rogers's theatrical conclusion curiously rhymes with historian Gregory Dowd's assessment that "Pontiac's War . . . forced even the highest levels of the British government to consider, if only briefly and inconclusively, the place of Indians in the empire" (*War* 275).

28. Note in this context Richard Slotkin's telling statement about power: "The most striking quality of life in the New World was the relative absence of social restraints on human behavior, the relative ease with which a strong man could, by mastering the law of the wilderness-jungle, impose his personal dream of self-aggrandizement on reality. In Europe all men were under authority; in America all men dreamed they had the power to become authority" (34). In a sense, everybody could be a king.

CHAPTER 7. THE AESTHETIC DIMENSION

1. Origins of such a discourse of liberty can already be found in the *Concise Account*: "In short, the great and fundamental principles of their policy are, that

every man is naturally free and independent; that no one or more [*sic*] on earth has any right to deprive him of his freedom and independency, and that nothing can be a compensation for the loss of it" (233). Note that at times Ponteach's rhetoric also sounds like Tom Paine: "And now's our Time, if ever, to secure / Our Country, Kindred, . . . all that's dear, / From these Invaders of our Rights, the *English*" (2.2.32–34). And later, when it comes to convincing Hendrick of the uprising: "Urge ev'ry argument with Force upon him, / Urge my strong Friendship, urge your Brother's Love" (4.3.14–15). On urgency in Paine, see Ferguson (382).

2.   I owe the Shakespeare references to my colleague Regula Hohl. See Hamlet: "Like Niobe, all Tears" (*Hamlet* 1.2.149).

3.   See York: "You are more inhuman, more inexorable, / O, ten times more, than tigers of Hyrcania. / See, ruthless queen, a hapless father's tears" (*3 Henry VI* 1.4.154–56).

4.   This incident can actually be read as another ethnographic example: Indian narratives tend to see human origins from below, and traditional Indian dancing seeks stomping contact with the earth, whereas Western metaphysics clearly originates in the above—hence classical European ballet tries hard to overcome gravity. Conversely, some Indians place the bodies of their dead on scaffolds or in trees, while Europeans bury them underground.

5.   "Over the Hills and Far Away" was a popular tune well known from George Farquhar's 1706 play *The Recruiting Officer* and John Gay's *Beggar's Opera* of 1728. For the tune, visit https://www.youtube.com/watch?v=7bso7 OvqXp4.

6.   According to White (see chapter 5), there may also be a historical inspiration for these double scalps.

7.   This statement could be read by contemporaries as a threat to Johnson and/or Gage.

8.   Such rituals would become very popular in American literature, as exemplified in the long "funeral obsequies" for Uncas in Cooper (*Last of the Mohicans* 3:266–89).

9.   Chekitan's madness is especially touching because he began as the most humane and rational of the Indians, when he refuted his brother's accusations of cowardice:

> Is there no Courage in in delib'rate wisdom?
> Is all rank Cowardice but Fire and Fury?
> Is it all womanish to re-consider
> And weigh the Consequences of our Actions,
> Before we desperately rush upon them?
>
> (2.2.202–6)

10.   Wallace Stevens would have been impressed by this noisy reflection of wilderness.

11.   Though Rogers's storm imagery is conventional, it may have influenced

the later history writing about the uprising, as in the title of Marquis's chapter 3, "The Gathering Storm."

12. The diction is more conventional when signaling Indian nobility. Thus Ponteach speaks in lofty English prose, and so do his chiefs. For example, the first chief complains about the governors' meager gift: "We think it very small, we heard of more" (1.4.154).

13. See the conclusion of his famous *Tractatus*: "Wovon man nicht sprechen kann, darüber muss man schweigen" (115).

14. Significantly, when the loquacious priest is arrested by Chekitan, he stays "dumb," and Monelia comments: "May he be dumb and blind, and senseless quite, / That has such brutal Baseness in his Mind" (4.2.12–13).

15. Brooks find the origins of melodrama in the "context of the French Revolution and its aftermath. This is the epistemological moment which it illustrates and to which it contributes: the moment that symbolically, and really, marks the final liquidation of the traditional Sacred and its representative institutions (Church and Monarch), the shattering of the myth of Christendom, the dissolution of an organic and hierarchically cohesive society, and the invalidating of the literary forms—tragedy, comedy of manners—that depend on such a society" (14–15). Rogers's artistic hybridity stands for similar new, intercultural challenges.

CHAPTER 8. IMPORTANT ISSUES

1. Tiffany Potter also notes "the play's movement from private encounters between private citizens, to semi-private military encounters, and finally to public political exchanges between Ponteach and the three governors of the colony" (43).

2. Vizenor writes: "My presence is a native trace. / My names are forever in the book. / My tease is natural reason. / My memory endures in stories. / My vision is survivance" (6–7). Like the real Pontiac in Peckham's account, Ponteach does not yield to victimhood.

3. The cultural significance of this teaching concern is comparable to, for example, the late twentieth-century plays of David Mamet. See the older-younger relationships of the male couple Danny and Bernie as well as the female couple Deborah and Joan in *Sexual Perversity in Chicago*; see also the relationship of Walter Cole (significantly called "Teach") and Bob in *American Buffalo*.

4. It is interesting to know, in this context, that the real Pontiac had two secretaries, in order to avoid spying on his correspondence. Parkman quotes General Gage that Pontiac "keeps two secretaries, one to write for him, and the other to read the letters he receives, and he manages them so as to keep each of them ignorant of what is transacted by the other" (1994 ed. 255–56).

5. Drama critics specializing in gay studies may also see a bit of the "Restoration fop" (see Andrew Williams) in this odd frocked figure.

6. Previously the French priest has described his favorite saint as follows: "Our great St *Peter* is himself a Warrior; / He drew his Sword against such Infidels" (3.2.61–62). The phallic imagery is fairly explicit.

7. Bissel recognizes the English ideology in the description of the French priest: "The wily Jesuit is here pictured, not at all as he was, but very much as he was viewed by the English of the eighteenth century" (135).

8. On the merely instrumental function of Indians for the Puritans, see Slotkin: "Indians become instruments of God for the chastisement of his guilty people" (99).

9. Later Monelia uses the Christian label to explain what is wrong with rape as well, calling the French priest a "cruel barbarous Christian" (4.2.8).

10. This contradiction in Monelia's character may again have its origin in the interference of Rogers's American knowledge with European stage expectations. As Walter L. Williams writes: "American Indians offer some of the world's best examples of gender-egalitarian societies. . . . Native American women were (and are still, to a great extent) independent and self-reliant personalities, rather than subservient dependents" (65–66). See also John Tanner's courting of Red Sky of the Morning (116–18).

11. Echoes of this can still be read in Parkman, who notes: "These nominal Christians of Father Pothier's flock . . . soon distinguished themselves in the war" (1994 ed. 243). Worse, they wanted to "be allowed time to hear mass, before dancing the war-dance" (243).

CHAPTER 9. OPEN QUESTIONS

1. "Mr. Colden" is probably the New York governor Cadwallader Colden (1668–1776), author of *The History of the Five Indian Nations* (1727).

2. In the 1938 novel *Northwest Passage*, the novelist Kenneth Roberts makes exactly this claim. He has Rogers and Potter delightedly read reviews of the *Journals* and the *Concise Account* (424–27). His narrator, Langdon Towne, notes: "I took the clipping: 'The picture drawn by Major Rogers of the Emperor Pontiac,' it read, 'is novel and interesting, and would appear to vast advantage in the hands of a great dramatic genius'" (426). This fiction writer obviously did some library research.

3. See Dillon on the hypocrisy of such colonial behavior: "If Londoners were unable to view the sixty-nine slaves who were tortured to death in Antigua, in 1736, they were nonetheless able to view Oroonoko tortured and killed on stage at Drury Lane, Covent Garden and Lincoln's Inn Fields, [and] they might have viewed Montezuma tortured on the rack in performances of John Dryden's *Indian Emperour* at Lincoln's Inn Fields and Goodman's Field's" (34). She adds that "torture thus appears as what has 'disappeared' into the colony" (34). Because her book focuses on theater and performance, it unfortunately does not discuss the never-staged *Ponteach*.

4. As soon as the Indians were no longer a threat, the savages became noble. Also see my Pocahontas article on the changes in the image of the Indian from the early republic to the urbanization of the United States, and my entry on Native Americans in *Imagology: The Cultural Construction and Literary Representation of National Characters*.

5. When Rogers proposes that they'll "make Indians the fashion in London" and, "Natty, do you think we could get Garrick? Garrick's the man—Garrick as Pontiac!" (426), the fictional Potter in Roberts responds: "The play's the thing, wherewith to catch the notice of the King!" (427). Garrick was a most popular actor in London at that time. One of his monologues is printed in the same issue of the *Gentlemen's Magazine* as its review of the *Concise Account* (576).

6. The text is based on "Jerem. VIII.20. / The Harvest is past, the Summer is ended, and we are not saved."

7. As a Swiss I remember the Marxist journalist Niklaus Meienberg, who was trained in a monastery school in Disentis and would never forget his instruction. He returned on a regular basis to visit his old teachers in the mountains with his motorcycle.

8. Ossian could be appropriated by all: "Even though there were early claims of forgery against Macpherson, the Ossianic poems turned out to be a great success across Europe and were one of the first significant works of the Romantic movement. Mighty figures such as Goethe and Napoleon were fascinated by Ossian" (Gibbs n.p.).

9. Curiously, this association already existed even before permanent settlement in America by the English. Thus in 1585 John White's pictures of tattooed Algonquian Indians from Roanoke were published together with pictures of Scottish Picts in the same volume; see Smiles on the "five engravings of Picts and ancient Britons, included as a supplement at the end of Harriot's *A briefe and true report of the new found land of Virginia*" (106). Carver writes: "The manner in which these hieroglyphicks are made is breaking the skin with the teeth of fish or sharpened splints, dipped in a kind of ink made of the soot of pitch pine. Like those of the ancient Picts of Britain, these are esteemed ornamental" (164–65). Another reference to Native American "Picts" appears in John Slover's captivity narrative: "I was taken from New River in Virginia by the Miamese, a nation of Indians by us called the Picts, amongst whom I lived six years" (Brackenridge 20). I have not found this naming anywhere else, though, and Brackenridge is not our most reliable source on Indians.

10. The commentary on the painting in Lord Nelson's Gallery reads as follows: "When the Highlander was summoned to the American frontier to fight on behalf of The Crown, he formed an instant kinship with his Native American counterpart. Tribe and clan were remarkably similar in temperament and philosophy and both cultures produced highly skillful and courageous fighters. In this scene, a Cherokee warrior and Highlander scout in advance of Grant's disastrous expedition against Fort Duquesne. Sadly, both cultures eventually

crumbled beneath the oppressive weight of British expansion." See https://
www.lordnelsons.com/gallery/frontier/griffing/33.htm.

11. I owe this suggestion, including Algonquian stress on the second syllable, again to Wolfgang Hochbruck.

CHAPTER 10. CENTRIFUGAL INSIGHTS

1. Here is my favorite example from Harriot: "There is an herbe which is sowed apart by it selfe, & is called by the inhabitants Uppowoc: in the West Indies it hath divers names, according to the severall places and countreys where it groweth and is used: the Spanish generally call it Tabacco. The leaves thereof being dried and brought into pouder, they use and take the fume and smoke thereof, by sucking it thorow pipes made of clay, into their stomacke and head, from whence it purgeth superfluous fleame & other grosse humours, and openeth all the pores and passages of the body: by which meanes the use thereof not only preserveth the body from obstructions, but it also if any be, so that they have not beene too long continuance, in short time breaketh them: whereby their bodies are notably preserveth in health, & know not many greevous diseases, wherewithall we in England are oftentimes afflicted" (16).

2. See *Concise Account*: "In the late war of his, he appointed a commissary, and began to make money, or bills of credit, which he hath since punctually redeemed. His money was the figure of what he wanted in exchange for it, drawn upon bark, and the shape of an otter (his arms) drawn under it. Were proper measures taken, this Indian might be rendered very serviceable to the British trade and settlements in this country, more extensively so than any one that hath ever been in alliance with us on the continent" (244). This is the very postwar prominence of Pontiac that would finally lead to the "jealousy" of other Indians and his untimely death.

3. The novelist Roberts quotes this section at length when he has Rogers meet Pontiac at Oswego (501–5)—no wonder Bales mentions that the famous Bernard De Voto criticized "the exhaustive research that was a trademark of every Roberts novel" (221). But also historian Michael A. McDonnell confirms this vision in his recent 2015 study *Masters of Empire*: "For centuries, Michilimackinac was one of the few strategic entry points into and out of continental North America. Any nation, European or Native, wishing to pass back and forth from east to west, or even from north to south, would have to come through either Michilimackinac or the Sault sixty miles to the north" (12–13).

4. Regarding Rogers's memorandum, Nevins writes in a footnote about his "proposal for a new form of government at Mackinac": "This petition contains more than six thousand words, and is phrased as carefully as it is planned. As Potter himself is authority for the statement that it was composed secretly by Rogers, and during Potter's own absence, the document alone is sufficient to

refute Johnson's allegation that Rogers was illiterate" (*Ranger* 102n). This is interesting information for our judging of Rogers's writing abilities, and it leans in the major's favor.

5. Sir William Johnson's biographer James Flexner writes: "Johnson's policy was greatly embarrassed by Robert Rogers, [who] had gone to England where, in the general rooms of country houses, he had played so successfully the early-romantic role of a natural hero that he had returned with orders to Gage that he be appointed military commandant and administrator for the Indian department at Michilimackinac. . . . Sure enough, [Rogers] spent huge sums, which he wished the Indian Department to reimburse, to serve the ends of partners in the fur trade who disobeyed the regulations he was supposed to enforce" (323).

6. See Todish: "Colonel Edward Cole, Rogers' counterpart at Fort DeChartres, who was appointed by Johnson, spent considerably more than Rogers during the same time period. The conference at Michilimackinac was attended by over seven thousand Western Indians, and was the largest ever held up to that time. The resulting peace saved the Crown costly military expenses and also advanced British trade" (19–20).

7. See also McDonnell: "Robert Rogers, . . . who had fought against [Charles] Langlade and his Indian kin only a few years previously in the Champlain Valley, routinely consulted with him about affairs of the post and Indian relations" (252).

8. On 5 May he notes: "Mrs. Carden & Mr Seely were employ'd as spies on a party of Indians at Sheboigan" and discovered that they "were going to war against the Soux" (26).

9. The fact that Rogers was well liked also shows in the protests by the local Indians after his Michilimackinac arrest by Captain Spiesmacher (McDonnell 263).

10. According to Widder, some of Sir William Johnson's own ideas were not so different from Rogers's: "Johnson started to chisel foundation stones for his policy for carrying on Indian diplomacy at Michilimackinac after it had been reoccupied: giving annual presents to Odawa and Ojibwe for the use of Michilimackinac; rewarding Indians who allied themselves with the British; having an army garrison with its commandant working in conjunction with Johnson's agents to oversee the fur trade; and recognizing the geographical, cultural, and strategic significance of Michilimackinac to British influence in the upper country and beyond" (*Beyond* 179). Widder describes Johnson's plans in great detail but mentions that Johnson's "Francophobia" made him fail to understand the "central role played by the Canadians in the fur trade and how intimately they were connected to every Indian village" (191). He also mentions George Croghan, who "assessed the human and financial cost of the violence of 1763 to Britain, arguing that it would be much less expensive to buy friendship with the Indians" (186).

11. Another possibility for the origin of this negative view may be the hand of the former Massachusetts clergyman Nathaniel Potter, who knew of course about Roger Williams's heresy.

12. A curious Jewish reference in the *Concise Account* can be found about the inhabitants of "Red Lake," in the area where the Mississippi originates (189). We read: "This fruitful country is at present inhabited by a nation of Indians, called by the others the White Indians, on account of their complexion, they being much the fairest Indians on the continent; they have however Indian eyes, and a certain guilty Jewish cast with them" (191). The origin of the muddy river is here associated with the lost tribe of Israel. Again this is possibly the work of Potter's hand.

13. Rogers seems to have had contact with some Jewish traders. See McCulloch: "The Montreal fur traders to a man signed a letter backing Rogers' proposal, the list of their signatures a rollcall of names famous in the annals of the Northwest fur trade: Alexander Henry, James Finlay, Isaac Todd, Ezekiel Solomon, Gershom Levy, Henry Bostwick, John Chinn, Forrest Oakes and James McGill" (24). See also Heineman on "the presence of Jewish traders in Michigan at a very early day" (31).

14. Ross suggests that when Rogers fought in the South for the first time, in Colonel Grant's brutal campaign against the Cherokees, he "certainly was surprised and dismayed by the response of the rest of the regulars to his Stockbridge rangers" (323).

15. This text strongly correlates with the damaged "Plan of Robert Rogers" in the William Johnson papers: "But I forbear any one of the Least Sensib[le] May Imagin somthing of the pain & Chagr[in] that a Commandant must feel when he see[s him] self obblidged to Answer that he Cannot permit Traders to Come Nearer to them then this Garrison and if they want Goods they Must Come hither for them and what must be the Consternation the Uneasiness the Displeasure, and Resentment of the tribes & Nations when their Chiefs Return with this UnExpected Malencholy" (43). And later: "Secondly Many Others must Leave their wives & Children to Starve & Perish in their absence and lastly the Situation and Circumstances of Some Nations and tribes are Such that were they obblidged to Carry to the Single Market of Michillimackinac the Produce of their Years hunt or any part of it, they must leave their wifes & Children not only in a distressd Starving Condition but Liable Every day & Hour to becom slaves and their Whole Country & substance be left a Prey to Neighbouring Savages, the Differant Nations and tribes are now often at war with Each other" (55).

16. One gets a sense of parody when Kenneth Roberts's fictional Pontiac tries to convince the fictional Rogers of ideas that sound copied and pasted from the real Rogers: "What'll happen, Brother, if English traders are forbidden to travel to those tribes and live among them? . . . One family can't travel for

three months, in winter, to reach Michilimackinac and replace a gun lock: to buy another package of powder" (502).

17. Dixon writes: "In November 1747, a group of tidewater land speculators that included Thomas Lee [the famous Robert E. Lee's ancestor] and Lawrence Washington [George Washington's older half brother] formed a partnership called the Ohio Company and petitioned King George II to grant them title to half a million acres of land 'on the branches of the Allagany'" (16).

18. This is the later Colonel Crawford, who in 1782 was tortured and executed in a much-publicized act of brutality (see Brackenridge) in retaliation for the murder of ninety-six peaceful Indians at Gnadenhutten. Crawford, White remarks, "ironically, was no Indian hater," but "Indian hating determined Crawford's fate; it drew lines across which friendship could not pass" (395).

19. This is confirmed by Dixon: "Lastly, the Proclamation Line infuriated wealthy and influential land speculators who hoped to reap a fortune in the development of the trans-Appalachian frontier. Thomas Jefferson, George Washington, Richard Henry Lee, and Patrick Henry, to name a few, were poised to obtain lucrative land grants from the king at the end of the war" (246).

20. According to Volwiler, after the 1768 Treaty of Fort Stanwix, plans by the Great Ohio Company for the foundation of a new colony with the telling name "Vandalia" never materialized. The territory would later be split up between the states of Pennsylvania and Virginia. It mainly overlaps with today's West Virginia (268–77).

21. Ultimately, most loyalists lost their real estate in the newly founded United States, as Sjurson notes: "Though there were no guillotines in Philadelphia or Boston, there were, by war's end, more land cessions and flight by loyalists (mostly to Canada), per capita, than in the later French Revolution" ("Whose Revolution?" n.p.).

22. Stark has copied this sentence verbatim from Rogers himself (see *Journals* viii).

23. This fits well with Mark Twain's assessment of Cooper: "In his little box of stage-properties he kept six or eight cunning devices, tricks, artifices for his savages and woodsmen to deceive and circumvent each other with, and he was never so happy as when he was working these innocent things and seeing them go. A favorite one was to make a moccasined person tread in the tracks of a moccasined enemy, and thus hide his own trail. Cooper wore out barrels and barrels of moccasins in working that trick. Another stage-property that he pulled out of his box pretty frequently was the broken twig" (n.p.).

24. Interesting footprint lore can also be found in Jonathan Carver's *Travels*. Rogers's cartographer in Michilimackinac writes that Indians can "distinguish not only whether it is a man or woman who has passed that way, but even the nation to which they belong" (160).

25. Parkman writes that "the brave old savage, unable from age and corpulence to fight on foot, mounted his horse and joined the English detachment with two hundred of his warriors" (1994 ed. 116).

26. I sense a similar unease in Glover, who sees the Rangers as "agents of sanctioned male violence, and it is this collocation of wilderness and violence that emerges so powerfully from Rogers' *Journals*" (185). She regrets that the "'heroic' Rogers continues to fuel male fantasies" (186).

Bibliography

Adams, John. *Adams Papers*. "1760 Decr. 18th. Thurdsday." https://founders
.archives.gov/?q=potter&s=1511311111&r=2.

———. "Dec. 27th 1765. Fryday." https://founders.archives.gov/?q=potter&s
=1511311111&r=4.

Addison, Joseph. *Cato: A Tragedy*. 1713. Edited by Christine Dunn Henderson
and Mark E. Yellin. Foreword by Forrest McDonald. Indianapolis: Liberty
Fund, 2004. http://oll.libertyfund.org/titles/addison-cato-a-tragedy-and
-selected-essays.

America's History. "Rogers' Rangers and the French and Indian War—June
11–14, 2016—Past Tour." http://americashistory.com/2013/rogers-rangers
-and-the-french-and-indian-war-june-11-14-2014/.

Anderson, Marilyn J. "*Ponteach*: The First American Problem Play." *American
Indian Quarterly* 3, no. 3 (1977): 225–41.

Andrews, Clarence A. *Michigan in Literature*. Detroit: Wayne State University
Press, 1992.

Armour, David A. *Colonial Michilimackinac*. Mackinac Island, MI: Mackinac
State Historic Park, 2000.

———, ed. *Treason? at Michilimackinac: The Proceedings of a General Court
Martial Held at Montreal in October 1768 for the Trial of Major Robert Rogers*.
1967. Mackinac Island, MI: Mackinac State Historic Park, 1990.

Axtell, James, ed. *The Indian Peoples of Eastern America: A Documentary History of the Sexes.* New York and Oxford: Oxford University Press, 1981.

Bakhtin, M. M. *The Dialogic Imagination: Four Essays.* Edited and translated by Michael Holquist. Austin: University of Texas Press, 1981.

Bales, Jack. *Kenneth Roberts.* Twayne United States Authors Series. New York: Twayne, 1993.

Bland, Celia. *Pontiac, Ottawa Rebel.* New York: Chelsea House, 1995.

Bishop, Morris. "Four Kings in London." *American Heritage* 23, no. 1 (1971): n.p. https://www.americanheritage.com/content/four-indian-kings-london.

Bissell, Benjamin. *The American Indian in English Literature of the Eighteenth Century.* 1925. North Haven, CT: Archon Books, 1968.

Black, Albert. "The Pontiac Conspiracy in the Novel, 1833–1954." *Michigan History* 43 (1959): 115–19.

Brackenridge, Hugh. *Narratives of the Late Expedition against the Indians; with an Account of the Barbarous Execution of Col. Crawford; and the Wonderful Escape of Dr. Knight and John Slover from Captivity, in 1782.* Philadelphia: Francis Bailey, 1783.

Bradbury, Osgood Esq. *Pontiac—or the—Last Battle of the Ottawa Chief: A Tale of the West.* Boston: F. Gleason, at the Flag of our Union Office, 1848.

Brant, Clare. *Eighteenth-Century Letters and British Culture.* Basingstoke, UK: Palgrave Macmillan, 2006.

Brooks, Peter. *The Melodramatic Imagination: Balzac, Henry James, Melodrama, and the Mode of Excess.* New York: Columbia University Press, 1985.

Brown, Thomas. *A Plain Narrative of the Uncommon Sufferings and Remarkable Deliverance of Thomas Brown of Charlestown in New England.* 2nd ed. 1760. New York: William Abbatt, 1908.

Brumwell, Stephen. *Redcoats: The British Soldier and War in the Americas, 1755–1763.* Cambridge: Cambridge University Press, 2002.

Bunce, William H. *War-Belts of Pontiac (Red Wampum and White).* Illustrated by I. B. Hazelton. New York: E. P. Dutton, 1943.

Calloway, Colin G. *The Scratch of a Pen: 1763 and the Transformation of North America.* New York: Oxford University Press, 2006.

Canavan, Michael Joseph. *Ben Comee: A Tale of Rogers's Rangers 1758–59.* Illustrated by George Gibbs. New York: Macmillan, 1899.

Carver, Jonathan. *Jonathan Carver's Travels through America, 1766–1768: An Eighteenth-Century Explorer's Account of Uncharted America.* 1788. Edited and introduced by Norman Gelb. New York: John Wiley & Sons, 1993.

Castillo, Susan. *Colonial Encounters in New World Writing, 1500–1786: Performing America.* London: Routledge, 2006.

Cavazzano, Giorgio, and François Cortegianni. *Capitain Rogers: Le calumet de la guerre.* Brussels: Edition du Lombard, 1988.

Cavazzano, Giorgio, and G. Pezzin. *Capitain Rogers: Alles roger, Rogers?!* Stuttgart: Ehpha Verlag, 1987.

Church, Major Thomas R. *Operational Art in Pontiac's War: 1763 Pan-Indian Movement Attack on British Forts in Great Lakes Region, Pay d'en Haut and the Ottawa Chief Pontiac, Bradstreet and Bouquet Campaigns.* Fort Leavenworth, KS: CGSC Foundation, Department of Defense, 2015. Approved for public release.

Classics Illustrated. *Rogers' Rangers: French and English Soldiers Fight for Every Square Foot of Land in North America.* Berkshire: Classic Comic Store, 2010.

Clements, William L. "Rogers's Michillimackinac Journal." In Rogers, *Journal of Major Robert Rogers* (1918), 3–10.

Clifford, James. *The Predicament of Culture: Twentieth-Century Ethnography, Literature, and Art.* Cambridge, MA: Harvard University Press, 1988.

Cochrane, Mary Rogers. *A Battle Fought on Snow Shoes.* Derry, NH: self-published, 1917.

Cockings, George. *The Conquest of Canada; or The Siege of Quebec. An Historical Tragedy of Five Acts.* London: J. Cooke, 1766.

Colden, Cadwallader. *The History of the Five Indian Nations Depending on the Province of New-York in America.* New York: William Bradford, 1727.

Cooper, James Fenimore. *The Chronicles of Cooperstown.* Cooperstown: H. & E. Phinney, 1838.

———. *The Last of the Mohicans: Narrative of 1757.* 3 vols. London: John Miller, 1826.

Costopoulos, Philip J. "Jefferson, Adams, and the Natural Aristocracy." *First Things,* May 1990. https://www.firstthings.com/article/1990/05/jefferson-adams-and-the-natural-aristocracy.

Crane, Hart. "For the Marriage of Faustus and Helen." *White Buildings.* New York: Boni & Liveright, 1926.

The Critical Review: or, Annals of Literature. Review of *A Concise Account of North-America,* by Major Robert Rogers. No. 20, November 1765, 387. Reprinted in Rogers, *Ponteach* (2010), 202–3.

———. Review of *The Journals of Major Robert Rogers,* by Major Robert Rogers. No. 20, November 1765, 387–88. Reprinted in Rogers, *Ponteach* (2010), 205.

———. Review of *Ponteach.* No. 21, 1766, 150.

Cuneo, John R. *Robert Rogers of the Rangers.* New York: Oxford University Press, 1959.

de Fries, Caspar. *Aufstand der Indianer: Pontiac.* Parts 1 and 2. Munich: Book Rix, 2015.

D'Emilio, John, and Estelle B. Freedman. *Intimate Matters: A History of Sexuality in America.* New York: Harper & Row, 1988.

Dillon, Elizabeth Maddox. *New World Drama: The Performative Commons in the Atlantic World, 1649–1849.* Durham, NC: Duke University Press, 2014.

Dixon, David. *Never Come to Peace Again: Pontiac's Uprising and the Fate of the British Empire in North America.* Norman: University of Oklahoma Press, 2005.

Dowd, Gregory Evans. *A Spirited Resistance: The North American Indian Struggle for Unity, 1745–1815*. Baltimore: Johns Hopkins University Press, 1992.

————. *War under Heaven: Pontiac, the Indian Nations, & the British Empire*. Baltimore: Johns Hopkins University Press, 2002.

Dryden, John. *The Conquest of Granada by the Spaniards: In Two Parts*. London: Herringman, 1672.

Dryden, John, and Sir Robert Howard. *The Indian Emperour, or the Conquest of Mexico by the Spaniards, being the Sequel of The Indian Queen*. 2nd ed. London: Herringman, 1668.

————. *The Indian-Queen, a Tragedy*. London: Herringman, 1665.

Eccles, W. J. *The Canadian Frontier, 1534–1760*. Hinsdale, IL: Dryden Press, 1969.

Egan, Grace. "Corresponding Forms: Aspects of the Eighteenth-Century Letter." PhD diss., University of Oxford, 2015.

Elliott, T. C. "The Origin of the Name Oregon." *Quarterly of the Oregon Historical Society* 22, no. 2 (June 1921): 91–115.

Ellis, Edward Sylvester. *The Life of Pontiac the Conspirator, Chief of the Ottawas: Together with a Full Account of the Celebrated Siege of Detroit*. Beadle's Dime Biographical Library. London, New York: Beadle, 1861. New York: Hurst & Company, 1910.

———— [Col. H. R. Gordon, pseud.]. *Pontiac, Chief of the Ottawas: A Tale of the Siege of Detroit*. New York: E. P. Dutton, 1897.

Engel, Elmar. *Pontiac—Häuptling der Ottawa*. Göttingen: Lamuv Verlag, 1999.

Engelhardt, Emil. *Pontiac im grossen Indianerkrieg*. Potsdam: L. Voggenreiter, 1944.

Ferguson, Robert A. "The American Enlightenment, 1750–1820." In *The Cambridge History of American Literature*, vol. 1, *1590–1820*, edited by Sacvan Bercovitch, 345–469. Cambridge: Cambridge University Press, 1994.

Fleischer, Jane. *Pontiac, Chief of the Ottawas*. Illustrated by Robert Baxter. Mahwah, NJ: Troll Associates, 1979.

Flexner, James Thomas. *Mohawk Baronet: A Biography of Sir William Johnson*. 1959. Syracuse: Syracuse University Press, 1989.

Franklin, Benjamin. "Information to Those Who Would Remove to America." Pamphlet. Passy, 1784. https://founders.archives.gov/documents/Franklin/01-41-02-0391.

————. "To the Printer of the *London Chronicle*." May 9, 1759. Printed in *London Chronicle: or, Universal Evening Post*, May 10–12, 1759, 449–451. https://founders.archives.gov/?q=%20Author%3A%22Franklin%2C%20Benjamin%22&s=1111311111&r=768.

Friedrichs, Michael. "Ein wenig gewürdigtes Protest- und Erbauungstück: Rogers' *Ponteach; or, The Savages of America* (1766)." *Zeitschrift für Anglistik und Amerikanistik* 34, no. 2 (1986): 145–57.

Frost, Robert. "The Gift Outright." 1942. Read on President John F. Kennedy's inauguration, January 20, 1961. https://www.youtube.com/watch?v=XInL2uoDP88.

Fulford, Tim. "Prophets of Resistance: Native American Shamans and Anglo-phone Writers." In *Transatlantic Literary Exchanges, 1790–1870: Gender, Race, and Nation*, edited by K. Hutchings and J. M. Wright, 77–99. Burlington, VT: Ashgate, 2011.

Gasparro, Joseph D. "'The Desired Effect': Pontiac's Rebellion and the Native American Struggle to Survive in Britain's North American Conquest." *Gettysburg Historical Journal* 6 (2007): 38–62.

Gelb, Norman. "Introduction: The Life and Times of Jonathan Carver." In Carver, *Jonathan Carver's Travels through America*, 1–51.

The Gentleman's Magazine and Historical Chronicle. On Robert Rogers in the French and Indian War. No. 28 (1758): 498–99.

————. On the Battle of Ticonderoga. No. 28 (1758): 44–46.

————. "Particulars of Major Robert Rogers's Last Expedition against the Enemy." No. 29, May 1759, 203–4. Reprinted in Rogers, *Ponteach* (2010), 207–9.

————. On Major Rogers taken prisoner in Michilimackinac. No. 38 (1768): 301.

————. On Rogers arrested in Michilimackinac. No. 38 (1768): 348.

————. Review of *A Concise Account of North America*. No. 35, November 1765, 584–85. Reprinted in Rogers, *Ponteach* (2010), 201–2.

————. Review of *Ponteach*. No. 36, February 1766, 90. Reprinted in Rogers, *Ponteach* (2010), 199–200.

Gibbs, Chris. "The New Britons: Scottish Identity in the 18th and 19th Centuries." August 2006. https://www.napoleon-series.org/research/society/c_scottish identity.html.

Gill, Harold B., Jr. "Colonial Germ Warfare." *Journal of Colonial Williamsburg*. 2005. http://www.andallthat.co.uk/uploads/2/3/8/9/2389220/colonial_germ_warfare.pdf.

Glover, Susan. "Battling the Elements: Reconstructing the Heroic in Robert Rogers." *Journal of American Culture* 26, no. 2 (2003): 180–87.

Grant, Matthew G. *Pontiac: Indian General and Statesman*. Illustrated by Harold Henriksen. Gallery of Great Americans. Chicago: Children's Press, 1974.

Green, Mary M., and Irma Johnson. *Three Feathers: The Story of Pontiac*. Chicago: Follett, 1960.

Gustavson, W. "Marching through a Thousand Prints: The Invention of the 'Famous' Major Robert Rogers." In *The Image of the Hero in Literature, Media, and Society*, edited by W. Wright and S. Kaplan, 187–93. Pueblo, CO: Society for the Interdisciplinary Study of Social Imagery, 2004.

Hamilton, Milton W. Review of *Robert Rogers of the Rangers*, by John R. Cuneo. *Michigan History* 43, no. 3 (1959): 382–83.

Harlan, Robert Dale. "William Strahan: Eighteenth Century London Printer and Publisher." PhD diss., University of Michigan, 1960.

Harriot, Thomas. *A briefe and new report of the new found land of Virginia*. Frankfurt am Main: De Bry, 1590.

Hearting, Ernie [Ernst Herzig]. *Pontiac: Sendung und Schicksal eines grossen Indianerhäuptlings.* Einsiedeln: Waldstatt Verlag, 1961.

The Heath Anthology of American Literature. General editor, Paul Lauter. Boston: Cengage Learning, 2014.

Heineman, David E. "The Startling Experience of a Jewish Trader during Pontiac's Siege of Detroit in 1763." *Publications of the American Jewish Historical Society* 23 (1915): 31–35.

Henry, Alexander. *Alexander Henry's Travels and Adventures in the Years 1760–1776.* 1809. Edited by Milo Milton Quaife. Chicago: Lakeside Press, 1921.

Hernlund, Patricia. "William Strahan, Printer: His Career and Business Procedures." PhD diss., University of Chicago, 1965.

Hewitt, Barnard. *Theatre U.S.A.: 1668 to 1957.* New York: McGraw-Hill, 1959.

Hiller, Lejaren, and Robert Rogers. *Ponteach: A Melodrama for Narrator and Piano.* 1977. Philadelphia: Kallisti Music Press, 1992.

Hodge, Frederick Webb, ed. *Handbook of American Indians North of Mexico.* Part 1. Washington, DC: Government Printing Office, 1907.

Hollmann, Clide. *Pontiac, King of the Great Lakes.* New York: Hastings House, 1968.

Hough, Franklin B., ed. *Diary of the Siege of Detroit.* Albany, NY: Munsell, 1860.

Howells, William Dean. *Stories of Ohio.* New York: American Book, 1897.

Hubbard, Jake T. "Americans as Guerilla Fighters: Robert Rogers and His Rangers." 2009. http://mymilitaryhistory.blogspot.com/2009/06/robert -rogers-and-his-rangers.html.

Jefferson, Thomas. Letter to James Madison, January 30, 1787. http://www.let .rug.nl/usa/presidents/thomas-jefferson/letters-of-thomas-jefferson/jefl 53.php.

Jennings, Francis. *Empire of Fortune: Crowns, Colonies and Tribes in the Seven Years War in America.* New York: W. W. Norton, 1988.

Johnson, Sir William. *The Papers of Sir William Johnson.* Vol. 6. Edited by Alexander Flick. Albany: University of the State of New York, 1928.

Lahontan, Baron de. *New Voyages to America.* 2 vols. 1703. Edited by Rueben Gold Thwaites. Chicago: A. C. McClurg, 1905.

Loescher, Burt Garfield. *The History of Rogers Rangers.* 4 vols. San Francisco: self-published, 1946.

———. *Rogers Rangers: The First Green Berets.* San Mateo, CA: self-published, 1969.

The London Magazine, or Gentlemen's Monthly Intelligencer. Review of *A Concise Account of North America,* by Major Robert Rogers. December 1765, 630–32, 676–77.

———. "Foreign Affairs." June 1768, 330.

———. On Rogers' arrest in Michilimackinac. July 1768, 384.

Lucier, Armand Francis, ed. *French and Indian War Notices Abstracted from Colonial Newspapers.* Vol. 4, *September 17, 1759 to December 30, 1760.* Westminster, MD: Heritage Books, 2007.

————, ed. *Pontiac's Conspiracy & Other Indian Affairs: Notices Abstracted from Colonial Newspapers, 1763–1765*. Berwyn Heights, MD: Heritage Books, 2013.

Ludwig, Sämi. "America: Native North Americans." In *Imagology: The Cultural Construction and Literary Representation of National Characters; A Survey*, edited by Manfred Beller and Joep Leerson, 82–86. Amsterdam and New York: Rodopi, 2007.

————. "Ideology and Art: Pocahontas in Three Early American Plays." In *US Icons and Iconicity*, edited by Walter Hölbling, Klaus Rieser, and Susanne Rieser, 93–114. Münster: LIT Verlag, 2006.

Macomb, Alexander, Jr. *Pontiac: or The Siege of Detroit; A Drama, in Three Acts*. Boston: Samuel Colman, 1835.

Mamet, David. *Plays—One*. London: Methuen Drama, 1994.

Mante, Thomas. *The History of the Late War in North-America, and the Islands of the West-Indies*. London: W. Strahan & T. Cadell, 1772.

Marquis, Thomas Guthrie. *The War Chief of the Ottawas: A Chronicle of the Pontiac War*. Toronto: Glasgow, Brook, 1920.

McConnell, Michael N. "Introduction to the Bison Book Edition." In Parkman, *Conspiracy of Pontiac* (1994), vii–xviii.

McCulloch, Ian. "Buckskin Soldier: The Rise and Fall of Major Robert Rogers." *The Beaver* 73, no. 2 (1993): 17–26.

McDonnell, Michael A. *Masters of Empire: Great Lakes Indians and the Making of America*. New York: Hill & Wang, 2015.

Meserve, Walter J. *An Emerging Entertainment: The Drama of the American People to 1828*. Bloomington: Indiana University Press, 1977.

Middleton, Richard. *Colonial America: A History, 1585–1776*. Oxford: Blackwell, 1996.

————. "Pontiac: Local Warrior or Pan-Indian Leader?" *Michigan Historical Review* 32, no. 2 (2006): 1–32.

————. *Pontiac's War: Its Causes, Course, and Consequences*. New York: Routledge, 2007.

The Monthly Review, or Literary Journal. Review of *A Concise Account of North America*, by Major Robert Rogers. No. 34, January 1766, 9–22. Reprinted in Rogers, *Ponteach* (2010), 203–5.

————. Review of *Ponteach*. No. 34, March 1766, 242. Reprinted in Rogers, *Ponteach* (2010), 200–201.

Moore, Charles. "Memorials of the Great War." *American Magazine of Art* 10, no. 7 (1919): 233–47.

Morgan, Latoya. *Turn: Origins*. Graphic novel illustrated by Steve Ellis. 2014. https://www.amc.com/shows/turn/exclusives/origins-comic-book.

————. *Turn: Rivals*. Graphic novel illustrated by Chris Hunt. 2015. https://www.amc.com/shows/turn/exclusives/rivals-comic-book.

Morsberger, R. E. "The Tragedy of *Ponteach* and the Northwest Passage." *Old Northwest: A Journal of Regional Life and Letters* 4 (1978): 241–57.

Moses, Montrose, ed. *Representative Plays by American Dramatists.* Vol. 1, *1765–1819.* New York: Benjamin Blom, 1918.

———, ed. *Representative Plays by American Dramatists.* Vol. 2, *1815–1858.* New York: Benjamin Blom, 1925.

———, ed. *Representative Plays by American Dramatists.* Vol. 3, *1856–1917.* New York: Benjamin Blom, 1921.

Nagel, Joanne. *Race, Ethnicity, and Sexuality: Intimate Intersections, Forbidden Frontiers.* New York: Oxford University Press, 2003.

Nanda, Serena. *Gender Diversity: Crosscultural Variations.* Prospect Heights, IL: Waveland Press, 2000.

Navarre, Robert de. *Journal of Pontiac's Conspiracy, 1763.* Edited by M. Agnes Burton. Translated by Clyde Ford. Bilingual ed. Detroit: Speaker-Hines Printing, 1912.

Nester, William. *Haughty Conquerors: Amherst and the Great Indian Uprising of 1763.* Westport, CT: Praeger, 2000.

———. *The Struggle for Power in Colonial America, 1607–1776.* Lanham, MD: Lexington Books, 2017.

Nevins, Allan. *Ranger: The Adventurous Life of Robert Rogers of the Rangers.* Military Commanders Series. N.p.: Leonaur, 2011.

———. Introduction to Rogers, *Ponteach* (1914), 11–15.

———. "Introduction to Rogers' 'Ponteach.'" MA thesis, University of Illinois, 1913.

Northwest Passage. Directed by King Vidor. Featuring Spencer Tracy, Robert Young, and Walter Brennan. Metro-Goldwyn Mayer, 1940.

———. NBC TV series. 26 episodes. Featuring Buddy Ebsen, Don Burnett, and Keith Larsen. Metro-Goldwyn Mayer, 1958–59.

The Norton Anthology of American Literature. General editor, Nina Baym. 8th ed. 5 vols. New York: W. W. Norton, 2011.

Ong, Walter J. *Orality and Literacy: The Technologizing of the Word.* London: Methuen, 1982.

Ohio History Central. "Washington, George." http://www.ohiohistorycentral .org/w/Washington,_George.

Orians, G. H. "Pontiac in Literature: Part I, 1764–1915." *Northwest Ohio Quarterly* 35 (1963): 144–63.

———. "Pontiac in Literature: Part II, 1916–1964." *Northwest Ohio Quarterly* 36 (1964): 31–53.

O'Toole, Fintan. *White Savage: William Johnson and the Invention of America.* New York: Farrar, Straus & Giroux, 2005.

Parkman, Francis, Jr. *The Conspiracy of Pontiac and the Indian War after the Conquest of Canada.* Vol. 1, *To the Massacre of Michillimackinac.* 1870. Introduced by Michael N. McConnell. Lincoln: University of Nebraska Press, 1994.

———. *The Conspiracy of Pontiac.* Classics Illustrated. New York: Gilberton, 1967.

————. *The Oregon Trail & The Conspiracy of Pontiac*. Edited by William R. Taylor. New York: Library of America, 1991.

Peckham, Howard H. Introduction to Rogers, *Journals* (1961), v–ix.

————. *Pontiac, Young Ottawa Leader*. Childhood of Famous Americans Series. Indianapolis: Bobbs-Merrill, 1963.

————. *Pontiac and the Indian Uprising*. 1947. Detroit: Wayne State University Press, 1994.

Perrot, Nicolas. "Memoir on the Manners, Customs, and Religion of the Savages of North America." 1864. In *The Indian Tribes of the Upper Mississippi Valley and Region of the Great Lakes*. Translated and edited by Emma Helen Blair, vol. 1, 25–275. Cleveland: Arthur H. Clark, 1911.

Potter, Nathaniel. "Mr. Potter's Discourse on *Jeremiah* 8th 20th. Preached on the Lord's-Day Morning, *Jan.* 1, 1758, at Brookline. Wherein is briefly attempted—A Discovery of the *Causes* of our late national Calamities, Disappointments, and Losses—That *they* are owing to our Sins, *which*, not only render us obnoxious to the divine Indignation and Wrath; but in their own Nature tend to produce such *Distresses* and *Ruin*—That the only probable way to *Peace*, *Safety* and *Prosperity*, is to remove *them*, and turn to God and Goodness—Several Considerations proposed to rouse and awaken our Attention to *it*." Boston: Edes & Gill, 1758.

Potter, Tiffany. "Introduction: Staging Savagery and Fictionalizing Colonialism in Robert Rogers' *Ponteach: A Tragedy*." In Rogers, *Ponteach* (2010), 3–54.

Quaife, Milo M. Review of *Ponteach*, edited by Allan Nevins (1914). *Mississippi Valley Historical Review* 2, no. 1 (June 1915): 146–49.

Quasha, Jennifer. *Robert Rogers: Rogers' Rangers and the French and Indian War*. Library of American Lives and Times. New York: Rosen, 2002.

Richards, Jeffery H., ed. *Early American Drama*. Harmondsworth, UK: Penguin Books, 1997.

Richardson, John. *Wacousta; or, The Prophecy: A Tale of the Canadas*. 3 vols. London: T. Cadell, Strand; Edinburgh: W. Blackwood, 1832.

Roarke, Mike. *Silent Drums: Pontiac's Rebellion (1763–1765)*. New York: St. Martin's Paperbacks, 1994.

Roberts, Kenneth. *Northwest Passage*. London: Collins, 1938.

Rogers Island Visitors Center, Fort Edward, NY. "Welcome to Rogers Island Visitors Center!" http://www.rogersisland.org/Rogers%20Island.htm.

Rogers, Major Robert. *The Annotated and Illustrated Journals of Major Robert Rogers*. 1765. Annotated and with an introduction by Timothy J. Todish. Illustrated with captions by Gary S. Zaboly. Fleischmanns, NY: Purple Mountain Press, 2002.

————. *A Concise Account of North America: Containing a Description of the several British Colonies on that Continent, including the Islands of Newfoundland, Cape Breton, &c. as to Their Situation, Extent, Climate, Soil, Produce, Rise, Government, Region, Present Boundaries, and the Number of Inhabitants supposed to*

be in each, also of the Interior, or Westerly Parts of the Country, upon the Rivers St.
Laurence, the Mississippi, Christino, and the Great Lakes. To which is subjoined,
An Account of the several Nations and Tribes of Indians residing in those Parts, as
to their Customs, manners, Government, Numbers, &c. Containing many Useful
and Entertaining Facts, never before treated of. London: J. Millan, 1765. Internet
Archive, https://archive.org/details/aconciseaccountoorogeuoft/page
/n5.

————. *A Concise Account of North America.* Dublin: J. Milliken, 1769.

———— (Königl. Grossbritannischen Major). *Eine kurze Nachricht von Nord-*
Amerika. Sammlung neuer Reisebeschreibungen aus fremden Sprachen besonders
der Englischen in die Teutsche übersetzt, *und mit Anmerkungen erläutert von*
Johann Tobias Köhler. Vol. 1, section 1. Göttingen: Johann Christian Dietrich,
1767.

————. "First Proposal [to find the Northwest Passage]. A Proposal by Robert
Rogers Esq. formerly Major Commandt. of His Majesty's Rangers in North
America, founded on his Observations and Experience, during the Space of
Eight Years in the least known parts of that great Continent. Humbly Submitted to the Wisdom of the Kings most Excellent Majesty and his Ministers." August 1765. Reprinted in Elliott, "Origin of the Name Oregon,"
101–5.

————. *Journal of Major Robert Rogers (Michillimackinac Journal).* 1766–67.
Edited by William L. Clements. Worcester, MA: American Antiquarian Society, 1918.

————. "Journal of the Siege of Detroit." In Hough, *Diary,* 121–35. See also
Rogers, *Annotated and Illustrated Journals,* 272–77.

————. *Journals of Major Robert Rogers: Containing an Account of several Excur-*
sions he made under the Generals who commanded upon the Continent of North
America, during the late War. From which may be collected the most material Cir-
cumstances of every Campaign upon that Continent, from the Commencement to
the Conclusion of the War. London: J. Millan, 1765. Internet Archive, https://
archive.org/details/cihm_40213/page/n7.

————. *Journals of Major Robert Rogers [. . .]. to which is Added an Historical Ac-*
count of Colonel Bouquet's Expedition against the Ohio Indians in the Year 1764,
under the Command of Henry Bouquet, Esq; Colonel of foot and now Brigadier Gen-
eral in America, including his Transactions with the Indians, relative to the Deliv-
ery of the Prisoners, and the Preliminaries of Peace. With an introductory Account
of the Proceeding Campaign, and Battle at Bushy-Run. Dublin: J. Milliken, 1769.

————. *Journals of Major Robert Rogers.* 1765. Introduction and notes by
Franklin B. Hough. Albany: Joel Munsell's Sons, 1883.

————. *Journals of Major Robert Rogers.* 1765. Introduced by Howard H.
Peckham. New York: Corinth Books, 1961.

————. Letter to W. Davies Archibeto. Fort Edward, 2nd June 1758. Clements
Library, University of Michigan, Ann Arbor.

————. Letter to Mr. Henry Apthorp. New York, 19th July 1761. Clements Library, University of Michigan, Ann Arbor.

————. Letter to his wife, Betsy. "On Board the Ship," 27th [month unknown] 1765. Clements Library, University of Michigan, Ann Arbor.

————. Letter to Sir William Johnson. Michilimackinac, 4th September 1767. Clements Library, University of Michigan, Ann Arbor.

————. "Plan of Robert Rogers." 1767. In Johnson, *Papers*, 43–58.

————. *Ponteach: or, The Savages of America: A Tragedy*. London: J. Millan, 1766. Internet Archive, https://archive.org/details/ponteachorsavageoooroge/page/n6.

————. *Ponteach: or, The Savages of America: A Tragedy*. 1766. Introduction and biography by Allan Nevins. Chicago: Caxton Club, 1914.

————. *Ponteach: or, The Savages of America*. 1766. In Moses, *Representative Plays by American Dramatists*, 1:109–208.

————. *Ponteach: or, The Savages of America: A Tragedy*. 1766. Edited by Tiffany Potter. Toronto: University of Toronto Press, 2010.

————. "Second Proposal [to find the Northwest Passage]." February 1772. Reprinted in Elliott, "Origin of the Name Oregon," 106–9.

Rogers, Walter. *Rogers, Ranger and Loyalist*. Ottawa: Royal Society of Canada, 1900.

Rose, Alexander. *Washington's Spies: The Story of American's First Spy Ring*. New York: Bantam Books, 2006.

Ross, John F. *War on the Run: The Epic Story of Robert Rogers and the Conquest of America's First Frontier*. New York: Bantam Books, 2009.

Rowlandson, Mary. *The Sovereignty & Goodness of God, together, with the Faithfulness of His Promises Displayed, Being a Narrative of the Captivity and Restoration of Mrs. Mary Rowlandson. Commended by her, to all that desires to know the Lords doing to, and dealings with Her. Especially to her dear Children and Relations*. Cambridge: Samuel Green, 1682.

The Royal Proclamation—October 7, 1763. http://avalon.law.yale.edu/18th_century/proc1763.asp.

Sayre, Gordon M. *The Indian Chief as Tragic Hero: Native Resistance and the Literatures of America, from Moctezuma to Tecumseh*. Chapel Hill: University of North Carolina Press, 2005.

————. *Les Sauvages Américains: Representations of Native Americans in French and English Colonial Literature*. Chapel Hill: University of North Carolina Press, 1997.

Schatzer, Jeffery L. *Chief Pontiac's War*. Professor Tuesday's Awesome Adventures in History. Ann Arbor, MI: Mitten Press, 2009.

Schuessler, Jennifer. "A New Museum of the American Revolution, Warts and All." *New York Times*, April 13, 2017. https://www.nytimes.com/2017/04/13/arts/design/a-new-museum-of-the-american-revolution-warts-and-all.html.

The Scots Magazine. "British North America." No. 29 (1767): 99.

Sears, Priscilla F. *A Pillar of Fire to Follow: American Indian Drama, 1808–1859.* Bowling Green, OH: Bowling Green University Popular Press, 1982.

Silbersack, John. *Rogers' Rangers.* New York: Ace Science Fiction, 1955.

Sjurson, Major Danny. "American History for Truthdiggers: Whose Empire?" *Truthdig.* March 3, 2018. https://www.truthdig.com/articles/american-history-truthdiggers-whose-empire/.

————. "American History for Truthdiggers: Whose Revolution? (1775–1783)." *Truthdig.* April 7, 2018. https://www.truthdig.com/articles/american-history-for-truthdiggers-whose-revolution-1775-1783/.

Slotkin, Richard. *Regeneration through Violence: The Mythology of the American Frontier, 1600–1860.* Middletown, CT: Wesleyan University Press, 1973.

Smiles, Sam. "John White and British Antiquity: Savage Origins in the Context of Tudor Historiography." In *European Visions, American Voices,* edited by Kim Sloan, 106–12. London: British Museum, 2009.

Smith, Bradford. *Rogers' Rangers and the French and Indian War.* Illustrated by John C. Wonsetler. Landmark Books 63. New York: Random House, 1956.

Smith, Rev. William. *An Historical Account of Colonel Bouquet's Expedition against the Ohio Indians in the Year 1764.* 1765. Attached to Rogers, *Journals* (Dublin 1769). See also Rogers, *Annotated and Illustrated Journals,* 236–71.

Sollors, Werner. *Beyond Ethnicity: Consent and Descent in American Culture.* New York: Oxford University Press, 1986.

Solomon, Richard. "Sexual Practice and Fantasy in Colonial America and the Early Republic." *Indiana University Journal of Undergraduate Research* 3 (2017): 24–34.

Southerne, Thomas. *Oroonoko: A Tragedy as It Is Acted at the Theatre-Royal, by His Majesty's Servants.* London: H. Playford & H. Buckley, 1696.

Spero, Patrick. *Frontier Rebels: The Fight for Independence in the American West, 1765–1776.* New York: Norton, 2018.

Spring, Ted. *Sketchbook 56.* Vol. 1, *Rogers' Rangers.* Elk River, MN: Track of the Wolf, 1991.

Steckley, John. "For Native Americans, Sex Didn't Come with Guilt." *Fair Observer,* March 30, 2015. https://www.fairobserver.com/region/north_america/for-native-americans-sex-didnt-come-with-guilt-21347/.

————. "Huron Kinship Terminology." *Ontario Archeology* 55 (1993): 35–59.

Steckley, John, and Bryan D. Cummings. *Full Circle: Canada's First Nations.* Toronto: Prentice Hall, 2001.

Stockdale, James. *Thoughts of a Philosophical Fighter Pilot.* Stanford, CA: Hoover Press, 1995.

Strahan, William. *The William Strahan Archive from the British Library, 1738–1861.* 121 vols. Microfilm Reading. Berkshire UK: Research Publications, 1989.

Stark, Caleb, ed. *Memoir and Official Correspondence of General John Stark [. . .] also a Biography of [. . .] Col. Robert Rogers, with an Account of His Services in America during the "Seven Years War."* Concord, MA: Parker Lyon, 1860.

Sweetser, Kate Dickinson. *Book of Indian Braves*. New York: Harper & Brothers, 1913.

Tanner, John. *Narrative and the Captivity and Adventures of John Tanner, during Thirty Years Residence in the Interior of North America*. Prepared by Edwin James, M.D. New York: Carvill, 1830.

Tanner, Laura E., and James N. Krasner. "Exposing the 'Sacred Juggle': Revolutionary Rhetoric on Robert Rogers's *Ponteach*." *Early American Literature* 24 (1989): 4–19.

Tebbel, John William, and Earl W. De la Vergne. *Red Runs the River: The Rebellion of Chief Pontiac*. New York: Hawthorn Books, 1966.

Thoorens, Léon. *Pontiac, Prince de la prairie*. 1953. Brussels: Editions Labor, 1999.

Todish, Timothy J., ed. Introduction to Rogers, *Annotated and Illustrated Journals*, 13–22.

Todish, Timothy J., and Todd E. Harburn. *A "Most Troublesome Situation": The British Military and the Pontiac Indian Uprising of 1763–1764*. Fleischmanns, NY: Purple Mountain Press, 2006.

Trump, James. *Rogers Rangers and the Raid on Fort Michilimackinac 1758: A Novel of the French and Indian War*. Bloomington, IN: XLIBRIS, 2014.

———. *Rogers Rangers and the Search for the River Ourigan: A Novel of the Northwest Passage*. Bloomington, IN: XLIBRIS, 2017.

Turn: Washington's Spies. Developed by Craig Silverstein. 40 episodes. AMC Network, 2014–17.

Turner, Charles Yardsley. "A Mural Decoration by C. Y. Turner." *Art and Progress* 4, no. 12 (1913): 1150–51.

Twain, Mark. "Fenimore Cooper's Literary Offences." 1895. University of Virginia. http://twain.lib.virginia.edu/projects/rissetto/offense.html.

Vanderwerth, W. C., ed. *Indian Oratory: Famous Speeches by Noted Indian Chieftains*. Norman: University of Oklahoma Press, 1971.

Vizenor, Gerald. *Native Liberty: Natural Reason and Cultural Survivance*. Lincoln: University of Nebraska Press, 2009.

Voight, Virginia Frances. *Pontiac, Mighty Ottawa Chief*. Illustrated by William Hutchinson. Champaign, IL: Garrard, 1977.

Volwiler, Albert T. *George Croghan and the Westward Movement, 1741–1782*. Cleveland: Arthur H. Clark, 1926.

Wheeler, Jill C. *Forest Warrior: The Story of Pontiac*. Famous American Indian Leaders. Bloomington, MN: Abdo & Daughters, 1989.

White, Richard. *The Middle Ground: Indians, Empires, and Republics in the Great Lakes Region, 1650–1815*. Cambridge: Cambridge University Press, 1991.

Whitney, Edson Leone, and Frances M. Perry. *Four American Indians: King Philip, Pontiac, Tecumseh, Osceola; A Book for Young Americans*. New York: American Book, 1904.

Widder, Keith R. *Beyond Pontiac's Shadow: Michilimackinac and the Anglo-Indian War of 1763*. East Lansing: Michigan State University Press, 2013.

———. "The 1767 Maps of Robert Rogers and Jonathan Carver: A Proposal for the Establishment of the Colony of Michilimackinac." *Michigan Historical Review* 30, no. 2 (Fall 2004): 35–75.

Williams, Andrew P. "The Centre of Attention: Theatricality and the Restoration Fop." *Early Modern Literary Studies* 4, no. 3 (1999): 1–22.

Williams, Raymond. "Dominant, Residual, and Emergent." In *Marxism and Literature*, 121–27. Oxford: Oxford University Press, 1977.

Williams, Walter L. *The Spirit and the Flesh: Sexual Diversity in American Indian Culture*. Boston: Beacon Press, 1986.

Williams, William Carlos. *In the American Grain*. 1925. New York: New Directions, 1956.

Wilmeth, Don B., and Christopher Bigsby, eds. *The Cambridge History of American Theatre*. Vol. 1, *Beginnings to 1870*. Cambridge: Cambridge University Press, 1998.

Wittgenstein, Ludwig. *Tractatus logico-philosophicus*. 1921. Frankfurt: Edition Suhrkamp, 1982.

Index

259